Praise for *Trouble Shooter* and George Jesse Turner

At the 1999 BAFTA awards, George Jesse Turner won best documentary cameraman. He doesn't mention it in his book but that's the sort of modest man he is. We started our careers at Granada at the same time and our paths have crossed many times, most fruitfully in the *Up* series of films. I couldn't do them without him – his warmth and sensitivity in awkward situations and his unobtrusive skill in capturing the images that illuminate the subjects' lives go to the heart of the matter. So it's a bit of a shock to read about the George of *Trouble Shooter* – the other George, the George who gets shot up the backside by Israeli commandos in Jordan; who's chummy with Yasser Arafat; who does battle with Pol Pot and the dreaded Khmer Rouge.

He never told me any of this – he was too busy getting on with the job in hand, but now it's all out there in this rousing book. It's about his time on *World In Action*, the series that revolutionized current affairs and put the very best 'in your face' journalism onto television. George worked on 600 editions and probably never had the time to put his feet up and watch any of them; Vietnam, Northern Ireland, the Middle East; Thalidomide, Mad Cow, Chernobyl; Nelson Mandela, the Beatles, Rodney King and on and on. He's had an exciting life and George gives us a candid and authoritative insight into what it takes to get those images that burn into our brain. He's paid a price, a near-fatal and lengthy attack of cerebral malaria and a workload that would make anyone a stranger in their own home. You can feel his pain when he tells of others who didn't make it, like Dan Eldon, a young news photographer who was beaten to death while working in Somalia. But the rewards have been thrilling because *World In Action* didn't just report, it got things done, most famously the release of the Birmingham Six. There were successes great and small and George was in the middle of it all.

Those of us lucky enough to have worked with him will recognize in the pages of *Trouble Shooter* the boyish enthusiasm, the almost foolhardy courage and the total commitment that George brings to everything he does. For the rest, know that the skills of George and his colleagues in throwing light in dark corners have made this naughty and perilous world a little safer for all of us.

Michael Apted, Director: *Coal Miner's Daughter, Gorky Park, Gorillas In The Mist, World Is Not Enough,* and the *7-Up, 14-Up . . . 42-Up* series

The remarkable story of one of the greatest journalists/cameramen. And a nice guy too.

Michael Parkinson

There is no one like George Jesse Turner, Ace Cameraman.

John Pilger

Dedication

In memory of my father,
George Jesse Turner Snr

TROUBLE SHOOTER

Life Through the Lens of *World In Action*'s Top Cameraman

George Jesse Turner with
Jeff Anderson

First published in Great Britain in 2000
by Granada Media
an imprint of André Deutsch Ltd
in association with
Granada Media Group
76 Dean Street
London
W1V 5HA

www.vci.co.uk

A catalogue record for this book is available from the British
Library

ISBN 0 233 99867 5

Jacket Design by Slatter Anderson
Plate Section design by Design 23

1 3 5 7 9 10 8 6 4 2

Typeset in Liverpool by Derek Doyle & Associates
Printed and bound in Great Britain by
Mackays of Chatham.

Contents

Introduction

Twenty-five minutes and five seconds. That's the length of a half-hour ITV current affairs programme once the advertisers have taken their chunk. It doesn't sound enough time in which to tell someone's life story, or expose a dictator's brutal regime, or help spring an innocent prisoner from the cells. Can you really cram in the details of a baffling financial scam or unravel the complex background to a far-off civil war? And is it possible to explain a political revolution in the same time it takes to watch a single episode of *Coronation Street*?

The answer is, of course, yes. Skilled producers are masters of storytelling, able to distil months of research down to the basic essentials that any viewer can understand and follow. They push their story along with sharp commentary and carefully chosen sound bites from their interviewees. Then there are the pictures. If we cameramen have done our jobs properly, one minute's worth of images should be worth ten of script.

What producers *can't* convey in such a limited time slot is the sheer adventure involved in getting their programmes on air. Usually what the viewer sees is the tiniest tip of the iceberg. The effort, the danger, the luck – good and bad – are all hidden. Journalists and crew may build up a fund of anecdotes with which to entertain our friends and families when we return home, but the wider audience never gets to know the full picture.

Now, however, I'd like to fill in some of the blanks. The

stories here come from my life on the road with *World In Action* – the series which, till its demise in 1998, became synonymous with fearless, investigative journalism. Born in the early 1960s, when current affairs coverage was ponderous and deferential, *World In Action* broke new ground by challenging authority. The phrase 'hard hitting' could have been invented for it, exposing – as it did – wasteful defence projects, price-fixing cartels, and the hidden ingredients of processed food. But, at the same time, it was entertaining, broadening the current affairs agenda to include profiles of soccer stars, and charting the progress of strange new social phenomena such as supermarkets and motorways.

In all there were 1,400 editions on ITV and, by my reckoning, I worked on some 600. I wasn't around for the first three years. And, if I missed some during the next thirty-two, it was because I was shooting other editions, or the occasional special series such as *The Christians*, *The Spanish Civil War*, or the long-running *Seven-Up* documentary project. As a result, this isn't a run down of the programme's 'greatest hits'. Several of the most famous editions went on air without any input from me. Others that I did work on may have been journalistic triumphs, but – from my point of view – they involved little more than filming interviewees behind their desks.

For this book I've chosen the programmes that not only made exciting, and often moving, television: they also provided me with some unforgettable behind-the-scenes experiences. If some old colleagues are disappointed that their own contributions have been missed out, I apologize. However, I have not set out to write the definitive history of *World In Action*. That is another book.

I was a raw twenty-one-year-old when I landed the job as a camera assistant on the series. For the following three years I filled up my passport while working on a mind-boggling array of stories. Back home in Southport my parents would ask me what I'd be covering next, but I was never able to tell them. The agenda was impossible to predict. One week we would look at the search for oil in the North Sea; the following Monday we would examine how people spent their increasing amount of leisure time. I travelled to Africa and the Middle East, working alongside producers who were attempting to explain major international developments. Then I'd spend a week filming with child prodigies to find the secret of a high IQ; or meeting the scientists who were working on ways to control the weather.

With a group of predominantly young producers on board the series reflected the spirit of the times. We were entering the late sixties and giving voice to the concerns and interests of the new generation. We made films about pirate radio, LSD and sexually transmitted diseases. And when Mick Jagger was released from prison after a drugs charge, a new producer called John Birt brought him to meet the Archbishop of Canterbury and the editor of *The Times* to explain sixties youth culture.

With a global brief, it was inevitable we would turn our attention to the issue causing the biggest political debate among the young. By 1968 America's war in Vietnam was increasingly reviled, and university campus protests had spread from the US to the UK and the rest of western Europe. In March of that year students throughout Britain organized a mass anti-war demonstration in the centre of London. A rally was planned for Trafalgar Square, from where they would march to the American Embassy to hand in a petition of protest against US policy in south-east Asia.

The team knew the demonstration would be big, and possibly even violent. Researchers had spent some time with students from Manchester University and had got agreement to follow four busloads of them on their way to the capital to join the protest. They were a group disgusted by the war and incensed by our own Labour government's support for it. Travelling down the M6, one student fully expected trouble:

'Well, Martin Luther King has said that a riot is the voice of the unheard . . . and for me the demonstration is really a strengthening of my muscles for the sort of society I want to see later.'

Another warned: 'I shan't be at all surprised if there's violence today . . . I think that the state is generally allowed to push anybody and everybody about as much as it wants to. Now people are starting to fight back and that is a good sign.'

Sensing the potential scale of the event, executive producer David Plowright demanded six cameras to cover all aspects of the action. Four of them would have sound, but the others would supply mute pictures from fixed points. To my delight, I was put in charge of one of the mute cameras and assigned to get aerial shots from the top of Nelson's Column in Trafalgar Square. Discussions had taken place with Westminster Council, who had agreed to give us access. So, early that Sunday morning, I climbed the 170 foot high monument to get in position for the demo.

In fact, I climbed it twice. I was working alone and had no one to help me carry all the gear. Once I got to the top with the camera, I had to leave it there and go back down for the tripod. The Column was actually in the process of being cleaned at the time and was surrounded by scaffolding and tarpaulins. Standing in position next to Nelson's left eye, I felt the old admiral should have had a wash and scrub a lot earlier. The pigeon droppings encrusted on his face were at least a quarter of an inch thick, and the stench was foul.

Down below, 15,000 people had gathered for the rally. The sea of bodies swept outwards from the square into the main roads, bringing the traffic to a standstill. The crowd heard speeches from the student leader Tariq Ali and the actress Vanessa Redgrave. Thousands were signing petitions and handing out leaflets; hundreds were flying North Vietnamese flags. At around 3.30 p.m. the protestors started to move off, heading for the US Embassy three quarters of a mile away in Grosvenor Square. I had got the shots I had come for, but I wanted to get in on any further action at ground level. I clambered down the scaffolding and ladders with the tripod strapped to my back to avoid another double journey.

By the time I got to Grosvenor Square, the bulk of demonstrators had already arrived. Nearly a thousand policemen were on duty, and most had formed thick cordons in front of the embassy and the adjacent buildings. I met up with another producer, John Sheppard, who wanted me to get hand-held shots in and among the crowd as it was surging forward. I managed to get only a few minutes' worth of material before the scenes started turning ugly. Newly arrived protestors began chanting and throwing missiles. Suddenly a couple of dozen policemen appeared on horseback in an attempt to drive the demonstrators back. One officer spotted John and myself and shouted to us to get out of the mêlée. He then ordered a few of his men to lift me over a green privet hedge and a wire fence. From that moment on I had a unique perspective on what was happening.

And it was just at that moment that the real trouble erupted. The next twenty minutes brought London's most violent riot in living memory. Just a few feet in front of me I saw policemen being hit with stones and lumps of wood. They responded with baton charges as the mounted officers rode forward trying to break up the most violent sections of the crowd. Snatch squads went in attempting to arrest the missile throwers. When a group of demonstrators broke through in a bid to get to the embassy they were tripped and kicked. One was dragged away by his hair, while another was clubbed to the ground.

The noise resembled that of a football crowd urging its team to score the winner in the last minute of the game. There were shouts, screams and whistles. Every couple of minutes would come the sound of breaking glass as a missile shattered one of the embassy windows. And throughout it all was the constant chant of 'Ho-Ho Ho Chi Minh'.

As the violence continued I saw one young PC being struck on the head with a flagpole. Seconds later another was pulled from the crowd with blood pouring from his skull. Finally, as battle weariness took hold among the demonstrators, the police regained control, and the crowd began to disperse. By 6 p.m. on Sunday Grosvenor Square was bloody and strewn with debris, but the demonstrators had all gone, leaving the police to count their casualties: 117 of them had been injured.

World In Action was due on the air the following night. Another programme was already cut and on stand-by, but the events of the day were so dramatic that we simply had to rush out a newly edited edition. I hurried in the direction of Marylebone Road to get my rolls of film to Humphries Labs for processing. Then, adrenalin still pumping, I climbed into my new Cortina and sped north along the M1 towards Granada's Manchester HQ. At 3 a.m. I arrived in the Quay Street studios to find John and fellow producer Leslie Woodhead viewing some 20,000 feet of film. Over the next fourteen hours they would have to edit it all down to a half-hour programme called, simply, *The Demonstration*.

I have to say that I was lucky, but the material I came back with provided a new angle on the events of the day. Unusually for the programme, this edition would contain little commentary or interviews. Instead, the images of violence would speak for themselves. In all, thirteen minutes of *The Demonstration* were taken up with fly-on-the-wall scenes of the violence in Grosvenor Square – and seven minutes of that was shot by me from behind the police cordon.

Watching Leslie and John edit the pictures in the early hours of Monday morning, I succumbed to exhaustion and began to fall asleep. But by then I knew my own shots were about to be shown to a TV audience of millions. I could hardly wait for another opportunity.

CHAPTER 1
A YEAR OF LIVING DANGEROUSLY

KOREA

A huge fist hits your screen tonight, blacking out the whole picture as it swings towards you. It's no TV production stunt – the fist belongs to a North Korean border guard. Behind the camera is 23-year-old 'World In Action' cameraman George Turner, covering the Korean peace talks for tonight's programme. He got a black eye for his troubles.

Daily Mirror, 23 February 1969

In fact, I didn't have to wait too long to be back in the front line. The Grosvenor Square shots had gone down well with the programme's team, and, when the regular cameraman Ray Goode announced he was leaving later that year, a few of the producers put in a word for me. Just before Christmas, I got a call from Granada's head of film operations, Bill Lloyd. He told me I was being 'made up' to lead cameraman on the series and that I had three months to prove I could do it. If I didn't measure up, I'd revert to my old role as an assistant.

At the time I was taking a break from *World In Action* while working on a controversial Granada drama starring Peter Egan. *Big Breadwinner Hogg* was made by two up and coming directors who would later achieve major success in the film world – Mike Newell of *Four Weddings and a Funeral* fame, and Michael Apted, who went on to direct a string of Hollywood hits, plus the James Bond movie *The World Is Not Enough*.

As their early TV series was inspired by the killings and tortures carried out by the Kray and Richardson gangs in sixties London, it was always bound to be violent. However, the vivid and uncompromising way they reflected the gangland world provoked a huge number of complaints, and the series ended up being banished from peak time and put into the late-night schedules. But while Fleet Street worked itself up into outrage over this work of fiction, I was getting ready to witness twelve months of real-life violence.

It all began in Korea. By 1969 its civil war had been over for sixteen years, but tensions between North and South remained high. The US still had 50,000 troops based in the South, while half a million men from that country were under arms, ready for an invasion by the communist North. Producer Russell Spurr, who had covered the war as Far Eastern correspondent for the *Daily Express*, was fascinated by the region and had kept up many of his old contacts. When thirty-one North Korean agents were killed after infiltrating the South in an attempt to kill the President, he persuaded the series editor Jeremy Wallington to commission a programme. I was diverted from a short stint in Northern Ireland, jumped on a plane to Heathrow, and on 27 January 1969 boarded another bound for Seoul – my first foreign assignment as lead cameraman.

The journey took me via Anchorage, Alaska, but when I arrived in Seoul the weather was, if anything, colder: the country was in the grip of its worst blizzard for half a century. I met up with Russell at Seoul Airport, along with camera assistant Mike Thompson, and the sound recordist with whom I'd work for many years, Alan Bale. Together, the four of us headed out for Panmunjon, some fifty miles north. Normally the journey would have taken a little over an hour, but with snowdrifts and minus fifteen degree temperatures it took us nearly five.

In 1953, by when the war between North and South had cost three million lives, both sides called it a draw. Panmunjon is the town where they drew the border line. Inside Panmunjom there's a concrete hut that straddles the line. And inside that hut is a wooden table where, once a month, both sides had agreed to meet, talk, and try to settle their differences.

Unfortunately, neither seemed interested in settling anything, and every meeting would end in a slanging match. 'Your regime possesses no honesty, lacks good faith and is devoid of collective integrity,' went the South.

'You employ pernicious propaganda, faulty logic, and fraudulent twistings of the truth,' replied the North.

At either end of the hut were loudspeakers blaring out propaganda. The communist loudspeaker would send out messages inviting South Koreans to overthrow their American-imperialist backed government and join the glorious revolution that had proved so successful in the North. The other would talk of the goodies that capitalism had delivered to the South: new homes, shiny cars, well-paid jobs and a 12 per cent growth rate.

Russell wanted to start the film with a shot of the hut and an interior sequence showing the talks disintegrating into the monthly ritual of insults. We filmed inside first, then left to get the exteriors. By this time the snow was so thick it was impossible to see where the border line had been drawn along the ground. Thinking I was relatively safe with several hundred UN peacekeeping soldiers milling around, I moved forward to get my perfect shot of the hut. But I'd strayed a couple of feet too far and encroached on official North Korean territory. Seconds later one of its border guards strode towards me and, without a word, threw a right hook at the lens. The force pushed the camera backwards into my face and I felt a sharp pain under my right eye. I went around sporting a shiner for the next few days, but I knew I'd captured a terrific moment on film.

For the following two weeks, Russell lived up to his reputation as a producer with a highly visual sense, putting me into situations which he knew would result in great action sequences. He wanted to show how the South was on alert for a seaborne attack from the North, so he persuaded the navy to mount an exercise featuring a battleship and two minesweepers. He wanted to demonstrate how the air force had benefited from US training, and so fixed up some air-to-air filming aboard an F86 fighter plane. Before you can go up in this most awesome of machines, you need to put on a G-Suit to guard against sudden rushes of blood from the head during high-speed vertical acceleration. Unfortunately, I'm rather larger than the average Korean, and they didn't have one big enough to fit me. Russell's desire for a great sequence, and my own enthusiasm to experience the power of an F86, meant I went up anyway. Exhilarating, yes, but unforgettable for another reason: I vomited.

The leader of the UN forces in South Korea was an American with a name straight from Central Casting: General C.H. Bonesteel the Third. A fervent anti-communist, his pride and joy were the Special Forces of the South's own army – the ROKs, who took their title from the country's official name, Republic of Korea. With his permission we were able to film the ROKs in training, and quickly realized why they had built their reputation as the toughest men in the world. Genuinely concerned about getting frostbite in our testicles, we filmed them wading through chest-high snow, camouflaged in flimsy white suits and hats. We then went inside an unheated gym, filming them practising black-belt karate moves in forty degrees of frost.

Later, finally warming up inside an army drill hut, the soldiers were keen to show off their survivalist skills. When a fifteen-inch-long viper appeared inside, one particularly macho specimen ran over and stamped on it with a Special Forces boot. Seeing this was potentially too good to miss, we sprang into action: I fitted a special lens that enabled me to film in ultra-close-up, and Alan got ready to capture the sound.

Looking straight at the camera, the soldier bit the snake at the back of its head, then started to peel back the skin before feasting on its body. Watching through the eyepiece, I was transfixed, not just by the sight of what was happening, but by the sound. The hut had gone quiet while the soldier performed his party piece, and all I could hear was the crunching noise he made as he chewed. I remember thinking 'I hope to God this sound comes across on the film,' and made a mental note to ask Alan whether it had registered on his Nagra recorder. Just then, though, I had something more pressing to think about: the soldier had finished eating and was holding what was left of the snake in front of my face and smiling. It was clear what he was thinking – he'd given me great pictures and now I had to give him some fun in return. Well, these were the toughest men in the world, and I'd never been one to turn down a free meal so, yes, I ate it. And – in case you're wondering – it tastes like herring.

With the project over, we flew on to Hong Kong for another assignment, while our rolls of film were sent back to Manchester for editing. A couple of weeks later the programme – *War On Ice* – was transmitted, winning both a large audience and critical acclaim. (In fact it later won second prize in the Rank TV News Awards, a gong presented to us by the soon-to-be-disgraced Postmaster General, John Stonehouse.)

For me, though, the film provided an early lesson in the impact of sound, as well as vision. Arriving back at Heathrow, collecting our silver camera-equipment boxes by the carousel, a baggage handler asked Alan and I who we worked for. When we told him, he guessed exactly where we'd been and what we'd been up to: 'You must have done that film from Korea that was on telly the other night. I'll *never* forget the noise of that snake being crunched!'

JORDAN

Mr George Turner, a British television cameraman, wounded recently while covering Arab commando

> activities, has left Beirut by air for London. Members of the Granada *World In Action* team confirmed that Mr Turner was wounded during an action on the occupied west bank of the Jordan.
>
> *The Times*, 18 March 1969

In its early days *World In Action* had employed producers with predominantly journalistic backgrounds. Often recruited from newspapers, they were masters of words, but had limited understanding of pictures. Tim Hewatt, the original executive producer, allegedly used to write his script and give it to the film editor with the instruction: 'Find some crap to go with that.'

By the mid-sixties, things had begun to change and a new breed of producer was coming on board. Several of the new school had learned the craft of film-making and direction elsewhere. They had a handle on the mechanics of finding stories, but their real interest lay in visualizing them.

John Sheppard, who had filmed with me at the Grosvenor Square demo, was perhaps the most extreme example. He arrived on the programme as a pure director, having spent the previous few years in the studio calling the shots on a wide range of live series, including the hugely popular music programme *Ready, Steady, Go*. From the outset, he was a breath of fresh air, bringing invention and wit to all of his programmes. He also had his own interests and obsessions that led to the series broadening its agenda and widening its appeal. It was John, for example, who directed a Granada profile of the sixties rock star Jim Morrison, and filmed his band, The Doors, in concert. He was also one of the team behind an hour-long special on the famous free Hyde Park concert by the Rolling Stones. The 1969 classic – *The Stones In The Park* – went on to win several major awards and remains one of the most evocative documentaries of the era.

John may have been immersed in the sixties music scene but

he soon developed a taste for visiting the world's trouble spots. Spells in Vietnam and Israel had whetted his appetite, and he was always keen to fly off to the latest danger zone. His exploits were part of programme folklore. He once spent weeks out of touch, finally contacting the Manchester office with a hippy-style telex message: 'EMERGED UNDERGROWTH STOP MOVIE GROOVY STOP SHEPPARD.' After a research trip to south-east Asia, he submitted an expenses claim with the explanation: 'Ten thousand kip to opium party for Lao general.' Until 1969 I hadn't shared in any of John's foreign adventures. Then, in March that year, he was assigned to a film on the PLO fighters waging guerrilla warfare in the Middle East.

When Israel routed its Arab neighbours in the Six Day War of 1967, it redrew its boundaries, claiming the west bank of the River Jordan and making hundreds of thousands of Palestinians homeless. Many of them now lived in crowded refugee camps in Jordan itself, and these became a stronghold of the PLO's most disciplined and feared faction, Al Fatah.

I had visited the camps as an assistant cameraman a couple of years earlier and had witnessed the anger and sense of injustice felt by the Palestinians. Here, amid the rows of cardboard, tin and prefab huts, a new mood of militancy had set in, and the people were fully behind the guerrillas who were making repeated incursions across the river to attack the Israeli army bases.

We filmed at an Al Fatah training camp up in the mountains. Discipline was fierce and security vigorous, with all of the fighters known only by false names. One boy, who had already been on five operations across the border, was aged just thirteen. Although the guerrillas didn't acknowledge a single leader, they took their inspiration from a man who was emerging as an almost legendary figure in the refugee camps – Yasser Arafat, known in the Arab world as Abu Amar. When we said we wanted to interview him, they arranged to pick us up from the Intercontinental Hotel in Amman and take us to a secret location at midnight. The location, in fact, turned out to be a cave, in which Arafat sat at a desk, his face illuminated theatrically by a single light bulb.

He was well spoken and courteous, surrounded by armed guards who obviously held him in awe. He spoke eloquently of the Palestinians' fight to regain their homes – many of which had been confiscated when the state of Israel was born more than twenty years previously.

ARAFAT: We wait and wait for a long time, from 1948, waiting for the United Nations, and nothing has been done, except more refugees.

So we think that the only way is to carry our arms and to fight. We don't like fighting, war, but the person who has been kicked out from his home is obliged and he has the right to fight – to fight for everything, to fight for his future, for his children, for his people, and that is what we have been doing.

QUESTION: And are you going to continue fighting until you have your land back?

ARAFAT: All our land, and nothing else.

Arafat was keen to make the PLO struggle understandable to a British audience, showing a media awareness well ahead of his time. The United Nations had passed a resolution calling for Israel to withdraw to its pre-1967 borders, but his organization said this did not go far enough, and that Palestinians should be allowed to reclaim land taken off them in 1948.

ARAFAT: We want no half solutions. Suppose an enemy of the UK came and occupied Wales, then he occupied Scotland. Would you be happy if he left Wales only?

On Sunday 9 March – my twenty-fourth birthday – Arafat's guerrillas intended to show us how deadly serious they were in their attempts to inflict damage on the hated forces who had now occupied their homeland. They were taking us on a Commando mission across the River Jordan. Their object was to attack, penetrate and totally liquidate the Israeli military base of Tel Najjar on the west bank.

Some birthday it would turn out to be. The story is best told in a memo from John, later submitted to the programme's executive producer David Plowright, shortly after we'd arrived home.

Memorandum — to: PLOWRIGHT cc LLOYD WALLINGTON WOODHEAD

from: SHEPPARD — date: 27 March 1969

subject: GEORGE TURNER

File Plowright

As requested, a piece of paper on the above. Any resemblance to a citation is intentional.

On Saturday March 8, George Turner and I were picked up by jeep at our hotel in Amman and driven down to the Jordan valley. We walked a kilometre or so to the edge of the river and waited in the reeds for a rope to be put across. After five hours this proved impossible, owing to the particularly fast flow. We were returned to Amman. We got back at 0100 Sunday. I include that preamble mostly to emphasize that the next night, Sunday, we were 'going back!'

On Sunday afternoon, March 9, we were taken again, This time we had only a short wait on the East bank. By now it was pitch dark and several times we had to flatten because of Israeli flares. We then waded for 15 minutes through knee deep mud and tit deep water to reach the main channel. This was about forty feet wide, flowing at about forty miles per hour, too keep to think of walking. Each bank was a sheer ten foot cliff of mud. The mode of transport was a rubber tyre on which one lay - first dragged straight downstream then hauled back to the far bank by a guerrilla sitting on a tree trunk jutting half-submerged fifteen feet out into the stream. It was necessary somehow to slither along the trunk and up the bank - all without getting the equipment wet. Impossible. By the time we were again on dry, if occupied, soil we had each spent a minute or two fully submerged. Without complaint (while I swore quietly) George set to in pitch darkness and cleaned and dried all the gear, restoring it somehow, as the results show, to working order. When all our party of 21 was across we set off in Indian file at a brisk pace (of 'Life' magazine: '.... lung-searing') straight up and down the sand dunes for about two kilometres. Stopping and starting, we arrived inthe vicinity of the target around 10.45 pm.The attack began, catching us quite unawares, at 11.00. Within four minutes George (and the camera battery) were hit. When it became clear we could not film any more we moved off into a shallow depression with a small group of the Commandos and, after waiting for some others to join us, filtered back to the river. The firing continued, though no longer dangerous to us, for about another twenty minutes and provoked an angry Israeli-Jordanian artillery duel that lasted until approximately 0100. Our return was more uncomfortable than ourgoing; apart from again falling into the river, it rained for some two hours as we sat in the mud waiting for the patrol to re-form and be counted. Throughout this period George made such skimpy complaint of his condition that I thought he was jarred by the battery as it was hit. Only as we were nearly back to the heep did he finally relinquish the camera to a guerrilla (who, in the friendly manner of the Third World, had been nagging George for hours to let him carry it.) I did not discover the extent of the damage until, halfway back to Amman, we stopped for a call of nature and I took his pants down. We then took him to a nearby hospital

/over...

Memorandum to:

from: date:

subject: GEORGE TURNER (Contd..)

Page 2

where he was stitched (that, he characteristically says, was the most painful bit). Finally, needless to say, despite stern lectures from Doctors, nurses and us, George bulldozed his way back to the eyepiece within thirty six hours.

I gather from Tom that George (in terms of hours logged on his sheets) will have earned approximately £50 for his weekend's work. His spirit and cheerfulness were priceless to me, to you I urge they should be worth, ex gratia, £250.

JOHN SHEPPARD

In the event, they gave me £150, which left £94 and 15 shillings after tax!

It's difficult to explain the sensation of the bullet hitting my backside. At the time it felt like a hard smack, and I wasn't certain I'd been shot until I put my hand down my trousers and felt the blood. Back at Al Fatah's field hospital in Jordan they gave me a local anaesthetic and stitched the wound. As John reported in his kind memo, that actually hurt me more.

For the remainder of the filming inside Jordan we kept quiet about the shooting. We didn't want the authorities to know, and we were also worried that a *Panorama* crew – who'd recently arrived in Amman – might get to know what we'd been up to. It wasn't until a few days later, when we got to Jerusalem, that I realized how lucky I had been. John found a French doctor who examined the wound, and traced the trajectory of the bullet as it had passed through my buttock, up my back and out through my right shoulder, where it had blown the camera battery apart. Studying the wounds at either end, he smiled and said: 'You've been a very lucky young man. If the bullet had hit you just a quarter of an inch lower you would not be getting up from that bed and walking – you would be paralysed.'

The resulting film, *The Six Day War – Day 666*, opened with the sequence of the attack on the Israeli base. Any viewers who listened carefully will have heard the following exchange amid the soundtrack of flares and gunfire:

ME: I've been hit.
JOHN: Where?
ME: Up the f***ing arse!

The programme was transmitted on 31 March 1969, the day my three-month trial period as a cameraman was up. Despite my pre-watershed industrial language, I kept the job.

NORTHERN IRELAND

I may have spent much of the year globetrotting, but the world's biggest international story suddenly turned up on our own doorstep.

I had visited Ireland five years earlier, for a series of reports for Granada's regional evening magazine programme *Scene at 6.30*. Along with reporter Michael Parkinson, I'd spent a week making travel items, meeting north-westerners who'd made their home there, filming tinkers and generally capturing the lighter side of life. Back then, my image of the Ulster people was at one with the Irish as a whole: warm, friendly, fun-loving. The events of 1969 were about to shatter my perceptions.

By the beginning of that year Northern Ireland's civil rights movement had had major success in highlighting the discrimination against Catholics in the country. Mass marches had attracted photographers and TV crews from

Britain, Europe and America. Once there, they filmed evidence of the inequalities – the way Protestants were at least twice as likely to get a job or a decent council house, and how electoral boundaries had been drawn so Catholics were under-represented at the Stormont parliament.

But those marches were leading, increasingly, to violence. Often there were counter-demonstrations by Protestant Loyalists, who saw the civil rights movement as a front for the IRA, who were attempting to destroy the state of Ulster and force its people into a United Ireland. Fighting would break out between the two sides, marches were re-routed or banned, and widespread rioting would result. It was clear that the two communities were becoming polarized and ancient hatreds were resurfacing.

Producer Charlie Nairn was looking for a microcosm of the troubles and found it in Newry, a town where 80 per cent of the population was Catholic. On 11 January, a civil rights march was scheduled to go through the centre of town, including a small Protestant district. Sensing trouble, Charlie scrambled four crews to the scene and we stood by waiting for the action to start. While filming the demo, we saw the police mount a barricade preventing the marchers from going through the Loyalist area. Arguments developed as the march leaders demanded their right to demonstrate, and the police directed them to an alternative route.

Insults were hurled, then stones, then the odd petrol bomb. Within minutes, a row of vehicles that formed part of the barricade had been set alight. Seven buses were burnt out and the police made twenty-two arrests. A group of women began screaming at us, angry that we wanted to film the action rather than listen to their grievances. One ran forward with the metal lid of a dustbin and struck Alan Bale across the head as he recorded the sound. During the rest of the night the rioting grew more serious, and there were further copycat disturbances over in Derry.

Our film *All Change At Newry* showed how the civil rights movement – which had modelled itself on Martin Luther King's brand of peaceful protest – was now being blamed as the source of the violence engulfing Ulster. However, it sought to prove that much of the violence had been started by people who weren't even on the march. Whatever the true causes were, the frequent marches – by Catholics and Protestants – became the triggers for large-scale disturbances over the next few months. By mid-summer, the Stormont government was losing control; by August it was crying for help.

World In Action had come off air for its summer break in May, and I had been assigned to film a number of documentaries. One of these took me to Killarney in Southern Ireland where we were looking at overseas investment in the Republic. On 14 August, the producer Brian Armstrong got a call from executive producer David Plowright: British troops had arrived in Derry to help quell rioting, and they were expected to move in to Belfast the next day. This dramatic intervention would be the subject of *World In Action*'s first two programmes of the autumn run. We abandoned the documentary shoot, loaded our convoy of Ford Cortinas and set off on the 200-mile journey to Belfast.

Driving through the night, it was strange to see that the events in the North were making little impact on life in the South. We passed through a succession of towns where the bars were still lit, and where people were drinking and enjoying themselves as late as 3 a.m. Meanwhile, over the border, Ulster was experiencing its worst night of violence for years. There was widespread rioting in Derry, extremists on both sides had taken up firearms, the police were roaming Belfast's streets with machine guns fitted on to their Shorland armoured cars. Four people were killed, including a nine-year-old boy, hit by a bullet as he lay in his bed.

We arrived in Belfast around lunchtime. As we drove along the Falls Road – the main highway running the length of

Catholic West Belfast – we saw that the local baths had been destroyed in what looked like an explosion. Thousands of gallons of water were running down the steps and into the streets. Some distance ahead a large mill was on fire, spewing out thick black smoke.

By mid-afternoon we'd gathered outside a school playground at the city-centre end of the Falls. Then, at the appointed time the 3rd Battalion Light Infantry came into view. The soldiers were young, wearing camouflage helmets more suited to the jungle than to the streets of one of the UK's major industrial cities. They were confused by the road layout, turning left instead of right by the school entrance. When they finally got their act together they assembled in the playground, receiving their orders before taking up their positions in the nearby streets.

The air was alive with the clanging sound of metal as they threw down barbed wire, hoping to separate people in Catholic and Protestant streets so they wouldn't attack each other. But they didn't seem to have a clue about Belfast's complex religious dividing lines. Many of the streets were actually mixed, and behind the wire some families were being terrorized out of their houses. Throughout the next three days 1500 Catholic families, and 200 Protestant, would lose their homes.

Our plan was to make two programmes – one examining the disturbances from the Protestant point of view, the other through Catholic eyes. That meant spending lots of time on the most fiercely Loyalist and Republican estates, where mistrust of the media was rife. Hysteria was in the air. If a news bulletin had just portrayed one side in a bad light, those people would scream abuse, and often assault the first TV crew they came across. It was certainly no time for heroics. If we went into, say, a hardline Republican area such as Ardoyne we would stay in the car until Brian had made contact with a leading member of the local community. Only after he'd agreed to act as our minder would we leave the vehicle, set up the tripod and start to film.

Throughout our ten days there we witnessed almost continuous rioting. At night it was the norm to see youths – their faces concealed by scarves – throwing rocks and petrol bombs. The Victorian back-to-back streets were strewn with masonry and burnt-out vehicles. We could hear sporadic gunfire, along with the frequent wail of a police car or ambulance siren. But what we saw and heard constantly was the mistrust, fear and prejudice displayed by two communities who'd retreated into themselves. On one side, an interview with a Catholic woman:

> I'll fight to the last and if I thought they were coming to burn my home, I'd burn it myself. Quite honestly I wouldn't give them the satisfaction of it. Mr Paisley was on TV yesterday, but if he'd been here he wouldn't have got out alive, I'm telling you that much. That man isn't a man. You know what he is? He's an anti-Christ!

Then, a Protestant woman's view of the Catholics:

> They won't clean, their children run about, and they're not really the same as us. You can't expect them to have the best of clothes on them, but at least they could be clean. Lying against the walls, collecting £20 a week social security for lying against the walls, while my son has to work 40 hours a week to earn £9.

If the sight of heavily armed troops taking up positions in a UK high street was shocking, so was the extent of the bigotry. We interviewed one Catholic man who'd seen families burnt out of their homes in a mainly Protestant street:

> And then there was the man who started a pet shop. A little window of imagination in this great industrial

desert. He had tropical fish and parrots and lovebirds. He even had a piranha from the Orinoco. People loved this, but then he found an assistant who was a Roman Catholic. They threatened him over and over again that they would burn him out if he didn't sack his Roman Catholic assistant. He told the police but they won and they burnt him out and they killed all his budgerigars and all his Australian lovebirds and all his fish including his Orinoco piranha, which was the only one in Ireland. The man who burnt him out said: 'Those are Papist budgies and Roman Catholic goldfish – burn the bastards out'. And he did so.

Manchester was 150 miles and a fifty-minute plane journey from Northern Ireland. Working in Belfast that week, it seemed like a world away. By the time we arrived home fourteen people had been killed in Ulster. They would be listed as the first official victims of 'the Troubles'.

BIAFRA

When I started working in this field I knew I'd have to be prepared to go anywhere at any time. It can be tough on you, and more particularly on those at home, but to do the job properly work simply has to come first. When the call came it was usually from Tom Gill, the programme's legendary production manager. He was from a military background, frighteningly efficient, and completely dedicated to his job. If you were in a foreign jail, Tom would get you out. If you'd missed a plane on the other side of the world he would find a connection. Nothing fazed him: even telling you that your holiday was about to go down the pan.

Late in November I was filming in Newcastle. I was asleep

in my hotel room when the phone went shortly after midnight. It could only have been Tom: 'I've just got one thing to ask you,' he said. 'Will you go to Biafra for Christmas – yes or no?' I knew a negative answer wasn't an option so I just said: 'Sure – when?' His answer was typical Tom: 'Get some sleep – I'll tell you tomorrow.'

The next day he filled me in. I was to go to Africa – as soon as our visa applications were approved – with producer Vanya Kewley and sound recordist Colin Richards. We were to make a film showing the everyday suffering of a people who were being bombed and starved into submission in the latest phase of an awful civil war. It would be set in Christmas week – the same time that millions back home would be celebrating peace and goodwill on very full stomachs.

The state of Biafra – the eastern region of Nigeria – had declared itself independent in 1967. Its population was drawn from the Ibo tribe, a proud and independent people who believed they were under threat from other tribes in the control of the federal government. Nigeria wanted its eastern region back and was prepared to use the most brutal means to get it. Apart from continuous bombing raids, it mounted a blockade aimed at stopping all food supplies from getting into Biafra.

Nigeria was a former British colony and we still had major commercial interests there. UK firms also remained the main supplier of heavy weaponry to its government. As 1969 wore on, British viewers were outraged to discover we were supporting a regime that was deliberately starving up to two million people to death. Biafra became synonymous with pictures of emaciated, pot-bellied children with sunken eyes, matchstick limbs and pained expressions of hunger. Scenes like these had never been shown on British television before and the impact was massive.

When my visa came through I flew to Amsterdam to meet up with Vanya and Colin. From there we took a plane to the island of São Tomé, a small Portuguese colony situated in the

Gulf of Guinea, three kilometres off the West African coast. Here the aid agencies had set up their base, hiring mercenary pilots to fly in supplies to the Biafran capital, Enugu. The day before Christmas the Catholic charity Caritas agreed to let us board one of their planes. The tiny São Tomé airport was strewn with battered old aircraft that had been hired to make the hazardous journey over Nigerian airspace into Biafra. Some of these would never make it back, as the Nigerian forces would attack any plane suspected of ferrying aid to the rebels. Others were so dilapidated, you wondered if they would even make it into the air in the first place.

Our plane was loaded with grain and other foodstuffs and took off just before midnight with me sitting in the glass cockpit alongside the American pilot. A couple of hours later we began the descent into Enugu and I was amazed to discover that the airstrip we were heading for was in total darkness. On the final few hundred feet the pilot appeared to be flying blind but then, just twenty seconds or so before landing, he grabbed a walkie talkie and yelled his request for lights. Suddenly the airstrip lit up with a row of car headlights that were switched off the second we touched down, plunging us into complete darkness once more.

The charity workers told us to load our equipment inside a beat-up old VW Beetle and we headed off to the nearby town of Owerri. Our base was to be a Catholic aid mission where the priests and nuns would give us the latest information on the fighting, and advise us where it was safe or dangerous to film. Some of them agreed to take us the following morning to the front line, where we filmed shattered buildings, homes and roads. Throughout the day there were frequent sirens warning of attacks from Nigerian forces, and every few minutes we could hear the distinct sound of shelling. We stayed at another aid camp that night and were warned by a Biafran soldier that the Nigerians were advancing, and that we might come under attack. There was little hope of protecting ourselves if the worst did happen. His only advice was: 'Get out, turn left and keep running.'

We woke up on Christmas morning with our bodies intact. We then headed back to Owerri where the Catholic nuns had arranged for us to film at an orphanage. Our guide, Sister Gertrude, told us about the frustration felt by the charity workers who were trying to relieve the suffering. With the Nigerians successfully blocking aid supplies, all she had to give the starving children was a single vitamin pill each day. Sister Gertrude said:

> It's a terrible experience to come into a country and find a whole nation literally dying of starvation. At the moment, Christmas time, they're begging us every moment of the day to help them and we just have nothing to give them.
>
> It's not just the hunger these people are suffering. They've lost everything in life – they have no homes, no clothing, nothing. The other day I was going to one of our sick bays and saw a child picking grasshoppers off the bushes. I could see he was almost dying of malnutrition. I asked him who I should contact before taking him to a sick bay and he told me that he'd lost his parents in the war and he didn't belong to anyone. This is the case with thousands and thousands of children.

I'll never forget the orphanage. Inside were more than 200 babies, all just a few days old. None had any clothes; each had a banana leaf for a bed. When a baby gave a weak cry of distress, a nun or an aid worker would offer a loving cuddle. Vanya, who'd trained as a nurse before moving into television, offered to help the medical staff dispense what few drugs and medicines they had. I filmed one aid worker, a German medic called Dr Dychter, as he tried to show a Biafran mother how to breastfeed her newborn child. But the exercise was useless as she was severely malnourished and had no milk to offer.

Scenes like this are difficult to film because you know that many viewers will find them too harrowing to watch. On one level you're trying to get the most emotive shots, but at the same time you're trying to avoid lingering for too long on the suffering. Dr Dychter knew I was capturing immensely powerful and moving images that would be seen by millions of British viewers in just a few days' time. But he was sceptical of the power of TV, and angry that news pictures hadn't already forced Western governments to intervene:

> People in Europe see starving Biafran children, but you do not feel hungry with them, you do not sit down on this mat with them, you do not see it pitifully. It's not enough to see it on television. Films and photographs are nothing. You cannot see a starving child by looking at your television set with a bottle of beer beside you.

When he was asked how the Biafrans would mark Christmas he became even more angry:

> Christmas means nothing to them or to me this year – let it be something for Europe. All these people know is that they're hungry and they're in pain. People from the outside must help them, by finding a political solution to this war. At the moment the solution seems to be to starve them to death.

But for many of the stricken Biafrans Christmas did have a special meaning. Heartbreakingly, some of them found a chicken, cooked it and offered it to us at lunchtime. They were a Christian people and, as the day wore on, those who could manage it attended special services. We went inside one church to film carols and a sermon from the pulpit. The priest said: 'Now, today being Christmas Day, it is good for us to remember why Our Lord came on earth. God landed on the earth at Bethlehem and it was to set the world right for it had gone wrong.'

Outside a Nigerian jet screamed overhead firing at civilians in the street. One man was hit and badly wounded, and we followed a group of aid workers as they took him for emergency treatment. Owerri's International Red Cross Hospital had recently been bombed by the Nigerians, and the doctors had been forced to build an underground operating theatre that was relatively safe from attack. Once they got him there the surgeons gave him an anaesthetic and began to operate. But the treatment probably came too late. The man, who'd been shot through the lungs and stomach, died on the operating table. It was the first time I witnessed a death from war.

We arrived home in England two days after Christmas following another mercenary flight back to São Tomé. Vanya headed straight for the editing suite and our film – *Last Week In Biafra* – was watched by nine million viewers on New Year's Eve. A fortnight later a delegation of Ibos travelled to the Nigerian capital Lagos and formally surrendered. On 15 January 1970 Nigeria reclaimed its eastern region, thus ending the existence of the Republic of Biafra.

And so my first year as lead cameraman on the series came to an end. I'd witnessed war, famine, death and civil rioting. I'd been assaulted and shot. And, by the end of that year, I'd slept in about 200 beds. On New Year's Eve my own mattress back in Southport had never felt more comfortable.

CHAPTER 2
THE THRILL OF THE CHASE

All the best investigative programmes end with a confrontation: that electric moment when a villain is caught unawares and forced to answer questions about his unscrupulous past. In television, these surprise interviews are known as 'doorsteps'. While they may take up just thirty seconds of airtime they can be the result of days, weeks, or even months of behind-the-scenes preparation.

Producers who want to carry out a doorstep have to satisfy the broadcasting authorities that invading a particular person's privacy is justified. Usually they will have to have made a formal request for an interview, which the subject has then turned down. They will also have to show that the interviewee is guilty of criminal or serious anti-social behaviour. They may even have to argue that there's a good chance of the interviewee going missing once he becomes aware that a TV company is on his trail.

Throughout its thirty-five years *World In Action* had no trouble identifying large numbers of people with a criminal or anti-social past. The result was usually me jumping out in front of them with my camera whirring away while a producer hit them with a series of quick-fire hostile questions. Early on, I learned that there's no standard reaction to that situation. One person will stand and calmly answer the questions, brazening it out. Others will stay tight lipped, covering their faces or trying to put their hands over the lens. Some people become violent, like the shady City banker who grabbed my lens cap and flung it in my face, the Amsterdam pimp who set his vicious dog on me, or the British Nazi leader who promised to put a bullet in the producer's head.

Then there are the runners. We once confronted an industrial spy who bolted into a busy high street and almost got himself knocked down by a car. There was also the detective whose long-term sick leave neatly coincided with a disciplinary inquiry into his close relationship with gangland villains. Staking out his house, we noticed that his illness didn't stop him going for a five-mile jog every morning. After a few days of carefully logging his usual route, we decided to pounce at the start of his 6 a.m. exercise. Unfortunately his superior fitness got the better of all of us. He was actually in training for the London marathon. The sequence ended with the sight of him disappearing into the distance – and the loud sound of me wheezing.

Stakeouts usually involve acting incognito. Although this protects you from being spotted by the interviewee, it can lead to other problems. While making a programme about anabolic steroids, we got information about a dealer who picked up a daily consignment from a PO box at his local Bristol post office. The researcher, Roger Beam, had followed him for a week and knew exactly what time he would turn up for his early morning collection. The producer and I met Roger at the back of the post office at 8 a.m. The plan was for him to stand at the corner of the building, pretending to read the morning newspaper. Folding it would be the signal that our target's car was about to pull up. At that point we would jump out and film the doorstep.

The post office was part of a row of commercial premises, backing on to a gravel car park. Sitting in the back of our vehicle, I put the camera on my knee and hid it under a black sheet. Then, at about 8.15, Roger dropped the paper and began waving frantically. I was just preparing to jump out when there was the deafening sound of sirens. So much for our attempt at keeping a low profile: within seconds, we were surrounded by police cars, and an armed man in uniform was pointing a gun and telling us to put our hands on our heads.

Confused and frightened, we did exactly as he said. Then he pulled back the sheet . . . and burst into laughter. Apparently we had been picked up by a CCTV camera mounted on the building next to the post office – which just happened to be a bank. Watching the film, a security guard had guessed we were a team of armed robbers waiting to pull off a job at opening time. My concealed camera was assumed to be a shotgun.

Once the police realized their mistake, they wanted to know what we were really up to. When we filled them in they agreed to leave at once, as our dealer was due to arrive within the next five minutes. Sure enough he did, blissfully unaware of the commotion that had just taken place. But then he was to get a shock of his own, as Roger tapped him on the shoulder and hit him with a series of questions about his illegal business.

For all their problems and dangers, stakeouts and doorsteps still give me huge satisfaction. They are the culmination of patience, deduction and painstaking intelligence gathering. And, if they're to come off, teamwork and trust are crucial.

NAZI HUNTING

At first I couldn't believe it. Old Nazis – prime movers in the Holocaust – alive, free and enjoying the protection of another country's government. All the more galling when, in this case, the country was America – Britain's biggest ally in the fight against Hitler.

The story was told to me by John Ware, a young journalist

who had recently arrived on the programme from Fleet Street. He was tenacious and fearless, and had three main obsessions: bent policemen, IRA terrorists and – most of all – war criminals. It was the late seventies; films like *The Odessa File* and *The Boys From Brazil* had raised awareness of the subject. Public interest was high, and John prepared to satisfy it. He helped track down five former Nazis who between them were responsible for around a million deaths. All of them had escaped justice. And, in the words of our programme title, all were *Alive and Well in the USA*.

I went with John and sound recordist Phil Taylor to a town called Mineola in Long Island, New York. We were going to the home of Boleslavs Maikovskis who had been a policeman in Latvia some forty years earlier. When Germany invaded in 1941, many Latvians welcomed the Nazis with open arms. They had lived under the occupation of communist Russia, and saw the Germans as liberators. Many signed up to fight alongside the Nazis, and others – like Maikovskis – willingly co-operated with their plans to exterminate the country's Jews.

John showed me a 1941 photograph of Maikovskis in a Nazi uniform. Alongside it was a document, signed by him, confirming that an execution had been carried out. It was one of many mass executions that had taken place near Riga, the city housing most of Latvia's Jews. Between 1941 and 1943, around 25,000 of them had been driven to a forest, then ordered to dig their own graves before being shot.

Maikovskis had entered the United States in 1951. Fifteen years later a Russian court sentenced him to death in his absence, judging him guilty of playing a leading role in the extermination of 15,000 Jews, including 2,000 children. Yet, the American authorities had no interest in sending him back to face justice. The US Immigration Service closed their file on him in 1966. When two investigators attempted to reopen the case in the early seventies, they found their efforts blocked.

We parked outside Maikovskis' smart suburban home, hoping to catch sight of him in order to get some modern-day shots. Lights went on and off inside, and curtains twitched, but after a couple of days he had still failed to appear. John then decided to adopt the direct approach. Phil fitted him with a radio-microphone, and I filmed him going up the path and knocking on the door. After a minute or so passed he bent down and opened the letter box, yelling at Maikovskis to come outside and answer questions about his Nazi past. Although he failed to respond, he did manage to summon the Long Island police via his private alarm system. A few minutes later five squad cars arrived and ordered us to leave. Old war criminals, it seemed, were entitled to their privacy.

Apparently they were entitled to protection too. Throughout the shoot we came across cases where the authorities had stopped them being prosecuted or deported. There was the minister in Hitler's puppet Croatian government who had personally overseen the murder of tens of thousands of Jews and Serbs in extermination camps. Despite the overwhelming evidence against him, the US Attorney General ruled that he could stay in America on the grounds that he would be subjected to political persecution if he was sent back to Yugoslavia. Then there was the chief torturer at Riga Jail who was not only allowed to settle in California, but also recruited as a government agent, working for the CIA. Time and again we were told the same story: America's enemy was now the Soviet bloc, and it was not prepared to hand back anti-Soviet people to communist countries.

Despite the government's helpful attitude, many of the old Nazis remained paranoid about their security. One was Valerian Trifa, a former commander in Romania's Nazi army, known as the Iron Guard. During the early 1940s this Gestapo-trained unit was responsible for the deaths of thousands of Jews in the Romanian capital, Bucharest. When the war ended, Trifa fled to America. He joined the Romanian

Orthodox Church and, by 1952, had become its leader. To John he was the 'Butcher of Bucharest'. To his followers he had become His Grace Bishop Valerian.

Trifa was rarely seen in public, spending his days in hiding at his church headquarters sixty miles west of Detroit. The estate spanned 200 acres and was staffed by security guards, some of whom had served with Trifa in the Iron Guard. John was determined to get a shot of their leader, and spent many a night trying to think up a plan that would get him inside with a hidden camera. The day before we were due to go to Trifa's HQ we hired a beat-up van from a local fixer called Denny Debbaudt. I would drive it to the compound outside the gates of the HQ very early next morning. Then, after putting a black drape across the back window, I would cut a small slit through which I could film the entry gates.

It was the middle of winter and one of the coldest days I can remember. We knew the van would attract suspicion so we had to make it look as if it had just been parked there, with no one inside. As we couldn't leave the engine running, Denny had supplied us with a tiny heater. I placed this under the back window to stop it freezing over and obscuring the view. We couldn't talk for fear of alerting one of the guards, so after a few minutes John signalled that he was going to slip quietly outside the van and walk in the surrounding parkland with our production assistant Lynn Marriott.

After about an hour inside the freezing van, Phil and I were shivering and our lips were numb. To make matters even worse, we had drunk lots of tea at breakfast time and were by now sitting cross-legged. We couldn't even afford to wedge open a door to take a leak, because it would show up in the thick snow that surrounded the van. Lesson learned – take a bottle. Just as well we resisted the temptation, though. At around 10 a.m., one of Trifa's henchmen became suspicious and came out of the security lodge to check on the vehicle. His face came right up to the window, with me filming him behind the black drape. Then he moved around to the front of the van, jotting down the registration number.

Meanwhile John had hit on a mad idea while walking around the parkland. Despite the sub-zero temperatures, he was going to jump in a lake. Taking a deep breath and closing his eyes, he ran, leapt in the air and landed in the water, breaking the ice as he came down. He then went up to the security lodge and asked to go inside to get dried off. He told the guard that he and Lynn were a courting couple who'd slipped on some ice while taking an early morning lovers' stroll. I filmed his conversation with the guard – then watched the two of them go inside.

Of course, I didn't get the full story of what he had done until after he came out about three hours later. By then he had gained entry to Trifa's inner sanctum, getting covert film of him walking around the grounds. I had also picked up shots of the self-styled bishop, strolling about with another Iron Guard friend called Stelian Stanicel, responsible for leading an execution squad in Bucharest Jail. It was the result we all wanted, but by the time John ran back to the van all our thoughts were on more pressing matters. Phil and I were only concerned with getting to a gents. John was deeply worried that his private parts would never thaw out.

Happily they did, and John and I worked together again many times over the next few years. The most memorable assignment of all came in 1983 when he, and researcher Patrick Buckley, tracked down a Nazi much more infamous than Trifa or Maikovskis. In both their cases it could be argued that they were functionaries, merely obeying orders. But when it came to Walter Rauff, we were dealing with one of the true architects of the Holocaust.

In Nazi parlance, Rauff was in charge of 'automotive affairs'. To you and me, this meant he was the man who developed and produced the mobile gas van, an invention that killed more than 200,000 people. Rauff invented the van in response to a request from Heinrich Himmler, who was responsible for supervising the so-called Final Solution. Himmler was worried that mass executions of Jews by firing squad was too time consuming. It was also messy, and took a psychological toll on SS officers who pulled the triggers and pushed the bodies into the graves. Working in secrecy in his Berlin office, Rauff developed the prototype. It was then taken to a concentration camp and tested on forty Russian prisoners of war before an audience of SS men. The van was driven a short distance, then stopped. When the door was opened, the forty bodies that had been pressing up against it tumbled out. Their skin was pinkish, which indicated to scientists that the victims had been poisoned by gas, and not simply suffocated from lack of oxygen.

The van was deemed a great success as a result of this experiment, and Rauff organized the manufacture of thirty more which then went into service, sometimes disguised as Red Cross ambulances. Jewish families were herded into an airtight compartment on the pretext of being resettled. They were then driven off, with the driver pulling a lever in his cabin to redirect the carbon monoxide engine exhaust on to his human cargo in the back. The journey would continue until the banging and screaming stopped.

Rauff was immensely proud of his invention. He set about his work with zeal, concerning himself with every last detail of the design, and trying constantly to improve the efficiency of his product. One report he commissioned gave precise instructions to the vans' drivers:

> The application of gas usually is not undertaken correctly. In order to come to an end as fast as possible the driver presses the accelerator to the fullest extent. By doing that, the persons to be executed suffer death from suffocation and not death by dozing off as was planned. My directions have proved that by the correct adjust-

ment of the levers, death comes faster and prisoners fall asleep peacefully. Distorted faces and excretions, such as would have been seen, are no longer noticed.

Rauff's vans continued in service until 1942, when the Nazis developed an even more efficient extermination process – the gas chambers of Auschwitz and Dachau. He was posted to Northern Italy as SS chief, and awarded the German Medal of Honour by Himmler in recognition of his part in helping wipe out the Jewish race. In 1945, just weeks before the German surrender he was arrested by American troops, but managed to escape before his interrogation. He fled to Naples and was hidden away by a Catholic priest. Months later, when his family rejoined him, he went to work in the Middle East. Then, in 1958, he took a flight to his final refuge – Chile.

Although attempts had been made to extradite Rauff back to West Germany, the Chilean government had blocked them. At the age of seventy-seven he was now able to live out his days in comfortable retirement. He had been guilty of some of the most appalling crimes against humanity, but he remained a fugitive from justice. He had got away with it.

Patrick and John traced Rauff to La Condes, a smart suburb of Chile's capital, Santiago. He lived in a cul-de-sac just off the main road. His bungalow was guarded by a ferocious alsatian and all his errands were run by two housekeepers. We spent a couple of days driving around trying to find a vantage point where I could put a camera trained on his bungalow, without me being seen. The trouble was, all the surrounding streets were low-rise and there was nowhere I could go to get the shot we needed.

We decided instead to hire a little red Nissan van, which was a common works vehicle in the area. I came up with the thought of filling the back compartment with whisky boxes – the idea being that anybody who looked inside would think it was a normal delivery van. One of the boxes was for Johnnie

Walker Black Label which, for covert filming purposes, was ideal. I cut out the black strip, and replaced it with a thin black flap that I could pull back and poke a small lens through. With my camera disguised, we parked the van at the end of the road and prepared for our target to emerge from his home.

Unfortunately he wasn't in a hurry. Day after day we drove to the corner of the cul-de-sac. Patrick would jump out, dressed in a boiler suit to make himself look like a workman, then walk to another street to be picked up by Dave Woods, our sound recordist. John and I would stay in the van, watching and waiting. We were in a cramped, confined space and, as it stayed parked up in the South American sunshine, the vehicle would become extremely hot and stuffy. Unable to speak in more than a whisper, the only time we made a noise was to eat our little chocolate bars or open our canned drinks. When the time came to call it a day we would stand up, our legs and bottoms almost numb.

One day we got information that Rauff's son, who lived nearby, was going to arrive at the house to take his father for lunch. Again we took up our position in the van and waited for something to happen. Suddenly, around midday, there was movement: a podgy, bald, bespectacled old man appeared at the gate of the bungalow. I switched on the camera, but by the time the film started rotating, he'd gone. Rauff had appeared for literally five seconds before vanishing back inside his home. Then, despite our tip-off, his lunch date failed to materialize. After so much time in the van the frustration was deep, but at least we knew for certain that our man was there. We felt that the prize was dangling in front of our eyes – and none of us was prepared to leave until it had been grasped.

But the waiting just continued. Every morning at 7 a.m., we would park the van, and convince ourselves that today would be the day. One evening Patrick and John had a discussion and decided on a more direct attempt to flush out our target. The next day Patrick walked up to the door and, in perfect Spanish, requested an interview. But instead of getting Rauff, he was greeted by a housekeeper who denied all knowledge of his existence or whereabouts. Later Patrick went back up the path to hand in a letter, and found himself almost pinned to the wall by the guard dog. We reverted to the van option. By this time, Patrick and Dave had had enough of cruising around Santiago dressed as plumbers, so they had joined us inside our hot and stuffy vehicle.

On our second Saturday in the van it finally happened. Around lunchtime I saw the garden gate open and the man himself emerge. I gave a thumbs up sign to the rest of the team as the camera sprang into action. It was the first time this notorious Nazi had ever been caught on moving film. Rauff stood at the gate for a moment, pushed it forward and started walking up the cul-de-sac towards the main road, passing our van. From having nothing at all we now had about forty-seconds' worth of usable shots that would be like gold dust in the resulting film. John could hardly contain his excitement. He decided there and then to doorstep Rauff. He told Dave to start the engine and drive the van to the main road. We parked up, jumped out and intercepted Rauff as he turned the corner. For the first time in almost forty years, he was going to be asked to account for his crimes:

JOHN: Good morning, Mr Rauff. I'd like to talk to you about your activities in the war.

RAUFF: No, er, interview.

JOHN: You're a very lucky man still to be living here, don't you think?

RAUFF: Yes, Chile is a nice country.

JOHN: Do you feel any guilt for what you did in the war? Any regrets now you've had time to think about it?

RAUFF: That's all.
JOHN: Do you have any guilt, any conscience?
RAUFF: Please don't ask more, nothing.
JOHN: You felt safe here, didn't you?
RAUFF: Eh? Why are you waiting here?
JOHN: We're waiting for you, Mr Rauff. Did you read our letter?
RAUFF: Ja, I read it all.
JOHN: But you don't want to say anything?
RAUFF: No.
JOHN: Are you still a Nazi?
RAUFF: Eh?
JOHN: Are you still a Nazi?
RAUFF: Goodbye.

John carried on in this vein until Rauff managed to scurry inside his son's house about a hundred yards away. After eight days inside the van we had done what we'd set out to do. Even reading the script now brings back the sense of exhilaration we all felt at the time.

Colonel Rauff's Refuge was one of those powerful films that caught the public's imagination. The American networks all bought our exclusive footage of the war criminal, and there was renewed pressure on Chile to hand him over. But Rauff remained free until he died in May 1984 – nine months after the programme was transmitted.

Anyone who doubts whether he should have been pursued and punished all those years after the war should take note of a letter he sent to a friend shortly before his death. Time had clearly done nothing to change him; his remorseless anti-Semitism remained unchecked. 'Why can't people understand,' he asked, 'that everything in America is regulated by Jews?' And, explaining his decision to renounce the Catholic faith, he wrote: 'I don't need priests to get to God. Himmler was the greatest God – the SS my religion.'

KIDNAPPED

Detective agencies come in all guises – from the international anti-counterfeiters employed by designer-label companies, to the back-street gumshoes hired to spy on suspected cheating partners. Private eyes will take on all sorts of work, but they usually advertise one particular area of expertise. Ian Withers was typical of the breed, but his own speciality was far from common. He had become known as Britain's leading child-snatcher.

In the mid-eighties he was a very busy man. So-called 'tug-of-love' cases were a common sight in the newspapers, and it was clear that the custody laws were not being implemented properly. Particular problems arose when one of the parents hailed from abroad. If they snatched their child and took him to another country it was immensely difficult for the other parent to regain custody – even if the law was on their side.

Producer David Darlow wanted to highlight the failings in the system by focusing on one father's battle to track down his son. Working with researcher Steve Boulton he came across Joe Yusuf, an electrician who was brought up in London's close-knit Turkish community. Eight years earlier Joe had married Sofia, a nightclub singer from Greece. The couple went on to have two children, but their marriage was a stormy one. By 1980, Sofia had started a long-lasting affair with a known Greek criminal called Spiros.

As the marriage crumbled, a custody battle developed over their son Nichos ('Nick') and daughter Nazif. After hearing about the backgrounds of the two parents, the courts came to an unusual decision. The children should live with their father until the age of seventeen, with their mother being granted once-a-week access. But Sofia was angry at the ruling and vowed to fight it. One afternoon she came to collect the children, then failed to return them home. Using a false passport, she boarded a cross-Channel ferry with her boyfriend, and drove across the continent to Greece, taking Nick and Nazif with her.

It was late in 1984 when we took up Joe's story, and by that time he was frantic. He had spent an estimated £15,000 trying to get his children back. His electrical business had gone on hold while he made trips back and forth to Greece. The British Embassy were of no help, and – as he was now operating outside British jurisdiction – no legal aid was available. Joe had to rely on a friend remortgaging her house to help pay for a succession of lawyers and private detectives.

Six months earlier he thought the saga had come to an end. After tracking down his wife he managed to get his case heard in front of a Greek court which then ruled in his favour. But minutes after the hearing he was attacked by a gang of thugs who snatched Nick from him and passed him back to his mother. He kept hold of Nazif, but his son was again gone. Sofia skipped her last known address and went into hiding. He had no idea where Nick had been taken.

We flew to Athens where Joe was beginning a fresh search for his seven-year-old boy. We followed him around the fairgrounds and arcades of Piraeus, a nearby seaside resort, as he showed people photos of Nick and asked them whether they had seen him. Although these trips were fruitless he did get a lead from a local detective who had been following Sofia's boyfriend, Spiros. He had trailed him to Salonica, some 300 miles from Athens, where he owned a boutique.

We hired two cars and drove to Salonica, by which time Joe had already arrived and found where Spiros was living. Keeping watch on the house, he quickly saw that Sofia lived there, too. Over the next couple of days we discovered that Sofia ran the boutique in the centre of town. While it hardly had any customers, it was always guarded by local heavies. One afternoon we saw the probable reason why: playing in a back room, under the watchful eye of his mother, was Nick.

Having established where his son was, all Joe now needed was a court bailiff to accompany him to the shop. Under Greek law he would then be free to take his son back. But, as usual, there was a sticking point. Spiros was a violent character feared around the town, and Joe could find no bailiff who would agree to take on the work.

It was at this point that he called in Ian Withers, the detective who had already successfully 'recovered' about 400 children around the world. He agreed to take on Joe's case for £200 a day plus expenses, and also insisted that he brought along a minder should any trouble develop. The man in question was Ray Foster: ex-SAS, tall, silent and strong as an ox. He would be known to the rest of us throughout the shoot as 'The Bullet'.

Withers and Foster spent three days keeping watch on the house and the boutique. After weighing up the risks they decided that neither was the place to attempt the snatch. Instead their preferred option was the junior school that Nick attended each morning. Joe was nervous about going into a classroom and whisking his son away in front of all his schoolfriends, but he would do anything to be reunited with his boy. With money fast running out, he also knew that the snatch had to be done as quickly as possible. With just a few hours to go, we interviewed him about the possible psychological effects his actions might have.

QUESTION: Have you really thought about what you're doing? Many people watching, especially mothers, will wonder whether you're doing the right thing.

JOE: Oh yes, I'm doing the right thing. I have the law on my side and the law didn't work. The longer I leave it the worse it will get for my son. If I knew that my wife was capable of looking after my son I wouldn't worry so much. I am thinking of his future.

QUESTION: Aren't you perhaps thinking more of your own?

JOE: No, I'm not. I'm thinking of my son's future. He's got a sister waiting back in England. I spent six months here trying to recover him. No, I'm not thinking of me...I'm thinking of my son's future.

Early next morning we parked outside the school: Joe, Withers, The Bullet and me. I was to film the snatch covertly, so I had concealed a small camera inside a holdall. The camera contained just five minutes' worth of film and I knew I had only one attempt at capturing the forthcoming action. Shortly before 9 a.m. we saw Sofia pull up in her boyfriend's white BMW. She got Nick out of the car, took him to the gates, got back inside the vehicle and drove away. A moment later, Withers gave the signal: the snatch was on.

I will never forget the next few minutes. With Joe leading the way we entered the school building, looking straight ahead and trying to ignore the strange glances from teachers and children milling about in the corridors. As he got to each door, Joe put his face to the glass, scanning the classroom for the face of his son. At the third door he saw him. He pushed it open, walked straight to Nick, lifted him up and walked out. At first the boy was dumbstruck. He looked confused but said nothing as Joe carried him out to the waiting BMW. But, once inside the car, he became like a wild animal – screaming, banging the windows, hurling abuse, clawing at his father's face. Joe was pleading with him to calm down, but he carried on yelling, jerking his body and attempting to get out of the door. This child was seven years old and literally terrified. It was the most distressing scene I've ever filmed in my life.

When we arrived back at the hotel, I explained to David and Steve what had happened. They agreed that no more filming should take place until Joe had managed to calm his son down. None of us had expected this sort of reaction from the boy, and we all believed that the presence of a camera would only make him worse. But, incredibly, Nick's attitude did change very soon afterwards. It turned out that his mother had told him his dad had left them and then been killed in a war back in England. His young mind had been confused when the father he thought dead suddenly turned up in his classroom. Within a few hours the warmth between father and son was clear for all to see. Nick wanted to hear all the news from home, how his sister was, what his old friends were up to.

But there wasn't much time for Joe to savour these moments. Withers insisted that we should get out of town as quickly as possible. He was sure the airports would have been told about the kidnapping, but didn't think the remote coastal ports would be alerted for another couple of days. With that advice in mind we set off on a 450-mile journey to Igoumenitsa, a small town on the west coast, where we could catch a car ferry out of Greece. I led the convoy with sound recordist Harry Brookes. When we got to the quayside, we set up to take a shot of Joe passing through Customs and boarding the boat. But we could see things weren't going to plan. Thanks to the radio-microphone that Harry had fitted to Joe's clothes, we could also hear what was happening:

OFFICIAL: Family name?
JOE: Yusuf, Yusuf.
OFFICIAL: You have children?
JOE: Yes, one.
OFFICIAL: You must stay here. Not possible to leave.
JOE: Why?
OFFICIAL: Why – I don't know. You must wait here for my chief. You must stay here, okay?

The small port had been alerted. In fact Joe's wife had been to court to press criminal charges, and he was being put under arrest. David became worried that we would be taken into custody too. The officials would have had descriptions of the three men who walked into the classroom – one of whom was me. Concerned that our film would be impounded he decided that we should travel back to Athens and take a flight from there. So we set off on an horrendous 600-mile journey through the mountains, arriving at the airport with just twenty minutes to spare. We were booked on a plane to Turin, from where we got a connecting flight back to England, with our film safely in hand.

In the meantime, Joe faced more hurdles to bringing his son home. After questioning at Igoumenitsa he was driven back to Salonica and charged with taking a child without the presence of a bailiff. The next morning he appeared in court with the prosecution demanding he receive a five-year jail sentence. The judge decided he should serve six months in prison but then agreed to release Joe, pending an appeal. With Nick at his side he promptly fled the courthouse and appealed to the British Embassy for help. Finally, after two days of negotiations, officials there put him on a plane back to London.

I was at Heathrow when he arrived along with his son. We drove both of them to a hotel near Regents Park for the final interviews, then set off to Essex where Joe lived with his new partner. When we got to the street, I jumped out of the car and went inside the house where Nazif was waiting to greet her little brother. A minute later the front door bell rang and she bounded down the hall, opened the door and smothered him with hugs and kisses. Nick responded in kind. After witnessing the state he'd been in just a few days before, it was wonderful to see him so happy. For the rest of the day we filmed him playing in the garden and familiarizing himself with his old way of life.

Our programme raised many ethical questions, and – probably more than any other – put me through the emotional wringer. We all feel protective towards kids, especially when we have them ourselves. My own son and daughter were only young at the time and I couldn't help but wonder what effect a similar trauma would have had on them. Thankfully, Nick grew up safe and happy in the surroundings that he should never have been taken from in the first place. We still keep in touch, exchanging Christmas cards every year.

At the age of twenty-one, the problems of his past are now just distant memories.

LAMBS TO THE SLAUGHTER

When you spend your life on the road you can't be too choosy about your food, and I've had a few meals over the years that would make most people balk. They include the Korean snake, roast guinea pig in Ecuador, and grilled sparrow in Jordan. Once, while working in a remote part of Greece, I was served a plate of chips topped with a whole thrush. Luckily, I'm not a fussy eater, and I've certainly never been troubled by a vegetarian's conscience. On the other hand, like most confirmed carnivores, I see no reason for unnecessary suffering or cruelty down on the farm.

In the early nineties, many other meat-eaters were surprised to find themselves embroiled in a battle for animal rights. It followed a huge increase in the export of live sheep to the continent where they would endure long journeys to the slaughterhouse. On the way they would be denied food, rest and water. Often, many of the animals would be dead when they were pulled off the trailer at the other end – the victims of exhaustion, overcrowding and thirst.

Our production team had spent several weeks gathering evidence from former drivers who explained how their haulage companies encouraged them to break the feeding and resting rules in a bid to save money. They also had records of prosecutions brought against haulage firms by the RSPCA. However, to make our film come alive, we needed to persuade the charity to give us access to one of their undercover operations in which drivers were tailed across Europe.

Initially they weren't keen. The head of the undercover unit was worried that we would blow the identities of his officers who relied on anonymity. Eventually he was offered a trade. If he would let us join his team on an operation, we would give him some of the information we had from the drivers. He agreed. We passed on our file – which he could use in potential prosecutions – and we were given access to his officers.

The two undercover investigators we were to deal with were Andy Foxcroft and Brynn Pass. Their speciality was finding which farms were exporting the live animals, then following the delivery trucks taking them across the Channel, sometimes for thousands of miles. When the driver unloaded his haul at the other end they would pounce to take photographic evidence of the suffering that had been endured. Once, Brynn had trailed a lorry from Scotland all the way to Spain over a period of three days. When the vehicle arrived, half of the 300 sheep were dead – some from thirst, others from heat exhaustion. Brynn and Andy were more than happy for us to follow them on their latest operation, but they were insistent that we kept their anonymity. At all times they had to be filmed from the back so their faces couldn't be identified.

We met them both at a hotel in Taunton, in Somerset. They had information about a nearby farm that was about to send a shipment of lambs to an unknown location in France, and were now waiting for a call from a contact in the Ministry of Agriculture, who had to be kept informed of all live export movements. They warned us we could all be stuck there for another week before the call came. We went to bed that night prepared for a long wait. But, shortly after lunchtime the next day, I got a phone call in my room: the pick up was going to happen that afternoon.

We headed off towards the farm and found a field from where I could get a shot on a long lens. We got to within about 300 yards of the pens and could hear the sheep bleating. With the midwinter light fading fast I had to put a special attachment on the camera to boost the image. Then, once I'd got the shots, we headed back to the hotel to wait for further information from Brynn. By then he had taken up a surveillance position in a ditch and was watching the farm through an old pair of binoculars. It was early January, the temperature was below freezing, and standing still made your feet go numb with cold. Thinking of him stuck there for hours to gather his evidence made me realize how dedicated he and his colleagues were to their task. It may have been animals they were trying to protect, but they went about it with the professionalism of undercover agents guarding a VIP.

Around teatime, Brynn called to tell us the lorry was about to load up and leave. We drove back and I got the camera out in time to see the driver draw up, talk to the farmer, and begin herding the animals on to the back of his truck. We were a good half-mile away but we could clearly hear the sheep making their familiar 'baaa' sound across the freezing and misty fields. Then, when we saw the driver jump into the cab, we ran back to our own Renault Espace and waited in a lay-by for him to pass us on the main road leading to the motorway.

Andy and Brynn were ahead of us in a Vauxhall Cavalier that would serve as the main tail vehicle throughout the journey. An undercover colleague followed behind in a Ford Escort and would keep in contact with us by walkie-talkie. All three RSPCA men had received surveillance training by the police and used the terms with which any fan of cop series shows would be familiar: 'Black One, have you got the eyeball?' 'Yes, yes, Bravo Two.' Back in the Espace we agreed on a formula for keeping up with the undercover convoy: we would always stay three cars behind the Cavalier.

Driving down the A303 we still had no idea for which port the truck was heading. It wasn't until the driver took a turn on to the motorway that Brynn radioed over his hunch that the lorry was going to Portsmouth. A quick call to the harbour-master's office revealed that a ferry was indeed due to leave for Le Havre at midnight. Based on the farm's past export records it seemed most likely that our trucker was going to be on it, en route to his mystery location.

Following a quick walkie-talkie conference call we decided to ring the ferry company and book places for ourselves too. It turned out to be a wise move, as the driver ploughed on to the south coast and eventually led us to Portsmouth harbour. We followed on behind, dumping the Escort in the ferry compound, and settling into our cabins for the overnight crossing on *The Pride of Cherbourg*. Cramped in the tiny beds during the sailing it was virtually impossible to sleep. The engine noise was bad enough – but there was also the loud bleating of our sheep in the cargo hold below us.

When the ferry docked at around 6 a.m. it was the lorries that were let off first. Stuck in a queue of cars watching the truck driver disappear on to the quayside, we wondered if we would ever catch up. The undercover Cavalier disembarked in front of us and sped off after him. When it came to our turn I was so anxious to make up lost ground that I drove the Espace off the edge of the ramp. More haste, less speed: we were stuck there for another minute while the dock workers realigned the wheels. Despite this Keystone Cops moment, all wasn't lost. Seconds later the walkie-talkie crackled into life with Brynn's voice telling us he had caught up with the truck. He radioed the directions and they were all back within our sights shortly afterwards.

As we headed south through the countryside we still weren't sure where the pursuit would end. Early betting was on the small northern town of Artenay – a known drop-off point for British lambs. But then the lorry driver ignored the turn-off, leading Andy to guess he was headed for Sisteron in the south. If that was the case, we were in for a much longer journey. By now we had been on the road for sixteen hours, and Sisteron was another 300 miles away. Meanwhile I was beginning to realize the advantage of the undercover team's police training. At various points they would slow down and let the lorry get out of sight, only to speed up minutes later. When I asked Andy what they were doing he explained that they had studied the maps: if there was no turn-off for the driver to take, they preferred to drop back and stay out of his eyeline. Only when a turn-off was looming did they need to catch up and risk attracting the driver's suspicion.

A couple of hours after negotiating the gridlocked Boulevard Périphérique (the Paris version of the M25) we took another turning south towards Lyons. There the driver finally decided to make a stop at a service station, giving us the chance to grab a sandwich and answer some extremely urgent calls of nature. After about fifteen minutes the lorry was still parked up. Assuming the driver was inside the station having a meal, Andy got out his small video camera and walked up to the trailer to get film showing the condition of the sheep inside. We had fitted him with a radio-microphone so, as I filmed him collecting his video evidence, he was able to give us the following running commentary of what he was seeing.

> Right, these are the sheep on the vehicle that we've been tailing from Le Havre.
>
> I can see them in there, they're very quiet and subdued. I can hear some coughing, and the stench is unbelievable.
>
> And – oh shit – the driver's inside. I've just seen him in the wing mirror!

Luckily the driver didn't see Andy. He was asleep in his cab and would stay that way for another hour. Meanwhile the animals stayed in the trailer, freezing, and now without food, water or rest for twenty-two hours. We did a quick interview with Andy who explained why he felt so strongly about bringing the live export trade to an end:

> We are not against people eating meat or anything. If people want to do that, then fair enough. But what we do object to is the suffering these animals have to go through on the way to the slaughterhouse. Why can't they be killed at abattoirs near the farm instead of having to endure exhausting and freezing journeys like this?

The next few hours were exhausting for all of us, as well as the sheep. And as the tiredness set in, concentration began to wander and mistakes started to happen. A couple of times the Cavalier allowed itself to get too far behind the lorry, resulting in a mad 90 mph hour dash to catch up before the next turn-off. Then our Espace got stuck behind a cloth-capped Frenchman who insisted on driving well below the speed limit, leaving us a perilous distance behind the Cavalier. After a couple of these scares we got back on course and carried on with the journey, without incident, for another couple of hours. I had done my stint at the wheel and was happily dozing in the back of the Espace when I heard the familiar crackle of the walkie-talkie. I was expecting a routine update but instead got an anxious Brynn: 'Don't want to worry you guys, but we've been going for a while now and we can't see him. I've got an awful feeling he took that turn-off we just passed.'

Immediate panic. It was twenty-seven hours since we left Taunton. Now, after all the effort and concentration, there was the real possibility of us having lost the target. If we had, we would have to do the whole thing over again. We groaned at the thought – and grimaced at the potential cost. The RSPCA team pulled into a lay-by and flagged us down. We then had a quick 'what the hell do we do?' conference during which Keith Quirke, the soundman, scoured the map and suggested taking a country road that led into Sisteron. It was a long route but if we drove quickly we might actually get there before the lorry and then rejoin him as he headed into the town on the main road. It seemed a long shot but there was no other option.

An hour later we found ourselves on the outskirts of Sisteron, parked on the hard shoulder. If the driver had taken the motorway turn-off he would come out here. But were we too late? Had we missed him? In truth, we thought we had blown it. Heads were in hands, and emotions ranged from frustration to anger. Only Keith Staniforth, my assistant, was immune to the air of pessimism. Looking at his watch he noticed it was now past midnight, and told us all it was time we cheered up: 'Stop worrying, it's my birthday today. And I'm always lucky on my birthday.' I was just about to wish him many happy returns when – unbelievably – the lorry reappeared. The chase was back on. We went from despair to elation within seconds.

There was no way we were going to lose the lorry again after a scare like that. But, in the event, the last leg of the journey would only be short. We stayed on the driver's tail as he went through a deserted town centre and towards open country on the south side of Sisteron. It was 2 a.m. when he pulled on to a dirt track and headed towards some old farm buildings. We parked our vehicles in a lay-by, grabbed the camera and a portable electric light, and jumped out. It was a nerve-racking few seconds as we yomped across the farmland in pitch darkness. We could hardly see a thing – but we were only too aware of the loud barking dogs that were guarding the farm. Then, as we reached the buildings we heard a tap running. Keith turned on the light to illuminate a startled driver next to a standpipe, and I flicked on the record button to capture the confrontation.

KEITH: Hello, we're looking for the driver of that lorry.
DRIVER: That's me.
KEITH: Well, we're from Granada TV's *World In Action* programme – can you tell us why you've driven these animals for twenty-eight hours and forty minutes without any food, rest or water?

The driver stood open-mouthed for what seemed an age. It was obvious he couldn't believe that he'd been trailed all the way from Somerset by a full TV crew. Finally, he did the familiar hand in front of the camera routine and walked away, refusing to answer any more questions. Jumping inside his cab, he locked the door and got on to his mobile phone, presumably to tell his bosses back home what had happened.

As he was talking, we walked round to the back of his trailer where Brynn and Andy opened the doors. Inside were the 310 sheep that had been loaded at Taunton. All were alive, but they were so cramped that some were lying on top of others. Many were shaking in the sub-zero temperatures, others were coughing. Throughout the journey they'd been urinating and defecating – causing a smell that almost knocked you over. When the ramp was pulled down, a few of them could hardly get to their feet they were so exhausted. Those that could ran inside the farm pen and gulped down the food and water that had been prepared for them. In all probability that would be their last meal. They would be slaughtered the next day and their carcasses sold as locally produced lamb. Even confirmed meat-eaters like myself were appalled at the way they had been treated during their last couple of days of life.

We transmitted our film two weeks later, complete with secretly filmed sequences inside continental abattoirs. In a brilliant publicity stroke, the researcher Peter Trollope had persuaded the animal-loving actress Joanna Lumley to attend a special screening a couple of days earlier. She then

Left: Holding the microphone on one of my first assignments as a sound assistant.

Below and bottom: Leading film units at home (© Nicky Clarke) and abroad.

Above: On clapperboard duty with cameraman Mel Davies, 1966.

Left: Celebrating my Royal Television Society award with my wife Jackie.

Right: A journey on Hong Kong's Star Ferry in 1987 with Ian McBride.

Above: Filming with Mike Beckham.
© Alan Bale

Right: Michael Apted takes time off from Hollywood to direct the latest *7-Up* documentary, 1984.

Above: Preparing for take-off with Leslie Woodhead, 1979.

Right: EMERGED UNDERGROWTH STOP MOVIE GROOVY STOP – A camouflage-suited John Sheppard, with Russell Spurr, 1967.

Capturing the atmosphere at the start of Longnor's anti-smoking week.

Mounted police clear the demonstrators from outside the US Embassy in Grosvenor Square, 1969.

Cameramen get into position at the start of the anti-Vietnam war rally. I'm at the top of Nelson's Column.

On board a South Korean jet fighter in 1969, moments before throwing up.

Interviewing Yasser Arafat in his Jordanian hideaway, 1969.

PLO guerillas in training.

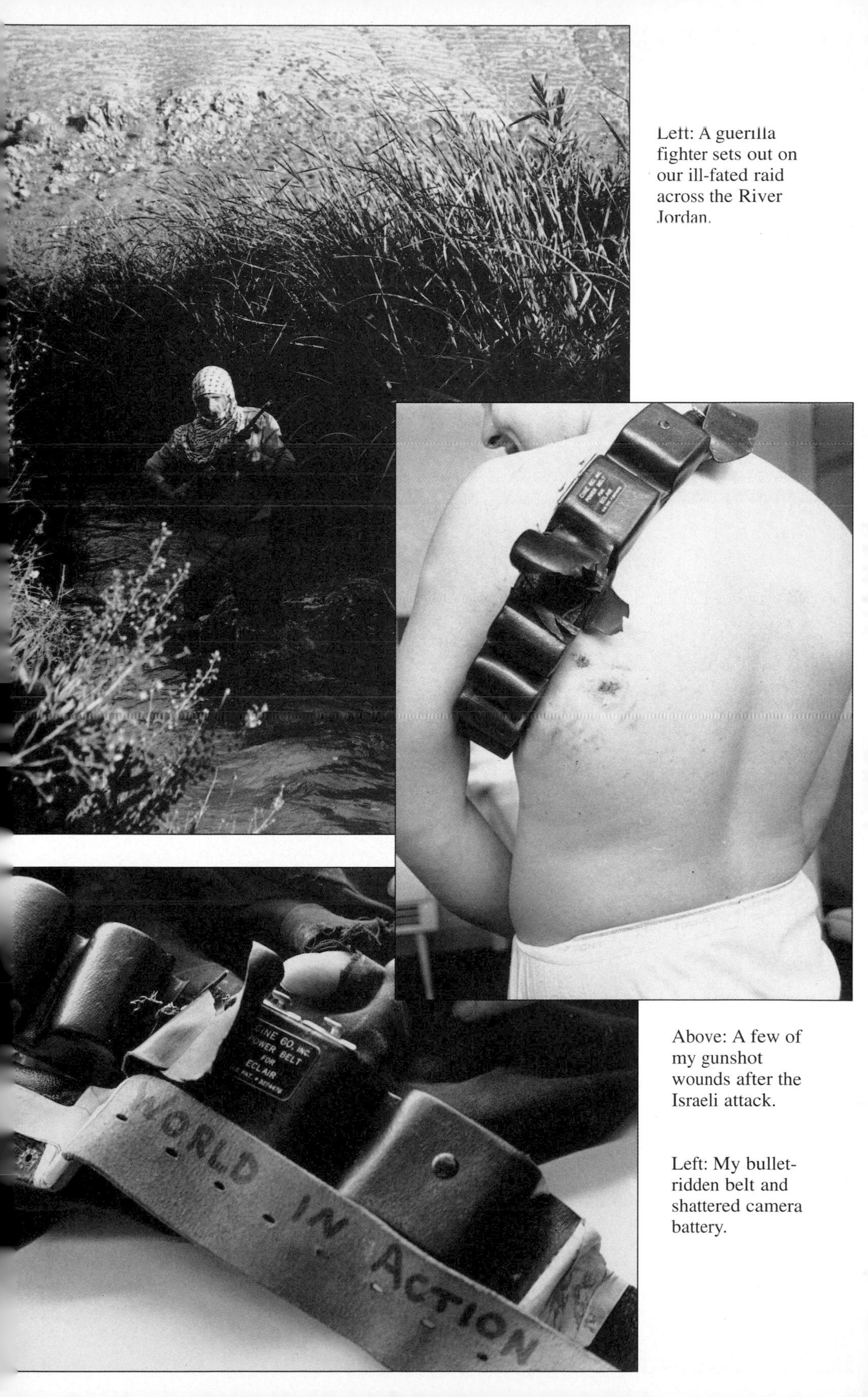

Left: A guerilla fighter sets out on our ill-fated raid across the River Jordan.

Above: A few of my gunshot wounds after the Israeli attack.

Left: My bullet-ridden belt and shattered camera battery.

Stephen Clarke and I search for Vietcong anti-personnel devices in the Laos jungle.

John Pilger with producer Charles Denton, Firebase Snuffy, Vietnam. © Alan Bale

held a press conference where, in front of the assembled newspaper photographers, she burst into tears: front page coverage was guaranteed. Within weeks the issue of live animal exports became huge, with mass demonstrations at the gates to the Channel ports. Several of them banned the trade, after passengers threatened to boycott their ferries. To this day the live export industry has never fully recovered.

For Andy and Brynn the programme provided ample visual evidence for another prosecution. They prepared their case and were able to show that the driver had broken every rule in the book. But just a week later they were on the road again – this time tailing another sheep lorry from Scotland to Spain.

CHAPTER 3
DECEPTIONS AND DISGUISES

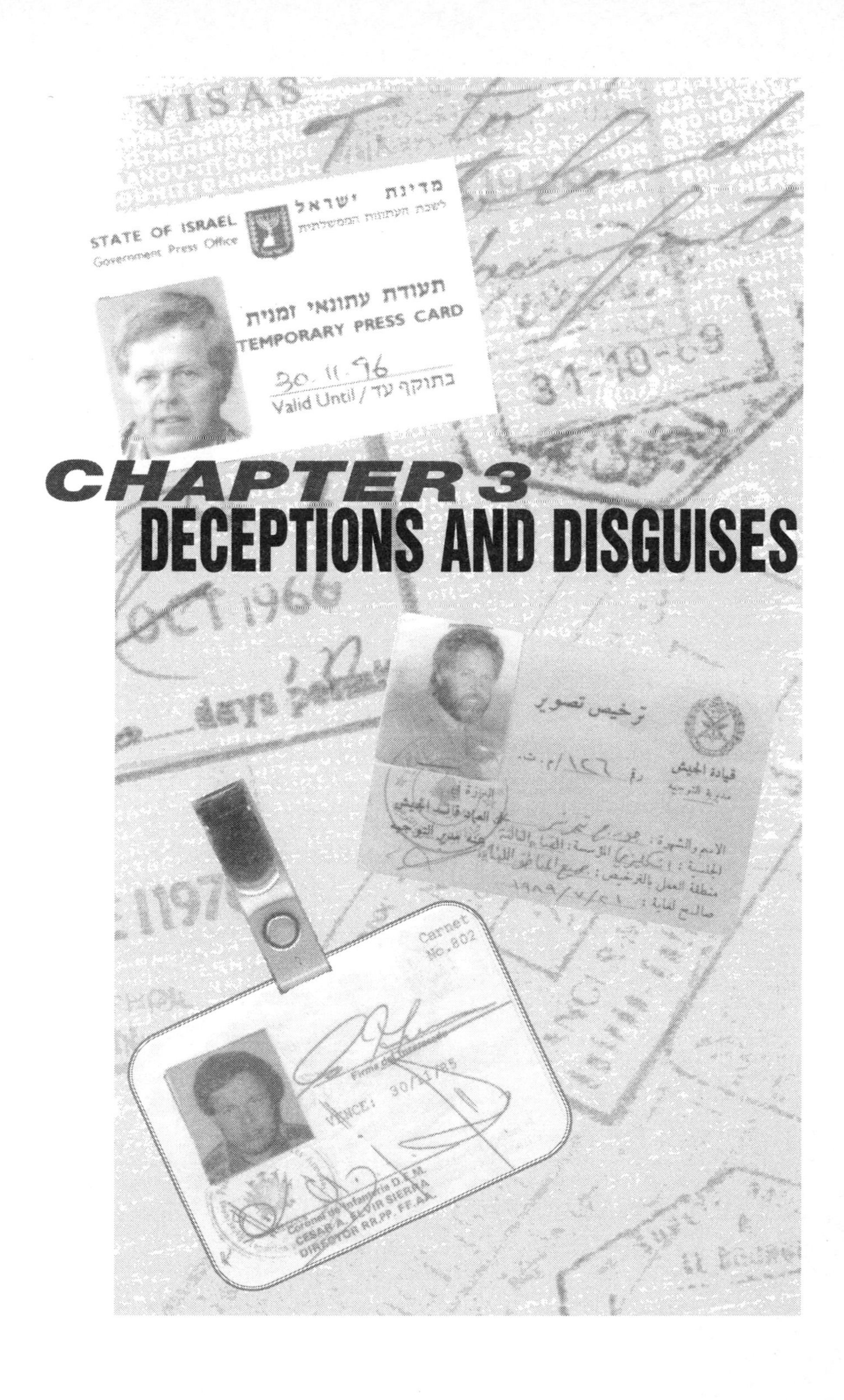

News has been described as 'something someone somewhere doesn't want published'. In the case of investigative journalism that someone will actively try to stop the story ever coming to light. It therefore follows that a certain economy with the truth is required while working on investigations. It ranges from little white lies about the emphasis of your programme, to full-scale whoppers about who you are and who you work for.

Of course there are ethical questions about tolling lies in order to gain access to somewhere, or concealing your identity so you can get close to someone. But I can honestly say that I've never been asked to take part in a deception that didn't have an ultimately good purpose. How can you bring a dictator's human rights abuses to light without going to his country to get first-hand evidence? Do you think he would let you in if he knew the real purpose of your visit? Would a dodgy salesman stick to the same law-breaking patter if I said I worked in TV current affairs, instead of the plumbing industry? And would he ever think to check my 'toolbag' for a concealed camera?

Deceptions can be elaborate and involve meticulous planning. However, despite your best efforts, a cover story can unravel and you can find yourself in real trouble.

Back in the seventies Paraguay was thought to be the hideout of Josef Mengele, the notorious Nazi doctor who carried out human experiments on concentration camp victims. The country was then under the right-wing dictatorship of President Stroessner. But while he provided a welcoming haven for war criminals and international terrorists, Stroessner certainly did not appreciate the presence of prying journalists.

Producer Mike Beckham and researcher John Ware led our hunt to track down Mengele. They decided we would enter Paraguay under the pretext of making an educational film about butterflies. Graphic artists made up special cards and leaflets promoting our mythical company 'Travel Films'. If we were ever challenged by the police or military these were to be produced. The cards listed Mike as the company director, with Alan Bale and myself as associates. They gave an address in London as our HQ and included made-up endorsement quotes from the likes of *Business Week* and *Educational Film Monthly*. They even contained a list of 'awards' that we'd supposedly won for our fictional films:

LAST SUMMER
(An hour-long documentary following deer hunters through Swedish Lapland)

1st Prize, Salerno International Film Festival
2nd Prize, Mannheim International Film Festival

THE INCAS
(An hour-long film on the lost tribes of Peru)

2nd Prize, Cork International Film Festival

THE SUN NEVER SETS . . .
(A film about South Africa's white settler farmers set in the beautiful province of Transvaal)

1st Prize, Berlin Film Festival

Armed with our new identities we set about trying to find Mengele, visiting Paraguay's border with Brazil and filming in and around the capital Asunción. There was a large German community in the city and it was here that many of the old Nazis had sought refuge after the war. Not surprisingly, they were also extremely suspicious of TV crews. So, when not pretending to film nature scenes in the park, I kept my equipment hidden in a black bag. A favourite trick was to pretend that a car had broken down. While I bent down to look inside the engine or fix a 'puncture', my camera would be taking shots of various buildings and people.

A week into the shoot we went to meet Mike at his hotel, only to find his car abandoned in the middle of the road with all the doors open. When Alan ran up to his room, there was no trace of Mike ever having been there. Only with the help of the US ambassador, whom we had interviewed a few days previously, did we discover what had happened to him. He'd been arrested by armed police and accused of being an American spy. Officers had taken him to an infamous government detention centre known as 'the pink building' for interrogation. While being held captive he was made to stand upright against a wall all night, with a gun-wielding guard watching him. During the night the police brought a Brazilian journalist into the cell and beat him up.

With the assistance of the ambassador, Mike was finally released, escorted on to a plane and barred from re-entering Paraguay. Alan and I destroyed a lot of paperwork and managed to get what material we had already shot out of the country. But we weren't there long enough to find Mengele. Despite our best efforts we had attracted suspicion and been rumbled. We later learned that about one in three people in the capital were in some way connected to the security services.

Fortunately, though, such experiences have been rare. Courage, confidence – and luck – have resulted in the vast majority of deceptions being successful. The viewers have seen some amazing sights. But producers and crews have had to lead double lives in order to bring them to the screen.

CANTERBURY TALES

> Film shot under the cover of the Archbishop of Canterbury's recent visit to South Africa has been smuggled into Britain by a Granada camera team. The Archbishop, Dr Michael Ramsey, knew nothing of the illicit filming, which is about starvation on special black reservations. But a Lambeth Palace spokesman said he will be watching the film with great interest when it is shown on Monday night.
>
> *Daily Mail*, 18 December 1970

Filming in South Africa was always risky during the apartheid years. On my first trip I was arrested, stripped to my underpants and thrown in jail. It was my début foreign assignment as a camera assistant, working alongside one of Granada's legendary current affairs producers, Brian Moser. The year was 1966 and he was making a film about the conditions in the former British protectorate of Basutoland. It had cut free from Britain a few years earlier and was now in the run-up to declaring itself the Republic of Lesotho.

Basutoland may have been independent in theory but, in reality, it was surrounded and dominated by its all-powerful white neighbour. While it had huge mineral wealth its people were impoverished. Around the gold and diamond mines we saw people frantically panning the rivers in an attempt to find a tiny nugget that would bring them some income. In a land that was so naturally rich, the people were eking out a meagre existence.

Towards the end of the project, we heard on the radio that South Africa's leader, Dr H.F. Verwoerd, had been asassinated. Verwoerd, who had been the architect of much of the country's most repressive apartheid laws, was widely reviled around the world for his white supremacist views. But, ironically, many whites had turned against him before his death, denouncing him as too liberal.

Brian led us on to the streets of Basutoland's main city, Maseru, to get people's reaction to the killing. One man was particularly keen to offer his views, denouncing Verwoerd as 'the devil himself' and saying that his death was the best news he had heard in a long time. Our cameras had attracted a sizeable crowd, and while this man's opinions were more or less typical, they drew the attention of a couple of South African sympathizers who had joined the throng. We later learned that they were informants who had immediately gone off to report the interviews to the authorities.

That afternoon I was in the Lancers Inn hotel with cameraman Mel Davies when there was a loud knock on our door. It was the police demanding to know where our film was. We were marched off to Maseru prison, along with our sound recordist Roy Minge. The guards frisked us and ordered us to undress. Then they led us across a dusty inner courtyard to our cells for further questioning. On the way we passed scores of black prisoners, most of them in chains, all of them in the classic hooped T-shirts. Although some had obviously been inside for a very long time, they wore expressions of disbelief as we walked by. White prisoners in this part of the world were simply unheard of.

I was just twenty-one, tense, frightened, and happy to leave all the talking to Mel and Roy. The trouble was, they couldn't help. Following the street interviews, Brian had collected up the rolls of film and disappeared. None of us knew where he – or the offending material – had gone.

After a few hours we were released and ordered out of

Basutoland with a warning not to come back. We drove across the border to Bloemfontein, only to be arrested by South African guards who then subjected us to a further round of questioning. After an hour they let us go, clearly furious at their failure to find our film. We drove away, checked into a local hotel and read about ourselves in the evening newspapers – a British TV crew allegedly attempting to stir up hatred on the streets of Maseru. The reports even accused us of bribing passers-by with bottles of whisky in order to get anti-Verwoerd quotes. We were treated like lepers during the rest of our stay, with the hotel staff insisting we ate our meals in a far corner of the dining room, with a curtain pulled around us.

While at the hotel, Mel managed to track down Brian back at the Lancers Inn. He warned him not to cross the border or he – like us – would be searched, and his film inevitably seized. To avoid the Bloemfontein guards, Brian then chartered a planc from Maseru to Johannesberg, with all the rolls of film concealed in a large tin trunk. When the plane touched down he convinced the Customs officers that he was a visiting geologist, and that the tins contained nothing more than harmless rock samples. Waved on his way, he caught a connecting flight back to the UK and edited a programme for an audience of millions. This experience taught me several important lessons about filming in South Africa – not least the need for complete secrecy when criticizing a reactionary government. It was a lesson I would put into practice four years later.

By 1970 the horrors of apartheid were plumbing new depths. The government was forcibly removing tens of thousands of blacks from their homes in the so-called European areas, wrenching 'non-productive' women and children from their husbands and dumping them in newly created reservations. Whereas their old settlements had been built next to rivers and on lush farmland, the new homelands were in the middle of nowhere, some on the edge of the Kalahari Desert. There were no jobs. Nothing could grow. People who had arrived fit and healthy were now impoverished and showing signs of chronic malnutrition. Children were beginning to die from starvation.

Leslie Woodhead and Stephen Clarke were two producers who had been monitoring the mounting crisis in the reserves. They had made contact with a number of British doctors and aid workers who were seeing at first hand the effects on the health of the black population. They were determined to bring the consequences of the government's resettlement policy to world attention, but they knew it would be impossible to make such a programme openly.

But, as often happens, an opportunity suddenly presented itself. Stephen read of an impending visit to South Africa by the Archbishop of Canterbury, Dr Michael Ramsey. He checked the itinerary with Lambeth Palace, then contacted the South African Embassy asking if it would be OK for a British documentary crew to follow the Archbishop as he toured the country, meeting his ministers. Within days the embassy said yes. We packed our Bibles and boarded the flight to Johannesburg.

Fascinating though his tour undoubtedly was, we had no intention of following the Archbishop around. We knew though that the South Africans were ultra-suspicious, and it was likely their agents would spy on us for the first few days to make sure our story checked out. So, when Dr Ramsey arrived at the government buildings in Pretoria, there we were, dutifully filming his every move. A minute or so after he went inside I was packing up my gear when I was tapped on the shoulder by a British cameraman called Mike Whittaker. He told me he was in town on a BBC project and, naturally, asked what we were doing. We gave him the cover story but Mike, who had recently completed a freelance stint on our programme, knew exactly what sort of agenda we followed.

'Archbishop of Canterbury? I don't think so, somehow,' he said with a smile. He agreed to ask no more questions, but wished us luck. We may have been rivals, but when it came to covering apartheid, the British media were on the same side.

And rightly so. The regime ruthlessly discriminated in favour of an élite minority, putting black Africans and Asians at a deliberate disadvantage. Everywhere you looked you saw the results: luxury mansions for whites, slum townships for blacks. The best schools and hospitals for those of European descent; illiteracy and low life expectancy for the black Africans.

Apartheid blighted lives on a grand scale but also reached into the most mundane areas. A couple of days after I arrived I bought a postcard to send home to my parents. I went into the main post office in the centre of Johannesburg and queued for a stamp, choosing the line that looked the shortest. But when I reached the front the woman behind the counter looked at me and shook her head, saying simply: 'Sir, I think you are in the wrong half.' I looked around and realized that everyone else in the queue was black. I had broken the segregation rule. If I still wanted a stamp I had to cross the hall and join the line reserved for whites.

But a little everyday discrimination in the big city was nothing compared to what was happening out in the countryside. A few days later we drove inland looking for one of the new settlements, known only by its impersonal government codename of 'Wyk 7'. We had been told about it by Donald and Rachel McKenzie, two British doctors who ran a mission hospital in the area. They had watched as 7,000 people were taken from their thriving little village and dumped in a desolate new homeland. Now they were dealing with the human consequences: a huge explosion of rickets, tuberculosis, pellagra, and – among children and the elderly – extreme hunger.

The McKenzies had got into trouble with the South African authorities when they started signing death certificates with the word 'starvation'. According to the state, such a condition didn't exist. They then risked further government wrath with an annual health report that concluded: 'The suffering witnessed in and around the hospital can only be described as a disgrace to the country.'

We stayed overnight in a town called Vryburg, about ninety miles from the settlement. Around four o'clock the following morning we left the shabby roadside motel along with the Rev. Cosmas Desmond who, as a priest, was allowed to go in and out of the reserve freely. He had warned us it was surrounded by security guards, so we decided to film at dawn before they awoke. During the drive we were all nervous. Simply straying from the main road in this part of the country was an offence for a white man. Entering the settlement with a camera would certainly have meant arrest and deportation.

After about an hour on the road, as dawn began to break, we saw a water tower on the horizon. As we got closer I started to make out the outline of a well, and a weather vane. Cosmos began to nod – we were about to enter Wyk 7. A minute or so later we turned off the dirt track, passed a security post and drove slowly through an entrance. We got out of the car as quietly as possible. Apart from the weather vane clanking in the wind there was no noise. But, as we continued to film, cockerels began to crow and dogs began to bark. All around us were little huts made of straw and grass. After about twenty minutes tiny faces started to appear at the doorways. These were the children who had been forcibly moved here. They faced a future on a reserve where the land couldn't support them. According to the McKenzies, many were suffering from kwashiorkor and marasmus – malnutrition disorders that led to weight loss, immune system depression, mental illness and, finally, death.

As far as we were aware, no one had ever filmed on one of the new homelands before. The images we were capturing were unique: proof that the South African government was dumping people in the wilds of the country, tearing families apart and endangering an entire race. But despite the power of the evidence, we knew we couldn't hang around. Less than half an hour after I'd set up the tripod, Leslie told me to pack it away. The wardens were still asleep but the sun was beginning to rise. And, as more people became aware of our presence, we were starting to attract a noisy and inquisitive crowd.

We jumped back in the car and drove out of the entrance. There and then Leslie made the decision to drive the 800 miles back to Johannesburg non-stop. Word of a white camera crew filming inside a settlement was bound to get out during the day, and eventually that news would seep back to the government. If we could get back to the city before nightfall and be seen filming the Archbishop, no one would think that we were the crew in question. And that's exactly what we did. Later that night, as Dr Ramsey toured a succession of churches, we tagged on behind. We were exhausted from the early start and the marathon journey, but we were providing ourselves with the perfect alibi.

As the night shoot came to an end I checked into the Sun Towers Hotel. I had seen the sickening face of apartheid close up and had had a bellyful of the officially sponsored racism that passed for government in South Africa. But I was in for one final reminder of the white attitude. The hotel receptionist – a recently arrived immigrant from Bolton – took my guest registration card and handed me my key. Then, gesturing to an elderly black bellhop, he yelled: 'Take the boss's cases to his room.' Not surprisingly, I was glad to check out the following day.

Back in Britain, Stephen sent a sample of soil collected at Wyk 7 for analysis. The lab came back with a report proving that the South African government had dumped large sections of its people in inappropriate areas, condemning thousands to a future of hunger and poverty. It concluded: 'The soil is totally unsuitable for crops or grazing in conditions of low annual rainfall.' During the previous twelve months it had rained just once at Wyk 7.

ITV showed *The Dumping Grounds* four days prior to Christmas. Before the annual holiday was over, I had received an official South African government notice banning me from entering the country again. It would be another sixteen years before I could return.

AT HOME WITH GENERAL PINOCHET

> It was a great pity that only 30 minutes could be devoted to this world scoop. It contained astonishing and horrifying material, and the highest praise is due to the programme team for their enterprise. Just how *did* they get their cameras into a women's prison?
>
> *Daily Mail*, 4 December 1973

Western students have long had a romantic attachment to Latin American revolutionaries. By the early seventies they had another hero to rank alongside the likes of Castro and Guevara. He had come to power in Chile, notable in South America for its commitment to the ballot box, and now making history with the election of an openly Marxist leader. Salvador Allende became President on a promise of sweeping nationalization and redistribution of wealth and land. He drew his support from the millions of working-class labourers who lived in the shanty towns around the big cities. For years they had been denied a share in the country's wealth, but now they had a leader who was committed to raising their living standards, and investing heavily in health and education programmes.

But three years into Allende's government Chile's powerful

middle class were in revolt, and looking to the army to smash their country's experiment with socialism. In September 1973 a four-man junta, headed by General Augusto Pinochet, duly obliged. In a ruthless coup, they led their troops on to the streets and assumed command. With Allende inside the Presidential Palace, they gave him an ultimatum: surrender within three minutes or be bombed. When he refused to come out they followed through with their threat, launching a ferocious bombing raid on the palace and reducing it to burning ruins. Allende was later found dead inside. Some say he was killed in the attack, others that he committed suicide rather than be captured.

Shortly after the coup I was watching a TV news report in which a Scandinavian cameraman was shot dead. He was filming on the streets of the capital, Santiago, when a soldier began shouting at him to stop recording. Undeterred, the cameraman carried on – only to be felled by a lethal bullet just seconds later. I was still thinking about how dangerous a place Chile had become for the media when I got the call to go to Santiago myself. By then, the country had been under the thumb of Pinochet and his generals for ten weeks.

Mike Beckham was again the producer. He had been in touch with opposition leaders in Santiago and was confident that we could make a film exposing the terrors that were being visited upon ordinary Chilean civilians. However, it would be almost impossible for us to go in as a current affairs documentary unit – particularly as we were becoming known for programmes on the subject of torture. Instead, we would visit the country as a freelance news crew, supposedly supplying pictures to the BBC and ITN bulletins back home. We applied for our visas and solemnly agreed that all the material we did shoot would be handed over to the military government for censorship.

We arrived in Santiago in the evening and went straight to the Carrera hotel in the city's main square. After checking in we went on to the roof to watch the capital descend into darkness and witness the last few frantic minutes before the 9 p.m. curfew. Bang on the hour, everything went still and all that could be heard was the distant sound of sniper fire. This came from the surrounding shanty towns like Neuova Matacona which housed some of Allende's most loyal supporters. They might have lost their leader, but a few of them were still putting up spirited resistance to the new regime. Suddenly, tanks appeared on the streets, and soldiers began setting up roadblocks. One of the purposes of the curfew was to cordon off the shanty towns so the troops could go in and search them house to house.

The following morning we saw some of the results of those searches. Bodies – bearing the scars of vicious beatings – were left dumped at the roadside. Others came floating, face down, along the city's main river. Independent observers told us that each day around 200 people were being admitted to the main Santiago mortuary with bullet wounds and head injuries. On a visit to Neuova Matacona we met a nun who said she had seen forty bodies in the week before we arrived. Like many others, she believed the troops had left the corpses on the streets in order to frighten people.

And frightened they were. Not only of being killed, but of being taken from their homes at gunpoint and being interrogated about their political sympathies. Thousands of Allende supporters, trade unionists and left-wing sympathizers from neighbouring countries had been rounded up and tortured by the new military rulers. Pinochet was determined to erase all traces of Marxism from the country. Anyone even suspected of supporting the previous regime was a target for his military thugs.

The most notorious of the torture centres was the national football stadium, where around 7,000 people were being detained. When we arrived outside, there were literally hundreds of women at the perimeter fence attempting to get information about their fathers, husbands and brothers who had simply 'disappeared'. Some told us they had been going there every day for weeks trying to find out whether their loved ones were still alive. A few days earlier, a group of women did get that news. But they were also told that their relatives had been sent to a new prison – down a disused coal mine.

The military commander at the stadium allowed us to go inside for just five minutes. He ordered us to film on a long lens and strictly forbade us to speak to any of the prisoners. I hurried in, setting up the camera on the turf. On the surrounding terraces sat thousands of men. All were waiting their turn for 'questioning'. We later learned that this would take place inside the three-storey complex of changing rooms that now served as a torture chamber.

The scale and brutality of that torture still has the power to shock. At a United Nations camp we spoke to several people bearing the physical and emotional scars from their time in the stadium. One man, who worked as an Allende press attaché, told us what happened after he was arrested inside the Presidential Palace.

> I really never dreamt of what man could do to man. They kicked me severely in the stomach. They hit me around the head, they poured water into my nose and mouth at the same time, and they gave me electric shocks. I was naked apart from the hood on my head – the beating lasted for around three hours.

Another man told us how his interrogation turned into a torture masterclass:

> I was tied up, hands and feet, in the infamous parrot perch position – it cuts into your wrists and ankles. From then on they went over to interrogating me, and tortur-

> ing me with electric shocks in the anus and genitals. This lasted for about two hours, during which a policeman gave a running commentary to the Chilean officers on what he was doing to me. The atmosphere was just like a lecture theatre, and a group of young Chilean officers who were on duty at the stadium came along to this particular torture session. The policeman kept them fully informed of what he was doing – and he was a specialist, I'll give him that.

One of Pinochet's fears was that Allende – even though dead – would remain a rallying figure for those on the Left. As a result, the final resting place of the murdered President remained a closely guarded secret. There were many stories about where his body had been taken, but no one had ever filmed his grave. About a week into the shoot Mike met up with the BBC correspondent Tim Ross. He was an expert on Chilean affairs, spoke the language perfectly and had many contacts. When Mike told him we wanted the first shots of the graveside, Tim got to work. A few days later he gave us the location – a cemetery in the small town of Vina del Mare.

When we got there we discovered that the gravediggers who knew the spot of the burial site had been sacked. However, we did come across an elderly woman who also had knowledge of the location. After some discussion she agreed to take a bunch of flowers to the adjoining plot, with me alongside her posing as a relative. Although there were no signs of any soldiers, we decided it was far too risky to take out a camera and tripod. Instead, I took along a small Beauliea camera concealed inside a black holdall. As we got to the unmarked site she laid the flowers and I switched on the camera. But the old lady was desperately nervous of being seen, and as soon as I got a few seconds' worth of material recorded, I agreed that it was time to go.

Back in the car we were jubilant – we had got the shot we

came for. I took out the film, put it in a tin and hid it under the rear carpet. We started the engine and prepared for the long journey back to the capital. Just then a military truck appeared from around a bend, heading towards us. There were about a dozen soldiers on board, with the leader in the front passenger seat. As he pointed a handgun out of the window we froze. Then, gesturing with the barrel, he ordered us to pull over and stop the engine.

After what we had witnessed over the previous few days we decided it was a bad idea to disobey Chilean soldiers. We pulled off the highway and screamed to a halt on the dusty hard shoulder. The man who'd been pointing the gun came up to the car, told us to get out and put our hands on the roof. For the next few minutes he and his colleagues frisked us and searched inside the vehicle. For a moment I thought they had mistaken us for Allende supporters, who had come to pay their respects at the graveside and were possibly armed. But it was just as likely they had been monitoring our movements from afar and were fully aware that we were a foreign film crew. Whatever they suspected, they finished their search and went back to their own truck with the leader gesturing to us to drive on. Luckily, though, they hadn't looked under the carpet. Our precious few seconds of film remained intact.

Back in Santiago, we made contact with various embassy officials who were helping Allende supporters flee the country. Some of these had extraordinary stories – like the Scandinavian official who was giving the dissidents false passports and dyeing their hair blonde. Then there was the Argentinian ambassador who had opened his doors to nearly 200 refugees – including five of Allende's former ministers. Although they were safe inside the embassy grounds, they faced arrest, beatings and probable death the very moment they stepped outside. And with Chilean soldiers waiting at the gates they could be trapped in there for years.

We were all pleased with the material we'd gathered, but

there was one more sequence we wanted to film before we left. Throughout our three weeks in Chile, we heard repeated stories about a prison where nearly all the inmates had been tortured simply because of their political sympathies. Descriptions of their injuries were legion. Some were said to bear burn marks, others had had their bones broken as a result of continuous beatings. Although we had come across such stories at the football stadium, these victims were different. According to our information, all of them were women.

After making inquiries at the UN camp Mike discovered the location of the prison, just outside Santiago. He also found a group of female visitors who were prepared to help us smuggle a camera inside. All we needed were false identities to enable us to get past the guards and make it appear as if we had a right to be there. The solution came from the International Red Cross. Local officials agreed to give us passes and vouch for us should we run into any difficulties while inside.

We met up with one particular woman who had agreed to carry my small Beauliea camera with her. Together we decided to place it at the bottom of a shopping trolley loaded with fruit for the prisoners. As the stone-faced Chilean guards opened the big steel gates at visiting time, our smuggler walked on ahead. I remember thinking how brave she was to be helping us expose the brutality of her country's new regime. A thorough search of her trolley could easily have led the guards to the camera and small audio-cassette recorder. And all around us were the reminders of what could happen to her if they found them.

Altogether there were ninety-two women in the jail. After being led across an internal garden we came to their dormitories. Just as we had been told, many of the inmates were battered and bruised. Most were lounging around talking, but others sat on their beds looking dazed and confused. All of them were being held without trial. According to UN officials, all but ten had undergone torture sessions.

As soon as our equipment was passed to us we began secretly filming the inmates. My small camera took only 100 feet of film at a time, which meant that each roll lasted just two minutes and forty seconds. Throughout the shoot I was watching the guards out of the corner of my eyes, and my heart was literally pounding. Pretending to be engaged in everyday conversation, we got some of the women talking about their recent experiences. One of them described what had happened while she was held at the stadium before being transferred to the jail:

> We were tortured more or less during eight hours. I was just hit. That's nothing in comparison with the things that have been done to other people. I was hit in the face and blindfolded. Other people were kicked, electricity was applied to them in different parts of the body, such as the tongue, breasts, genital organs and head. Ninety-five per cent of the women in this compound were tortured.

Another told us:

> First of all the police undressed me and then tied my hands together. Then, because I refused to say what they wanted me to say, they applied an electric current to my anus. I was blindfolded and they began to hit me on the head, just on the head, not in the face. I fainted. Then they trampled on my hands to wake me up and kept on questioning me.

We stayed inside the jail for about half an hour. I was so nervous of being caught that it felt like a day. When my rolls of film ran out I handed the recording equipment back to our smuggler. We then left through the steel gates showing our Red Cross passes, and hoping she would escape the suspicious eyes of the guards. Later that night she arrived at our hotel back in Santiago. She had come out safely, and our camera, film and sound recordings were all intact.

We arrived back in Britain with a scoop. For the first time there was hard evidence that the new military regime's use of torture was official government policy. But despite further exposés of Pinochet's brutality, the general stayed in power. Throughout his rule thousands of his opponents 'disappeared', and many more prisoners fell victim to his torturers. Perhaps he reflected on his record when he found himself under arrest in Britain twenty-five years later, holed up in a comfortable hotel, and enjoying regular visits from a former Prime Minister.

THE COST OF A CUPPA

> Most of this programme lay outside normal critical terms of reference because the team had to film it in secret, using home-made equipment and working at night . . . but it was tough, bloody-minded, excitable, and ready to defy government bans by sneaking into a country and spying, instead of relying on the official information services.
>
> *Daily Mail*, 18 March 1975

Of all the dedicated journalists I've worked with, Michael Gillard was probably the most driven. He arrived in the early seventies, choosing a current affairs TV career after a distinguished spell on the business desks of national newspapers. Within months of joining, he was providing us with the sort of exclusives that had made his name on Fleet Street. Michael was a mysterious character, often arriving at Granada's London HQ late in the afternoon as everyone else was preparing to leave. He was a loner who kept his own office door locked, rarely letting anyone know what stories he was working on. But when it came to financial matters, no one could touch him. He had built up the finest contacts in the business, and the result was a string of scoops about City scandals, white-collar frauds and crooked share dealings.

He also had an unrivalled talent as an interviewer. Physically intimidating in his black leather jacket and shades, he would dispense with any pre-filming small talk and go straight for the jugular. Many is the time I've set up the camera, arranged the lighting, and helped put an interviewee at ease, only for Michael to breeze in and reduce him to a gibbering wreck within minutes. Slick PR advisers would sit in the corner and squirm as he produced document after document to support his line of questioning. By the end the viewer was left in no doubt about their client's guilt. For me and other crew members, these verbal contests were always entertaining, but often brutal. I'm sure a boxing referee would have stopped some of them on grounds of cruelty.

If there was a criticism of business and finance subjects, it was that they were sometimes beyond the experience of the average viewer. But, in 1973, Michael turned up a story that had direct relevance to almost every adult in the land: even now, it's difficult to think of an edition that caused more widespread outrage. The subject was tea – and the conditions of the families working on the plantations to provide us Britons with our favourite brew. Before that programme the only images we had were the smiling faces that feature on the cartons of tea-bags in the supermarket. But by the time it ended, we knew that many of those workers were anything but happy. Some, in fact, were starving.

Michael's investigation, produced by David Hart, centred on a number of plantations in Sri Lanka, owned and operated by well-known British firms. It revealed how they paid men just 24 pence a day for picking 300lbs of tea leaves; for women, the daily wage was 18 pence. A doctor who examined the workers' children found widespread evidence of anaemia, malnutrition, rickets and hookworm. The companies, which were bound by law to provide accommodation, had crammed up to twelve people in tiny rooms designed for four. Sanitation was non-existent. Some families were getting their water from broken drains.

For British tea lovers, the programme was truly shocking. Newspapers cashed in on the outcry, publishing banner headlines about the workers' plight. A group of opposition Labour MPs – including the future Prime Minister Jim Callaghan – wrote an open letter to one firm describing how they were 'horror struck' by the conditions on its estates. Facing this barrage of bad publicity, the companies promised to investigate and improve matters. A year and a half later, it was time for us to check on their progress.

Although I had missed out on the first programme, I was around for the follow-up. This time Michael and David intended to broaden the story – looking at tea estates in India, as well as returning to the plantations of Sri Lanka. Such had been the worldwide condemnation after the first exposé, it had become impossible to film on any of the estates openly. The companies who owned them were now both secretive and security conscious. The Sri Lankan government was so sensitive that it had banned film crews. As a result, we decided to enter both countries undercover, filming only at night while the estate managers slept. Light equipment would be used as well – in my case a new Kodak 8mm cinecamera that recorded both pictures and sound and could be concealed quickly and easily.

We travelled first to Madras, then down to India's south-eastern province of Tamil Nadu, a lush, tropical peninsula between the Indian Ocean and the Bay of Bengal. Each night we would leave our hotel in Combiatore and travel the fifty or sixty miles to the tea estates that had been set up by the British colonialists a century earlier. Our car was the Ambassador, an Indian version of the 1950s Morris Oxford, complete with wooden fascia and bench seats. With seven of us on board I often elected to sit on the floor, cradling the camera and counting out the many three-minute-long rolls of film I would need for the shoot that lay ahead. Although this was an uncomfortable position, it made me less prone to heart failure than the rest of the team. Our Indian driver terrified them all when he insisted on hitting the pitch black country roads with his headlights off, on the grounds that it made him see better in the dark. He also had a tendency to drive at absolutely maximum speed, often swerving violently to miss the local ox-carts that travelled along the lanes laden with hay.

It was usually past midnight when we arrived at the plantations, slipping quietly past the darkened houses of the managers. We would then go into the workers' quarters, gently waking the parents and children and explaining to them what we were doing. As with the first programme, Michael and David had brought along an English-speaking doctor who could assess their overall health. For the next two to three hours he would talk to them and conduct full examinations.

From the beginning of these tests it was obvious that conditions were no better than those we had uncovered eighteen months earlier. Time after time the doctor would turn a child to my camera and describe the unmistakable signs of severe malnutrition: emaciated limbs, distended tummy, sunken eyes and scaly skin. After weighing and measuring dozens of youngsters he estimated that three-quarters of them were below the average bodyweight of other Indian children, some by as much as half.

Clearly the companies in India had put the bad publicity behind them and were getting on with the serious business of making money. When the first programme was transmitted, they had tried to blame the poor conditions on the collapse in the world price of tea. They said their estates were loss-makers; any profits they did manage to make were highly taxed. But since then tea prices had risen sharply, along with dividends to their shareholders. In India those benefits had not been passed on to the workers. Would it be any different in Sri Lanka?

Our journey to what was formerly Ceylon ended more than 6,000 feet above sea level in the highland town of Nuwara Eliya. As you drive in along the mountain roads, its surrounding countryside seems to have been covered with plush, deep green carpet. Only as you start to descend do you realize you're looking at thousands of tea bushes, freshly plucked. The town itself is a model of British Victorian architecture, with grand hotels, golf and country clubs. The days are hot and the nights cool with mountain mists bringing regular rains. Looking out over such a rich landscape I couldn't believe anyone could go hungry there.

That night, though, I was to see the reality. In home after home, the doctor examined children showing signs of chronic malnutrition and starvation. One five-year-old boy weighed little more than the average well-fed child of nine months; a two-year-old girl measured the same size as a premature baby born at thirty-six weeks. In one room we found a mother of five who had recently lost two children on the same day, due to starvation. Clinging on to her filthy robes, and letting out the weakest of cries, was her tiny daughter. According to the doctor she would also be dead within three months.

On the estates each family member received 3lbs of rice from the government each week – a third of it free and the rest of it subsidized. But this ration was enough to keep only one working adult above starvation level for two to three days. The cost of the subsidized portion was deducted from the workers' pay packets at the end of each month. The tiny amount they were left with had to provide food for the other four or five days. Usually they couldn't manage it, and their families simply went hungry. In turn, they were unable to fight off the many infections caused by overcrowding and lack of the most basic sanitation.

It was on our last night that we saw the most appalling example of the tea workers' living conditions. We had been filming on one plantation until around 2 a.m. when we were told of one man who was seriously ill. Until recently the company had provided him with a cattleshed where he lived with his two children. But when that collapsed, they had moved him to new quarters where all three were expected to eat and sleep. That accommodation, we were to discover, was a disused toilet.

Words can't really describe the scene inside that tiny, rancid cubicle. Suffice to say that even the Ceylonese doctor – well used to human misery – was visibly shaken. Unable to squeeze myself and the camera into the 4 x 5-foot room, I filmed from the doorway as he inspected the faeces-stained walls. He then examined the two young children, both of whom were diagnosed with anaemia and hookworm. The man, it turned out, had worked for his British company for twenty-six years. Asked why he didn't move out, he said the bosses had told him there was nowhere else to go.

As we drove away from the plantation our rented Peugeot got stuck in a ditch, leaving us to cadge a lift from a friend of one of our minders. Michael and David went into huddled conference about when to tell Hertz about their vehicle; letting them know too early could alert the authorities that a film crew had been snooping around again. But as they discussed the options, I was still in a state of shock. I had witnessed starvation in the likes of Biafra, Angola and Ethiopia. But here there was no war, the soil was fertile, and the people had jobs. It seemed unbelievable that while they provided us with drink, they themselves could not afford to eat.

Predictably the second programme caused a similar outcry to the first. On the night it was screened, Granada staged a live debate in which politicians, businessmen and aid workers put forward their own theories on how to change things for the better. Whether there was a real improvement is difficult to say. I find it hard to believe that people could still be starving to death on those estates twenty-five years later. On the other hand I recently read an article revealing that some tea workers were selling their children into domestic slavery because they couldn't afford to keep them.

Whatever the specific result of the tea exposés, they did mark out new territory for TV journalism. Before Michael's investigations, coverage of powerful multinationals was almost unheard of. Afterwards, every other current affairs series began to shine its light on Third World exploitation. As a result of the bad publicity, and ensuing consumer boycotts, many companies have been forced to clean up their act. But, without journalists committed to uncovering the truth, would they have carried on regardless?

BEARDS, BOOTS AND PANTALOONS

The end of the eighties saw communism collapsing throughout Europe. States from the Balkans to the Baltic were breaking free from Moscow's rule, and the cold war was coming to an end. But, away from the eastern bloc, another symbolic Soviet withdrawal was taking place. In 1980 Moscow had sent its troops into Afghanistan, in an attempt to support the communist government which was falling apart in the face of popular resistance. But, as the Americans had discovered in south-east Asia, a dedicated nationalist guerrilla force was impossible to defeat. After ten years the war was sapping the Soviet Union's economy and killing many of its brightest and best young soldiers. Moscow finally pulled out. No wonder Afghanistan became known as 'Russia's Vietnam'.

By the time I paid my first visit there the Red Army had been gone for almost a year, leaving in place a puppet government led by President Najibullah. However, despite financial backing and military training from Moscow, the new President's control stretched only to the capital, Kabul, and a couple of other major cities. A vast swathe of towns, villages and countryside was now in the grip of the Mujahedin, the Islamic fighters who had declared a 'holy war' against the Soviets, and who were now sworn to remove Najibullah.

David Bowen-Jones was a freelance producer who had visited Afghanistan many times since the start of the Russian occupation. Some years earlier he had made a film about one Mujahedin warlord who claimed direct descendancy from the prophet Mohammed, and so was revered as a saint – or *pir* – by his Muslim followers. Ismael Gaillani led a guerrilla group based just outside Afghanistan's second largest city, Kandahar. When word reached David that Ismael was on the point of taking control of the city he contacted our then editor, Stuart Prebble, and proposed a follow-up.

Stuart was particularly taken by Ismael's background – a rich playboy who had spent his young days loafing around Europe, gambling, driving fast cars and generally enjoying the good life. On one extended visit to London he had run into debt and taken a job managing the mini-bar supplies at the Kensington Hilton Hotel to help pay his bills. Stuart, who always liked to personalize big international issues, bought the idea. He hired David to make the programme as an independent producer, using me as his cameraman.

The idea of independents was still quite new to Granada in 1989. Even newer was David's approach to technology. As the producer, he decided he would also act as the sound recordist. Meanwhile I – who had used only small 16mm film cameras for the last twenty-five years – was about to be introduced to a whole new way of working. This would be the first *World In Action* to be shot entirely on videotape, using the electronic cameras that had been pioneered by news programmes. While I had no objection to trying something new I was nervous about the problems it could pose on this particular shoot. In the wilds of the desert I would be miles from any electricity supply, as well as out of range of any maintenance base. Then there was the dust. Who knew what havoc that would play with the sensitive wiring.

But there were other problems to overcome first. Getting to Afghanistan required a trip to Pakistan where we had arranged to meet with Gaillani family representatives. During phone conversations they had told David they would take us across the border to team up with Ismael and his fighters. But when we arrived in Islamabad, one of his relatives told us we were in for a lengthy wait. It was the holy month of Ramadan and it had been impossible to make contact with the guerrilla fighters over the border.

We kicked around for a few days, enjoying the sunshine, listening to the BBC World Service and reading the English language press. Then David paid a call to the British Embassy to let them know a UK crew was in town, and to ask for a security briefing. Just as he was leaving, the vice-consul asked him for the name of the programme he was working for. On being told it was *World In Action* he asked: 'Do you know a guy called George Turner?' David explained that he not only knew me, but that I was the cameraman on this project. 'Great,' said the man from the embassy. 'He's my cousin. You must all come round for lunch tomorrow.'

So it was that I found myself on the lawn of the British Embassy, catching up on old times with Alan Rogers, my mother's great-nephew. We hadn't been together for about twenty years but he had seen my credit on TV and knew where I worked. It was a great afternoon, during which we were able to bypass the anti-booze laws because we were drinking on what was officially British territory. Apart from the social side it also gave me the opportunity to get a full briefing on exactly what we were about to go into. Up to that point I had thought the Mujahedin was a single fighting force. According to Alan, 'the Muj' was hopelessly split, with the Gaillani family heading just one of seven different factions. Although they all wanted Najibullah out, it seemed they hated each other in equal measure. If our lives were in danger, the threat wasn't just from government forces – it came from other Muj groups too.

After a week in Islamabad we were told to go to the southern town of Quetta where more members of the Gaillani family would meet us. It was a typically chaotic Pakistani urban sprawl, unbearably hot and noisy. Child beggars lined the roads and drivers adopted the usual Third World motorist pose (one hand on the steering wheel, the other on the horn). Open sewers were a common sight, as were the kids playing in them. Down in the open air markets you could buy fly-covered sides of beef, unnamed antibiotics that promised a cure for everything, plus fake branded sports gear you could wear to impress your short-sighted friends back home (Adibas and Nikke were two of the most common names). Judging by the number of people carrying automatic weapons, Kalashnikovs were freely available too.

Two of Ismael's in-laws arrived at the hotel to tell us the arrangements. We would be taken to a village called Chaman, a few miles from the border, and smuggled past the UN soldiers who were controlling all traffic in and out of Afghanistan. To avoid suspicion we would have to look like the Pathans – the border race who for centuries had moved freely between the two countries. Their appearance was familiar to anyone who had seen news footage of the Mujahedin fighters: long flowing beards, head-dresses, waistcoats, boots and pantaloons. The Gaillanis said we'd be picked up the next day. We threw away our Bic razors and headed to one of Quetta's shopping bazaars to buy the necessary uniform.

In fact it was several days before two Toyota Land Cruisers turned up at the hotel to take us and our equipment to

Chaman. Once we arrived, there were further inexplicable delays. For two days the non-English-speaking Gaillani followers plied us with sweet tea and laid on huge banquets of freshly slaughtered sheep. In the early hours, while we lay in our sleeping bags under the stars, we could hear our Muj hosts singing, dancing and enjoying the delights of their hubble-bubble pipes. We never did find out exactly what they were smoking but the shouts and laughter were not consistent with Golden Virginia ready-rubbed.

Eventually, David's assistant – an Afghan called Habib – managed to persuade the guerrillas to get a move on. After a long and heated discussion with some of the senior Muj he was told that the preferred route through the border had been closed. The elders were simply taking their time discussing alternative ways in. The next morning they apparently reached their decision. The group's leader – a tall Biblical-looking man called Haji Latif – rounded us up into the two vehicles and led us off over the mountains. After about an hour of driving he turned his head towards me, raised his arms in triumph and shouted one word: 'Afghanistan!'

Haji may have been in his seventies but he wasn't averse to a loud tune. As soon as he announced our arrival inside his home country he ordered one of his fellow travellers to put on a tape of local music. For the next few hours it blared out at deafening volume, making any conversation with David impossible. The Toyota bounced up and down mountainsides, throwing us out of our rear seats, causing us to hit the roof of the vehicle repeatedly. Sometimes I swear this was happening in time to the music. Meanwhile, I wasn't sure which was going to bleed first – my head or my ears.

At least the noise helped take my mind off the heat. We were now travelling through a virtual desert with the earth scorched and plant life minimal. Inside the packed vehicle it felt as if we were being baked. I looked out of the back window to check on my equipment, laid out on a trailer and surrounded by around a dozen armed Muj. But through the clouds of dust I could barely make out their figures. My fears for the camera gear only heightened.

Finally, I got to test it out. After we had been driving for around ten hours we reached a wide river that on first sight looked impossible to cross. In the middle were several other vehicles that had been abandoned in the attempt, including a juggernaut lorry embedded into the far bank. To my immense relief the camera had stayed relatively clean under its blanket in the back and sprang into life as soon as I switched it on. I got shots of the wrecks in the river, then – holding the camera high – had to wade across the chest-level water to the other side. When I got there I began shooting another sequence. Our Muj party had attached ropes to the Land Cruisers and were pulling them both across. As David had warned me beforehand, these boys were tough.

Around midnight we got to our destination on the outskirts of Kandahar. Ismael's Muj fighters were based at a dam which formed part of a hydro-electric plant once controlled by the Russians. Much of the plant had been destroyed in the fighting, but the generator was still, amazingly, in working order. David and Habib were probably most relieved when they saw that our new home had a steady supply of hygienic running water. But for me the most pleasing sight was the generator. I had packed sixteen batteries for the journey, on the asumption that there would be no power once I got inside the country. Now here I was with probably the only reliable electricity supply outside Kabul.

Ismael came to greet us, surrounded by followers who clearly held their *pir* in awe. He was in his late thirties, dark, bearded, and wearing long-flowing white robes. By Afghan standards he was also clearly very wealthy, displaying gold chains, rings and a designer wristwatch. He spoke good English, had a natural authority and was keen to show his hospitality. Expecting our arrival he had ordered his men to fix us a meal which we all devoured while sitting cross-legged outside his HQ. Then with our stomachs full we headed off to our own base – a bomb-damaged building that had once housed maintenance machinery. This would be our home for the next week. Hot, dirty and fly-infested it may have been, but it was a welcome sight after an exhausting marathon journey.

The following morning we had a long meeting with Ismael, laying out the sort of activities we wanted to film. But if we were expecting to make a war movie we were in for a surprise. Ismael announced that he was no longer interested in fighting the Kabul regime. Instead he now saw himself as a peacemaker who could help bring the warring Mujahedin factions and the government forces together for the good of the country. It turned out that he had made tentative contacts with Kandahar's governor over the past few weeks. If we wanted, he could get us into the city to interview him. As usual, such a meeting would take a few days to organize.

In the meantime we followed Ismael and his men around, meeting up with his local leaders and visiting the villages that were now under his control. The countryside seemed to be a patchwork of Muj command: a Gaillani area here, a village controlled by the Jamiat group there. Once we passed a command post bearing the flag of a particularly extremist Muslim faction who believed the Gaillanis were too 'Western' in their outlook. The driver speeded up, Haji Latif fingered his rifle, Ismael looked tense. But thankfully any trouble was limited to a few catcalls from behind the razor wire.

Our Muj gang may have been spoiling for peace but they did like to use their weapons. It was usual to be driving through the country at high speed only for the vehicle to screech to a halt when they saw a bird or animal they could all shoot at. When one of them spotted a huge stray dog rambling along the road he told the driver to pull alongside so he could draw his pistol. Sensing our squeamishness at what was about to happen he made a gesture that suggested the animal might be rabid. Even if he was correct it was sickening to see the dog groan, collapse and die as the bullets were pumped into its body.

Later that day Ismael brought the convoy of vehicles to a stop at a ravine so his followers could jump in and cool down after a hard day on the road. As we stood around in the water he asked us what we were missing most from home. When one of us answered 'fish and chips' he went to his vehicle and came back with a large case filled with a stack of hand grenades. He then told us to get out of the ravine, pulled a pin and threw one of them in. Seconds later there was a massive underwater explosion, followed by hundreds of stunned fish floating to the surface. No prizes for guessing what was for tea that night.

The 'few days' before we could go to Kandahar turned into a week. Early in the morning Ismael drove us to a mountainside overlooking the city and handed us over to a lorry driver who was going all the way to the governor's residence. The main road into the city was littered with bombed-out tanks, the remnants of Russia's disastrous occupation. As we surveyed the damage the driver warned us that the road was also heavily mined. The chances of our own vehicle ending up as a roadside wreck were not remote.

In the end we did arrive in one piece. We were taken to a reception room and made to wait for half an hour before our new host appeared. The governor of Kandahar province was a big, striking man with a powerful handshake. At first he appeared bemused by our presence, looking with suspicion at our Mujahedin dress. But after hearing Habib translate our story he seemed to warm to us, impressed at our cheek, and offering to put us up for the night in a row of guest houses attached to his home. He also gave us an interview, explaining what it was like to be surrounded by hostile forces determined to turf him out and institute their own Islamic regime.

The following morning he summoned us to his office. He

said he'd had time to think about the programme we were making and now felt that we needed more material reflecting the government's point of view. He had been in contact with his political masters in Kabul: would we be interested in an interview with the President himself? The question was hardly out of his mouth before David said yes. Half an hour later we were being driven to board his personal military plane.

The airport itself resembled a scrapyard, and the Russian plane looked more like an American wartime model. We flew at around 10,000 feet passing over the most breathtaking mountains, rivers and unspoilt countryside. From the sky it looked sublime and peaceful. But, as we entered Kabul airspace, we got a sharp reminder of the reality. The pilot began releasing strips of tin foil that flew from the cockpit and trailed the aircraft. When I asked what was going on, Habib translated the pilot's explanation: this was a defence mechanism designed to deflect surface-to-air missiles.

Once we reached ground level there was a different hurdle. We were now in government-controlled territory – about to interview the President – but still dressed in guerrilla fighters' clothes. Plus, after three weeks without a shave I looked more Mujahedin than typical Lancastrian Boy. Spotting the etiquette problem, the governor ordered one of his aides to do a quick check on our waist and collar sizes. He then sent him into town to buy three Western outfits that we had to change into before being driven to the presidential palace.

Najibullah was a large, overweight man who had little to smile about as the Mujahedin surrounded his city determined to overthrow him. But when he heard our story he seemed genuinely amused. He invited us into his offices and gave David his exclusive interview. Ecstatic at our scoop, we made our way to the airport again and flew back to Kandahar. Once we arrived we changed back into our native gear, caught a lift to the mountainside and were picked up by Ismael. Hobnobbing with the President by day, eating with the Muj by night.

Our programme *Ismael's War* was an optimistic film showing how a large number of Afghans wanted to put the fighting behind them and work together for peace. Sadly though, that peace never came. The war against Najibullah's government continued until 1992 when he was overthrown by an alliance of Mujahedin factions. But, soon afterwards, the old tribal rivalries emerged and civil war erupted. Then out of the chaos emerged the Taliban, a fanatical Muslim group, supported by Pakistan. Quickly, they seized Kabul and declared their aim to set up the world's most pure Islamic state.

When I returned to Afghanistan in 1996 I was joined by the veteran ITN foreign correspondent Sandy Gall. Along with producer Mike Lewis we saw how the Taliban had taken control of 90 per cent of the country, and were still at war with the more traditional Mujahedin groups in the north. Back in Kabul life was bleak, with the people living under ultra-repressive laws. Female employment was illegal. Women could leave the home only if they dressed in ankle-length veils. Non-religious music was banned, along with movies and television. Multi-coloured signs were prohibited. Even many children's games were not allowed – just in case they distracted the youngsters from their religious studies.

At least with the Taliban in command, Western TV crews no longer had to disguise themselves as Muj. On my second visit I wore high street clothes and was clean shaven throughout – much to the relief of my daughter Joanna, who had insisted I remove the whiskers gained on my first trip. Afghan men, on the other hand, had to wear beards at all times. If not, they faced being thrown in prison until their facial hair grew back.

CHAPTER 4
NICE PLACE, SHAME ABOUT THE WAR

It's an irony that many of the world's most tortured countries are also the most beautiful. I've never seen more spectacular mountain ranges than on that treacherous drive into Afghanistan. The sunsets over the jungles of Nicaragua would take away the breath of the most seasoned traveller. And if you've ever found what you consider to be your perfect beach, I guarantee it has nothing on the Gaza Strip.

Sadly, most people never get to see these global beauty spots, except on TV screens. Even then, it's not the scenery that they'll be looking at. Instead it's the bombs and bullets, the refugees and the wreckage, the human despair and the dead.

I went to Uganda in the weeks after the savage dictator Idi Amin fled from power. The drive to the capital Kampala took us past sublime countryside where wildlife roamed. But lining the dirt track roads were the butchered bodies of his opponents. And during Angola's civil war I could look out over majestic African plains – the view spoiled by the rusting tanks that had been shelled and left to decay by the roadside.

Many of the chaotic troublespots I've visited have since found a sort of peace. I hope that in future they'll play host to tourists instead of war correspondents.

VIETNAM – THE QUIET MUTINY

By the time I arrived in Vietnam the war was six years old and there were 400,000 Americans under arms. But despite its numbers, the military might of the US was beginning to unravel. It was 1970 and the new wave of conscripts – or 'grunts' – were from the anti-war generation. They may have been given a uniform and a rifle but many of them were more interested in growing their hair, wearing love beads and rolling joints. Above all, they were interested in going back home in one piece. In the words of reporter John Pilger, we were witnessing 'the quiet mutiny of the greatest army in history'.

This was John's first TV programme, having spent all his previous career in newspapers. Then, as now, he was a committed journalist who had no truck with 'balanced' reporting. For him, the job of the journalist was to find the facts and tell the truth as he saw it, however uncomfortable it might be. On his début assignment for *World In Action* he wanted to bring back what he regarded as the great untold story of the war in south-east Asia.

I flew into Saigon in August. Tan Son Nhat was one of the busiest airports in the world, and – certainly to my ears – the noisiest. As I walked down the steps of my little Air Vietnam plane there were massed rows of C130 transporters, F4 Phantom Fighters and dozens of different types of helicopters. The sound of these scores of military craft taking off and landing was both awesome and frightening. This was serious military hardware and there was no doubt I was stepping into a combat zone that would instil fear in much more experienced media people than me.

My own fears weren't eased a few hours later when I went to pick up my accreditation pass from the US Public Affairs office. Within minutes I was photographed and fingerprinted, with the impressions of each finger stuck on a laminated card which read:

Turner, George J.
British Correspondent

The bearer of this card is a civilian non combatant serving with the armed forces of the United States, whose signature, photograph and fingerprints appear hereon. If the bearer of this card shall fall into the hands of the enemies of the US he shall at once show this card to the detaining authorities to assist in his identification. If the bearer is detained he is entitled to be given the same treatment and afforded the same privileges as a Major in the military service of the United States.

I read it over and over. 'Falling into the hands of the enemy' had a special meaning in Vietnam. Stories of torture were legion, Major or no Major. To this day, many American PoWs have failed to resurface.

My first taste of action came a couple of days later when we were allowed to film with a so-called 'long range mission'. These were fifty-five-day tours of combat undertaken by GIs. They took place out in the jungle where the enemy Vietcong fighters – the 'gooks' – were thought to be hiding out.

Journalists who wanted to join these tours were airlifted out from a helipad at Tan Son Nhat at 5 a.m. and flown back at teatime. It was the rainy season in August and as we flew over the vast swathes of jungle I could see that many of the craters caused by US bombing had filled with water. I was to learn later that such bombing was a tactical mistake by the Americans, as the craters had provided the enemy guerrilla fighters with instant fish ponds and, therefore, a ready supply of food.

After about an hour in the air we saw a clearing. A minute later a flare went up – the signal for us to land. The pilot told us he was going down and that we would have a maximum of fifteen seconds to get ourselves and all our gear out. Every additional second he was on the ground increased the risk of his being attacked by the enemy. We scrambled out in time and were met by the captain of the patrol. He was warm and welcoming but very strict about us keeping close to him and not wandering off on our own. To illustrate the dangers of an unscheduled walkabout he pulled back a section of undergrowth to reveal a booby trap. The enemy guerrillas had dug a pit underneath. It was only around four feet deep but at the bottom were dozens of bamboo shoots that had been sharpened and wedged in the mud so the points were sticking upwards. Anyone falling into the trap would be speared through the soles of the feet. According to the captain, several men had done so and bled to death.

Although there could be moments of intense and terrifying action on these patrols, the grunts spent the vast majority of their days in tense silence. Our patrol had been walking for four weeks, covering around a mile a day. They moved slowly, afraid of stepping on mines and trying not to make any noise for fear of alerting the enemy. They told us they were bored and craved some sort of excitement to break up the endless hours. Their greatest excitement on our day came when a member of the patrol spotted a chicken. As chickens don't live in the jungle, this could have meant the possible presence of gooks who had been fattening it up for dinner. So, bizarrely, the captain described it as a Vietcong chicken, and wrote up the incident in his daily report as an 'enemy sighting'.

Around 5 p.m. we were led back to the jungle clearing and our helicopter swooped down to pick us up and take us back to Saigon's Caravelle Hotel. A couple of hours later we sat on the veranda, freshly showered, drinking iced lime and soda. On balmy nights like these I would read up on the history of the war. How America had refused to recognize the North Vietnamese government of Ho Chi Minh after his country won its war against the French colonial rulers. How the US had created an alternative government in the South and financed its army to fight the so-called Vietcong (North Vietnamese communists). And how in 1965 it sent in its marines to attack the North, on the basis that Ho Chi Minh was planning to invade the South. Those first troops had landed in the spring of 1965. By the day I arrived, 43,418 American soldiers had been flown back home to the US in body bags.

Soldiers who were lucky enough to return from their tours of duty usually headed for Saigon's Tu Do Street, just round the corner from the Caravelle. This was a 250-yard thoroughfare packed with girlie bars and restaurants. Walk down there any night and you would see hundreds of GIs out to enjoy themselves in every way. Booze and drugs were available, and so were girls. They were both beautiful and friendly, eager to get to know the soldiers whom they saw as a meal ticket for the evening. They wore badges announcing their names – including the memorable 'Miss Lay Me' who used to haunt our table at the Palm Court Hotel, where we went for US-imported steaks. And they were hard to shake off, pestering the troops and media pack for drinks and meals throughout the night. Of course, there were some girls who would want to charge a soldier for a night's worth of entertainment and passion. There was no shortage of customers for those girls either, despite the obvious health risks they posed. After all, 'Saigon Rose' – as the local version of VD was called – was grounds for a medical discharge from the US Army. And some soldiers actively tried to catch it.

Next on our schedule was a flight to 'Firebase Snuffy', an American military stronghold eight miles from the border with Cambodia, deep in enemy territory. The base was about the size of two football pitches, heavily fortified. It provided a position from which howitzers could fire off their shells into villages controlled by the Vietcong. Once these villages had been 'softened up' the ground troops would move in hoping to mop up any resistance that was left. Snuffy was a mass of trenches, sandbags, barbed wire, and red mud caused by the endless rain. There were guns everywhere, and every three minutes there would be a deafening explosion as a howitzer fired off a shell miles into the jungle wilderness.

It was here that we came face to face with the 'quiet mutiny' that John wanted to reveal. Nearly all the troops were grunts – eighteen-year-old kids who had been plucked from the safety of home and forced to fight a war on the other side of the world. They were angry, frightened, and confused about why they were there. Some were determined to do as little as possible before being sent back home. One of them told us:

> They say we're over here to fight the spread of communism. Well, I don't want to see communism spreading all over the world but there's nothing I can do about it. I'm just going to do my time, get out of Vietnam and go back to the world I know.

Another said:

> I couldn't see any point in the war back home and no one's ever explained to me why we are actually here. I

mean I don't have anything against these people but I'm sent into the woods to shoot them, and I have to do it or they'll shoot me first. I still don't know why I'm here, that's the God's truth. Three months and I still don't know why I'm shooting at these people.

The military commanders did their best to keep morale high, drafting in the likes of Bob Hope and the newly crowned Miss America to entertain the troops. I also filmed the arrival of the 'Donut Dollies' – pretty girls from the American Red Cross who would fly in to host quizzes, play party games and hand out candy.

But the grunts still wanted out. They were contemptuous of the 'lifers', those who had signed up for action rather than wait to be conscripted. These men were rarely seen on the battlefield, preferring to sit in offices back in Saigon and bark the orders at the grunts who had to do the actual fighting. One conscript told us how he and his friends would be ordered into the jungle. Then, as soon as they got out of sight of their commanders inside the base, they would just sit down and go no further. Another said officers had been beaten up for pushing the grunts too far into enemy territory. They knew of one captain who had been shot in the back by grunts.

But despite the insubordination of their newest recruits, the American military machine continued to grind on. And as well as the fighting with guns and shells, there was also the war of words. At Firebase Snuffy there was a department concerned with 'psy ops' – code for psychological warfare. Their mission was to bombard the enemy with propaganda and trick him into believing that he was losing and on the point of defeat. Some of the 'psy ops' are still scarcely believable. One operation – called 'Wandering Soul' – involved flying over villages at tree-top level and blasting out a tape recording supposedly containing the voices of their North Vietnamese ancestors. These voices would tell the people below that they should stop their fighting, surrender and make peace. Who knows what was actually audible to the villagers on the ground – but up in the helicopter all I could hear was the sound of the engine and blades.

The helicopters also carried huge boxes of leaflets, on which were printed spurious figures about the damage America was inflicting on the Vietcong, plus threats to kill any guerrillas who remained in the area. Something like 800,000 of these leaflets would be dropped from helicopters into the jungle below every day. The army hoped they would be picked up and read by Vietcong fighters who would then be frightened into surrendering. As I filmed one soldier throwing them out by the fistful, John asked him if it was having any success. He said that a total of six people had surrendered in the last two months. He then confessed it would probably be more effective to drop the entire boxes with the aim of hitting the enemy guerrillas on the head.

Our film was the first to document the anti-war sentiments of American soldiers in Vietnam and, predictably, it caused a storm of protest. The US ambassador sent a letter complaining to the Independent Broadcasting Authority which then loudly denounced the film for being anti-American. But despite the furore it had revealed a fundamental truth. As John put it in a powerful piece to camera: 'The largest, wealthiest and most powerful organization on earth – the American army – is being challenged from within . . . the war is ending because the grunt is taking no more bullshit.'

Sadly, though, it would take another four and a half years before America's long disengagement from Vietnam would be completed. On the way its planes would bomb that beautiful country back to the Stone Age, destroying villages with napalm and turning fertile land into a moonscape. By the time they finally pulled out, nearly 60,000 of their own troops had been killed, along with more than a million Vietnamese.

CAMBODIA – THE SIEGE OF PHNOMH PENH

Before the Vietnam war ended, other countries became engulfed in the fighting – leading to tragedies just as large. In 1969 American planes carpet bombed Vietnam's border with Cambodia, in an attempt to wipe out Vietcong fighters who were based there. In the process they killed thousands of civilians. And instead of destroying one enemy, the US only created another. A new communist fighting force – the Khmer Rouge – emerged on the Cambodian side. It was a revolutionary organization, dedicated to overthrowing the country's own American-backed government. Led by the infamous Pol Pot, the Khmer Rouge was vicious and highly successful. By the beginning of 1975 it had captured 80 per cent of the countryside and was now advancing on the one remaining government stronghold – the capital, Phnom Penh.

In January that year I was filming a programme about faith healers, oot in the Philippines. A couple of days before the shoot finished, Alan Bale and I got the call from Manchester – would we fly on to Cambodia? I can't say we weren't worried. The TV news had been full of reports about the barbaric acts committed by the Khmer Rouge. Now they were laying siege to Phnom Penh in an attempt to force its people and government into submission. It seemed the city could fall to the guerrillas at any moment, opening the door to a new era of savagery.

Mike Scott, a Granada executive who sometimes doubled as *World In Action* presenter, was with us on the Philippines shoot. When it was over we flew together to Bangkok, where he was due to catch a connecting flight back to London. As we were parting he looked Alan and me in the eyes: 'You don't have to go, you know. If you think it's too dangerous just come back with me. Don't worry – I will support you.' It was a kind gesture from a senior company man who was genuinely concerned for our safety. But this was the major international story of the day, programme resources had already been committed, and we felt we had no option but to go.

When we arrived in the besieged capital we went straight to its main hotel, La Phnom. This was an ornate palace typical of the buildings in the centre of town. I could see why the French had fallen in love with the place. Just like the British colonials had done in India, they had turned it into a home from home, with wide tree-lined boulevards, low-rise villas and street cafés. If you ignored the rickshaws and just looked at the hordes of little Renaults, you could have been in France itself. No wonder it had been known as 'the Paris of the East'.

At the hotel we met up with producer Mike Beckham. Always keen on films with a sense of adventure and excitement, he was in his element in Cambodia. However, he was under no illusions about the dangers, warning us that the Khmer Rouge were planning to start rocket attacks on the centre of the city. He was right. That evening a six-foot-long metal tube packed with explosives was fired into a nearby street. Following a three-second high-pitched whistle it detonated, killing two bystanders and injuring seven others. During the ten days we stayed there, 185 more rockets would fall on Phnom Penh.

Mike also explained how the Khmer Rouge fighters were rapidly taking control of all the main highways leading to the city, in an attempt to stop supplies getting in. Crucially, they were also shelling the barges that sailed down the Mekong River loaded with food for Phnom Penh's two and a half million citizens. At least three quarters of those were refugees – having fled from the countryside that the guerrillas had captured. Now they were huddled in makeshift camps and in foxholes that they'd dug for themselves on the banks of the Mekong. The shelling of the barges meant they were going hungry. If it continued for much longer they would be starving.

After a meeting with his contacts, Mike got information about a village five miles out of town that had been attacked by the Khmer Rouge the previous night. We hired a car and set off down the highway. As we got nearer to our destination the road became very lonely and our local driver began to get visibly agitated. Seeing a sign for the village, we told him to stop and then got out. Mike, Alan and I clambered through some thick undergrowth for about a hundred yards before we saw what was left of the village. Nearly everything had been burnt and all that remained were a few tree stumps and some smouldering embers of what were once people's homes.

I put the camera on my shoulder and started to take some shots, lying low to get a nice effect of smoke rising from the ground. Seconds later there was a burst of machine gun fire that went over my head and crashed into the trees just behind me. I heard Mike shout, 'Get the hell out!' and the three of us ran for the waiting vehicle. No wonder the driver had been ill at ease. He had realized before us that this was now Khmer Rouge territory. The guerrillas had obviously been watching us while we walked around. Presumably it was only the sight of the camera that made them fire a warning shot instead of a fatal one.

A couple of days later we went to another settlement that had been burnt out and looted. This time it was a camp set up by the Catholic Relief Service which was providing temporary homes for the refugees. Here, around twenty miles from the city, the Khmer Rouge had arrived in the middle of the night, killing twelve people including a child. By the time we got there, the refugees were crowded into a nearby school. Eyewitnesses told us that the victims had been bayoneted to death. But they had no explanation for the four Khmer Rouge guerrillas who were also lying dead – with what looked like the backs of their heads blown off.

Back in Phnom Penh, the war against the Khmer Rouge was being run from the US Embassy. On the outside it was protected by wire rocket screens. Inside, around 200 military and CIA men effectively controlled every move made by Cambodia's army. The head of the government was Marshal Lon Nol who rode around the city in an armour-plated Rolls Royce and enjoyed the protection of personal bodyguards. But although his forces were supported by American cash they were ill-equipped to deal with guerrilla fighters who were dug deep into bunkers around the city. The result was horrific casualties, with up to 250 dead and wounded being ferried back from the battlefields each day.

I watched many of those injured arriving for treatment one afternoon at Phnom Penh's main hospital. Some had been hit by bullets, some by shrapnel, while others had stepped on land-mines. While filming, I heard a helicopter landing and dashed out to see Red Cross volunteers running towards it carrying stretchers. Suddenly a whole procession of wounded troops emerged from inside the helicopter – there was one with an arm blown off, another with both legs missing, a third covered in blood-soaked bandages. Inside, as they were seen by the doctors and surgeons, I listened to the awful sound of screaming and groaning. Several of the soldiers were obviously in agony. I don't know how many survived, but I'm sure a lot of them didn't live beyond that night.

If the Khmer Rouge were to finally take Phnom Penh they had to stop the convoys of boats and barges that sailed down the Mekong bringing the food supplies and ammunition. By this stage in the war, the guerrillas were lined along both banks of the river stretching all the way back to Vietnam. The convoys had to run a sixty-mile gauntlet of shells and bullets if they were to reach the docks in the Cambodian capital. Only one town on the riverbank – Neak Luong – was still in the hands of government forces. We flew there by helicopter to see how the army was trying to protect the convoys as they sailed towards Phnom Penh. Alongside us was a Catholic Relief Service medical team who were going to treat the casualties of the fighting. As we landed and got off, wounded soldiers and civilians got on – to be flown back to the hospitals in Phnom Penh.

At around noon we caught sight of the first supply convoy of the day. Each boat was shielded by empty barges on either side. These were fitted with wire screens to take the impact of rocket and shell fire. Within minutes the Khmer Rouge guerrillas began their shelling. In response, the government planes appeared overhead, dropping their bombs on the guerrilla positions. The battle continued as more convoys appeared throughout the day. By sunset, one boat had been sunk and an oil tanker was blazing in the water. The boats that did make it through arrived in Phnom Penh carrying 2,000 tons of ammunition, and 1,000 tons of rice – enough to feed the city for just two days.

As our shoot was drawing to an end, the Khmer Rouge had advanced still further on the capital. Guerrilla units were dug in around the airport and we thought it would be too risky to attempt to fly out. We'd seen how dangerous it was on a boat, but sailing now seemed the most viable way. Mike went to see one of the captains who did agree to let us on board during his journey back up the Mekong into Vietnam. But when we returned to confirm the arrangements the night before the sailing, we found that the captain had already gone. It was just as well he left without us: we later learned that his convoy had been shelled during the journey. Every boat was sunk, many of the crew killed, and the captain himself seriously injured.

With the sailing option closed, and a journey by road out of the question, it was back to the airport. We found a Cambodian pilot who was flying out that night and who agreed to take us. Conscious that the guerrillas would have him in their sights, he was going to make it as difficult as possible for them to try to shoot him down. As his engines roared into life we hardly moved across the runway. Instead, the plane spiralled skywards completely disorientating everyone outside the cockpit. It wasn't until we reached around 7,000 feet that the corkscrew movement stopped and the pilot began flying normally. We were dizzy and sick, but at least we were safe. When our stomachs calmed down, a member of the crew prepared a chicken dinner. After the acute food shortages of the last couple of weeks, we could start eating normally again.

As for the people we were leaving behind, they were about to experience unbelievable horrors. Phnom Penh fell six weeks after we left. The Khmer Rouge emptied the city, murdering anyone suspected of supporting the government, being middle class or having an education. This was Pol Pot's Year Zero. By the time he was deposed in 1979, his regime had killed an estimated three million Cambodians.

LEBANON, 1982 AND 1989 – HELL-ON-SEA

It is hard to believe now, but Beirut was one of the world's richest and smartest resorts when I first visited it. East met West, with domes and minarets lining the French style boulevards. Classy high-rise hotels looked out on to the sun-soaked Mediterranean beaches, while at night the smart set gambled in the casinos and ate in the sophisticated restaurants. It was the first time I had come across real wealth, seeing people bedecked with gold jewellery and driving round in fast cars. I remember thinking at the time that I could have been in Monte Carlo. That was in 1967.

Fifteen years on there were no tourists. Religion – not money – had become the main preoccupation in Lebanon. Israel had just mounted ferocious bombing raids on the southern half of the country, claiming they were the bases of PLO guerrillas planning terrorist attacks on its people. Now they were attacking West Beirut – home to 9,000 Palestinian refugees and headquarters of the PLO leader Yasser Arafat. Israel insisted that its raids were carefully targeted at terrorist positions, but reports were coming back of terrible civilian casualties. We set out to discover the real consequences of Israel's invasion.

To get to Beirut, we had to first fly to Cyprus, then jump on a freighter travelling from Larnaca across the Med to Lebanon. Joining me on board were the producer Simon Berthon, the researcher Paul Greengrass, plus Alan with the sound equipment. During the eighteen-hour crossing we heard that Israeli gunboats were patrolling the shores around Beirut, and were firing on any vessels that they suspected of supplying the PLO. Our freighter was unknown to the Israelis and we had a real fear that we ourselves could be blown out of the water.

Luckily, a pilot from Middle East Airlines was also on board. He had just flown his plane out of Beirut for safety until the airport could be reopened. Hearing of the threat he got on to the ship's radio and managed to contact someone in Lebanon who gave a promise that we would be safe. Nice though this reassurance was, none of us quite believed it. As we sat up on the deck through the night, paranoia set in. Every slight sound was mistaken for an approaching missile. Not until we safely entered the port of Jounie the following morning did we feel the full relief – and give the pilot the thanks he richly deserved.

Jounie was six miles north of Beirut. Looking at the hordes of people water-skiing and sunbathing on the beach, you'd never have guessed you were entering a war zone. Once on land, though, there could be no mistake. The air strikes had flattened many buildings, and scores of apartment blocks were now no more than piles of concrete rubble. One of our first stops was a block of flats that had been demolished by an Israeli bomb. Fifty people had been killed. One eyewitness described how he had tried to pull some of the dead from the wreckage. Two of them were members of his own family.

We were staying at the Bristol Hotel in Muslim West Beirut. Several times a day we had to cross through the 'Green Line' that separated the West from the Christian East of the city. The Line was about twice the width of a motorway with clearly defined crossing points. Gun-toting teenagers looked ready and willing to pull their triggers at either side. Although it felt relatively safe here in the day, going across at night was a different matter. Carrying our camera equipment in the darkness there was always a deathly silence, and a constant fear of being shot.

During the first few days Paul was keen to get an interview with Arafat, who was holed up at his headquarters plotting the PLO's response to the air strikes. We went to the street where he lived, jockeying for position with several other crews from around the world. When he emerged, surrounded by bodyguards, he walked towards a car, unwilling to stop and give interviews. Then, spotting me behind the camera, the PLO leader beamed a big smile, and pointed at me: 'Hello, my friend – and how are you?' It seemed he remembered me from all those years back at his former base in Jordan. Paul saw his opportunity and started firing questions, which Arafat happily answered on the way to his waiting limo.

Our own driver, Adjani, took us round the most devastated parts of the city as Paul and Simon gathered their evidence. They were able to show that the Israeli bombing had been largely indiscriminate – hitting houses, schools and refugee camps. American-made cluster bombs had also been used. Like land-mines, these would be picked up in the street by children who lost limbs when they exploded. At a Lebanese civilian hospital we went into a ward housing mentally handicapped children. A number of their fellow patients – aged between three and six – had been killed in a bombing raid. The survivors were in a room where the glass had been blown out of the windows. Flies crawled over their faces as they sat on burnt-out beds looking bewildered. A nurse told us that there was no running water in the hospital due to the bomb damage.

The next step was to put our findings to a representative of the Israeli government. Foreign Minister Yitzhak Shamir had agreed to an interview, but first we had to get over the border from Lebanon. Adjani took us out of Beirut past the airport, where we were picked up by some Israeli soldiers. From there we headed south on a well-bombed road that passed through gutted villages. There was no other traffic as we weaved round craters on the way to the no man's land that separated the two countries. Months of Israeli aerial bombardment had made ghost towns of the settlements that were once here. Town after town was flattened, with the apartments and houses looking as if they'd imploded.

We met Shamir in Tel Aviv. He was unmoved by our reports of civilian casualties, saying that his country was pursuing an enemy that wanted to destroy it. And he gave a warning of more attacks to come:

> We are fighting against a terrorist organization and we have to use military means. We are sorry there are casualties but it's not our fault. The goal of our military operation is to give security to our country. We want the PLO to leave Beirut – and they will leave it.

But the PLO weren't Israel's only enemies. And the constant bombing and invasion of its neighbour only created ever more extreme forces across the border. Over the next few years we would all become familiar with them – Amal, Islamic Jihad, Hezbollah. These extremist Muslim groups carved out their own territories in Lebanon, putting them at odds with other militias such as the Druze and Christian Phalangists. The country descended into a chaotic civil war, with daily bombings, shootings and kidnappings.

By 1989 there was probably nowhere more dangerous for

the Western media to operate. Reporters John McCarthy and Charles Glass had been taken hostage and were still being held alongside the likes of Terry Waite and Brian Keenan. Other journalists such as Alec Collett had been kidnapped and murdered by the Muslim fundamentalists. But the story wouldn't go away, and in July that year the programme editor Stuart Prebble asked me to go back to film a profile of the Christian warlord Michel Aeoun.

Aeoun was the Christian militia leader who, for the last three months, had been trying to drive his various Muslim rivals out of Beirut. Since beginning his 'war of liberation', he had only brought more devastation to his country and his people. The Muslim militias, backed by Syria, were going nowhere. They had pinned Aeoun and his Christian followers back into their East Beirut enclave with ferocious shelling. Food was running out and the electricity supply had been cut.

I linked up with reporter Andrew Jennings and the producer, Steve Boulton. To get into Lebanon, we again had to go to Cyprus, though this time we could fly by helicopter instead of sailing. In one of those bizarre filming encounters, we met up with another crew on board the same aircraft. But these weren't going to cover the war – they were joined by a female Lebanese pop star who wanted to make her latest video, using the shattered Beirut seafront as her backdrop.

We ourselves decided not to stay in Beirut this time around. We found a place up in the mountains that was relatively safe, and each day we would drive down to the city's Christian enclave to see what effects Aeoun's war was having. We found people huddled in shelters as the shells dropped each night, chronic food shortages, and drivers queuing for hours for precious petrol. At the roadside black marketeers were doing brisk business selling it for up to £14 a gallon.

Aeoun himself moved around in an armour-plated BMW, surrounded by his élite band of commandos. Outside, he wore a bulletproof vest and flak jacket, removing them only once he was back in his concrete command bunker. He could no longer live in his presidential palace which, over the preceding three months, had received 5,000 direct hits from rockets and shells.

It was a depressing few days filming the suffering of his people, and listening to him justify his war. And predictably, it was a war he lost. Who actually won when Lebanon's fighting finally came to an end in the early nineties is still not clear. The Muslim warlords, the Syrians and the Lebanese forces did a deal that would bring peace after almost twenty years of chaos. And under pressure from the US and Iran, all the remaining hostages were released. But by then the country that the militias had fought to control was little more than a shell.

SOMALIA, 1993 – DAN ELDON'S LAST ASSIGNMENT

Every war brings hundreds of media people to the scene. Writers, photographers, cameramen, radio correspondents and TV journalists vie for the big exclusive. In reality we usually come back with similar tales and images, each film and dispatch almost indistinguishable from the next.

But there are rare occasions when one individual's words or pictures bring the conflict vividly to life. When the definitive accounts are written, it is their work the historians will turn to for reference. In Somalia, it wasn't a grizzled TV reporter or a veteran newspaper correspondent who made other countries wake up to what was happening. Instead it was a young, fresh-faced photographer who, in just one year, provided the world's press with some of the most haunting images ever captured in wartime.

Dan Eldon was twenty-two. Although British, he'd lived much of his life in Kenya, developing a passion for Africa and an affinity with its people. Always artistic and creative, he became interested in photography, showing an immense talent for lighting and composition. He began submitting his work to magazines and soon started to receive commissions for fashion shoots and travel features. Then, after one trip to north-east Kenya to photograph Somalian refugees he came to the attention of the international media agency, Reuters. They were so impressed with his work they asked him to go to Somalia itself.

In 1992 Somalia was probably the most violent country in the world. For two decades it had been controlled by the dictator Siad Barre who ran a terror regime, but at least managed to keep a lid on the smouldering hatreds that existed between various warring clans. As his grip on power began to slip those ancient hatreds erupted again, with each clan putting forward its own leader as the man to take over the government. When Barre fled at the beginning of 1991 the country descended into total anarchy. On top of the vicious fighting came a catastrophic drought. Within a year, four million Somalis – a third of the population – were facing starvation. Efforts to get aid into the country were proving useless. Gunmen intercepted food containers at the port of Mogadishu, the capital. Warlords cut off transport links to rural villages so any supplies that were left couldn't get through. Thousands began to die of hunger.

Into this chaos stepped Dan. Within weeks he was taking photographs that made the covers and centre-page spreads of *Time*, *Newsweek* and the *International Herald-Tribune*. His stunning portfolio included a starving man against the background of a stone-faced soldier; a dying child with sunken eyes waiting for her first drink in days; a gunman in front of grain supplies at the port, brandishing his AK47 rifle to ward off the civilians the food was meant for. The effects of these images were swift. Newsdesks around the world were alerted to the story, and more journalists were sent in. As the coverage grew, so did the calls for action. Then, at the end of 1992, the UN responded by sending in a peacekeeping force led by 2,000 American marines. Their job was to end the famine by protecting food aid convoys, so the supplies could go directly to the people. The name of this humanitarian mission was 'Operation Restore Hope'.

Although the operation was initially successful, the warlords soon began to reassert their power. The most dangerous was General Mohamed Aideed who wanted UN forces out of the country so he could take power himself. He directed his followers to attack the military convoys and sabotage the roads making it impossible for them to deliver their supplies. In June 1993 he ordered an ambush on one convoy which led to twenty-three UN troops being killed.

Suddenly the whole purpose of Operation Restore Hope changed. The Americans assumed command, sending in helicopters to mount revenge attacks on Aideed's forces. In turn, the general's militiamen carried out guerrilla attacks on UN troops. Mogadishu became a battleground by day and night, with hundreds being killed or injured.

Dan's photographs, charting the worsening situation, continued to be wired around the world. But back in Kenya his parents Mike and Kathy were growing increasingly worried for his safety. After the publication of one picture – showing a row of bodies on slabs in a makeshift mortuary – Dan contacted his mother and told her he was having trouble coping with the terrible scenes he was witnessing day after day. He had just seen a mother cradling a baby who had been killed by a single bullet. Next to her was a young girl whose eyes had been blown out, and another who had lost both legs in an explosion. Both girls were alive and bewildered. Kathy told him to come home adding, with a mother's intuition: 'I think you've probably gone through a lot of your luck.' But Dan stayed. He had been in at the start of the story and wanted to be there when it ended.

On 12 July American gunships launched a ferocious air attack on a building thought to be housing General Aideed and his followers. It was a terrible mistake. Aideed wasn't inside, but several respected tribal leaders were: some reports suggested they were holding a meeting about food aid distribution. Estimates varied, but somewhere between fifty and seventy people were killed. Outside the building an angry mob gathered, bent on revenge against 'westerners'.

Back at his hotel Dan was watching the scene from the roof, along with a group of other journalists. He helped bandage up a reporter from the *Daily Telegraph* who had got too close to the crowd and then been attacked with rocks and clubs. While he was keen to get nearer to the action himself, Dan knew that he could easily find himself a target of the mob, too. Only after receiving an offer of protection from some of Aideed's armed followers did he decide to go to the scene, along with four other journalists.

Tragically, the protection that was promised was neither reliable nor effective. Their car was attacked by the baying crowd. Dan and his four colleagues got out and fled, but there was no escape. The young photographer was chased down an alley at the side of a house, dropping his camera equipment as he ran. When he fell to the ground in exhaustion, he was surrounded then beaten. A Reuters' driver who witnessed the attack knew there could be only one outcome: 'They were using stones and long iron bars, and they were shouting as they hit him. They were shouting "We don't need the white man – the white man is killing our people, our fathers, our mothers." '

A few minutes after that savage attack, the crowd dispersed. An hour later Dan's body was recovered by a UN helicopter.

I arrived in Somalia on 22 July, ten days after Dan Eldon's murder. We'd been sent to make a programme about his life, and the war as seen through his pictures. Alongside me on the plane was Mike Beckham, who had been moved by Dan's story, just as I had. Like Dan, we both knew the fear and the excitement of covering wars at a young age. Like him, we cared deeply about bringing the plight of the suffering to the attention of the wider world.

Mike and I had shared another experience: Vietnam. And flying into Mogadishu on a UN prop plane awakened memories in both of us. The airfield was like Tan Son Nhat all those years earlier: massed rows of US helicopters, soldiers and marines. In the sky above, the Cobra helicopters hovered, fighting for airspace alongside the UN choppers which were all painted white. Every few minutes a huge American transporter plane would land bringing supplies for the troops – food, blankets, medical kits and what appeared to be an inexhaustible supply of blue plastic bottles filled with purified water.

The city itself was a mess – a mix of rubble, sewage and teeming human wreckage. Every pane of glass seemed to be broken – including those in the only functioning hotel still standing (ours). Sleep was a near impossibility in the equatorial heat, so I would spend most nights on the roof with the camera trying to capture any shelling, helicopters or tracer fire. Meanwhile the American cable network CNN had comandeered half the entire building, installing satellite dishes, editing equipment, plus their own generators. In different buildings across the city, other US networks were doing the same, along with major broadcasters from across Europe, Canada and Australia. How different it must have been when Dan first arrived a year earlier. Back then journalists and camera crews were a rarity. It had taken his photographs to make us sit up and realize there was a story here at all.

Now, of course, the story had moved on from famine to full-scale war. The UN, which had gone in to feed the hungry, was now interested only in seeking out Aideed and his private army. Charities such as Save the Children, Concern and CARE were back where they started, trying to deliver food aid without being attacked by the militiamen. The UN wasn't providing armed escort convoys and, in most cases, the rural feeding centres weren't being protected either. One day we filmed with CARE's Field Director Hugh Hamilton as he drove along with a truck full of aid bound for one of the starving villages. Seeing a military convoy coming the other way he turned his vehicle around and sneaked in behind it. This was what he called 'unofficial protection' – at least there was the illusion of an armed escort to deter one of the countless gunmen from attacking.

When we left Mogadishu we were bound for Nairobi for an interview with Mike and Kathy, and for their son's memorial service to be held in Kenya's Rift Valley. At the house, Mike showed us around his room – 'Dan's Depot' – filled with mementoes from his adventures around Africa. There were carvings, ornamental spears, swords, ostrich feather headgear – everything that spelled his love for the continent and its people. When Mike had done his interview I spent some time alone in the room getting close-ups and looking through boxes and boxes of photographs that Dan had taken. It was a choking experience to see these wonderful pictures and think that a lad so young and so gifted had met such a terrible end. Like many journalists and photographers before him, Dan had paid the ultimate price for doing something he loved.

One of the key speakers at the memorial service was the late Mohammed Amin, the vastly experienced international cameraman who had covered dozens of wars around the globe, facing constant danger and losing a limb in the process. In the tranquil peace of the Rift Valley, Dan's friends and family gathered to hear his final tribute: seven years on, I still can't add to it:

> Somalia was always dangerous, but in the past few months it became the most dangerous place on earth for

Filming at an IRA training camp in the Irish Republic, 1969.

The shape of things to come – the terrorists set off a bomb for the benefit of the media.

A *World In Action* surveillance van in a Santiago street.

Inside the van, John Ware and I secretly film.

Our target, Walter Rauff, as a Nazi war criminal.

Rauff, when we finally caught up with him in the Chilean capital, in 1984.

Joe Yusuf bundles his son Nick into a car after snatching him from his school in Greece, 1984.

Later in the day, after Nick had recovered from the shock.

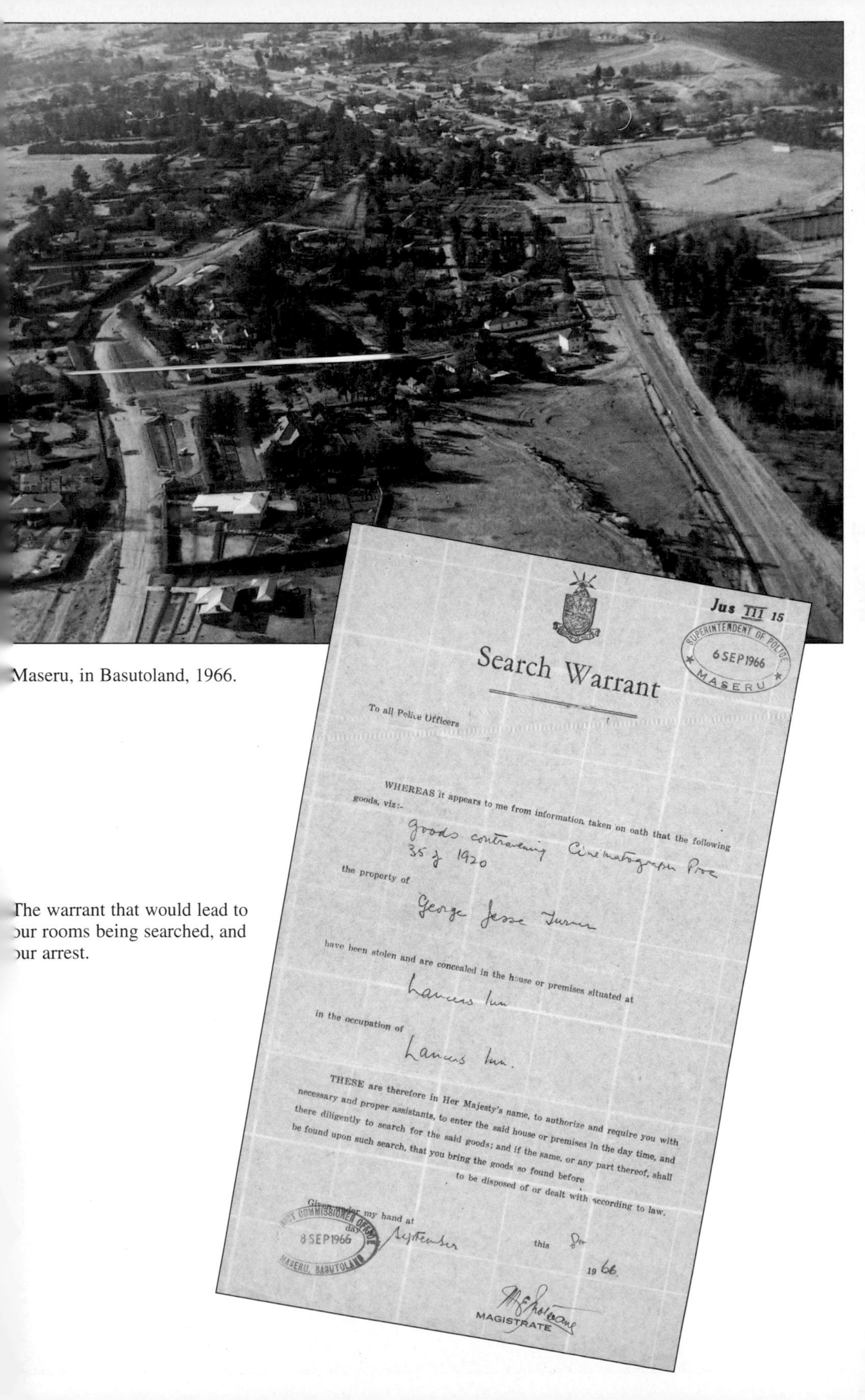

Jus III 15

SUPERINTENDENT OF POLICE
6 SEP 1966
MASERU

Search Warrant

To all Police Officers

WHEREAS it appears to me from information taken on oath that the following goods, viz:-

goods contravening Cinematograph Proc 35 of 1920

the property of

George Jesse Turner

have been stolen and are concealed in the house or premises situated at

Lancers Inn

in the occupation of

Lancers Inn.

THESE are therefore in Her Majesty's name, to authorize and require you with necessary and proper assistants, to enter the said house or premises in the day time, and there diligently to search for the said goods; and if the same, or any part thereof, shall be found upon such search, that you bring the goods so found before to be disposed of or dealt with according to law.

Given under my hand at this 8th day September 19 66.

DISTRICT COMMISSIONER'S OFFICE
8 SEP 1966
MASERU, BASUTOLAND

MAGISTRATE

Maseru, in Basutoland, 1966.

The warrant that would lead to our rooms being searched, and our arrest.

A typical sight during South Africa's apartheid years.

A family forced to 'resettle' at Wyk 7. © Leslie Woodhead

The Archbishop of Canterbury's visit to Johannesburg in 1970 provides us with a perfect cover story for the authorities. © Leslie Woodhead

The family who lived in the toilet, Sri Lankan tea estate, 1975.

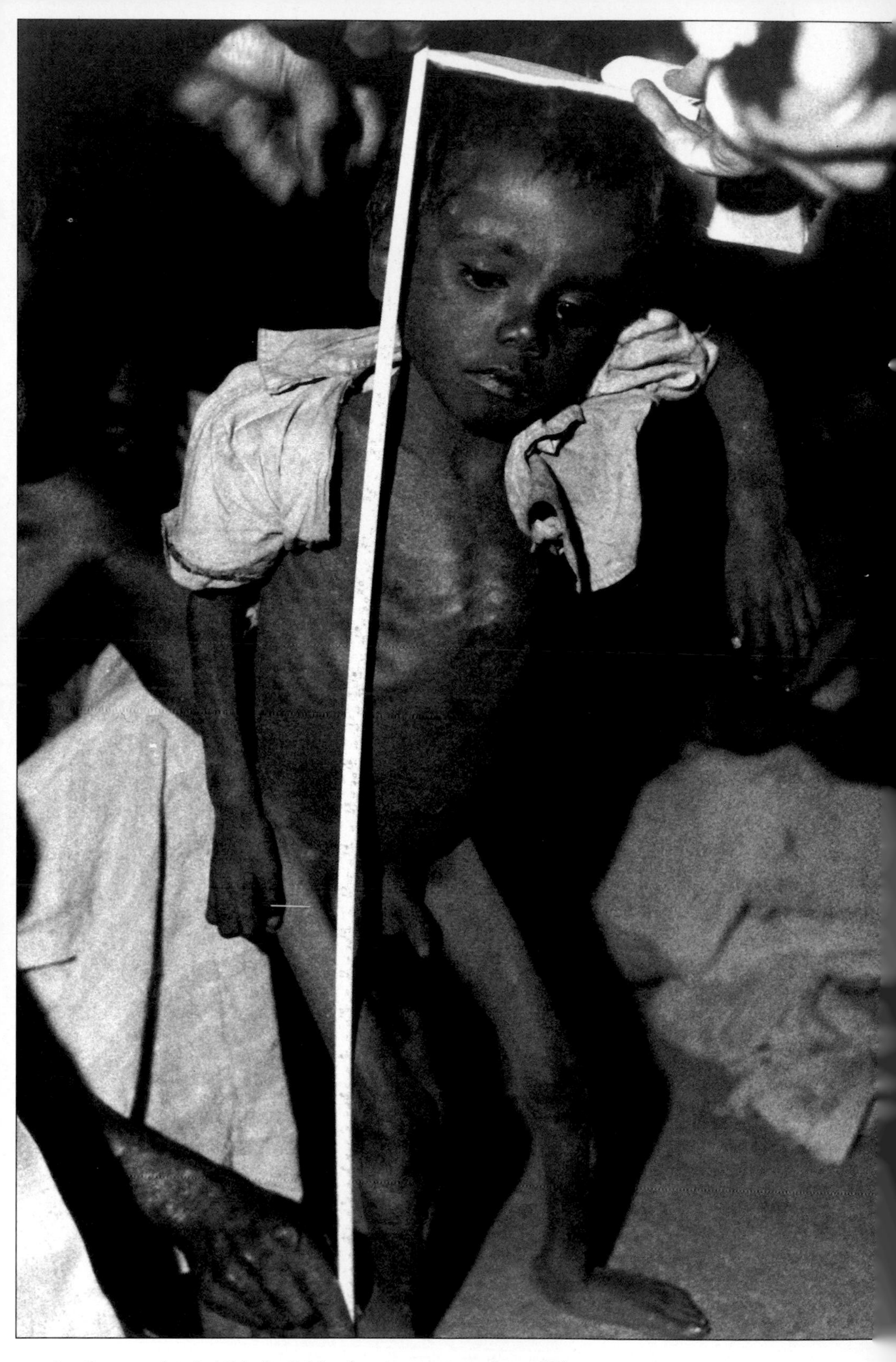

Another emaciated child of a Sri Lankan tea estate worker, 1975.

journalists. Many of the top war correspondents, veterans of several wars, dread going to Mogadishu. Some I know opted to go to Bosnia, to be out of the way so they did not get sent to Somalia.

But Dan stayed with the story. His pictures appeared on the front pages of the world's top newspapers and magazines. At the age of twenty-two when most people his age are still wondering what they want to do, he had already become a legend.

CHAPTER 5
IN AT THE BEGINNING

The two questions I get asked most often are:

a) Where do the programme ideas come from?
b) Why is your middle name Jesse?

The second is easy enough: I come from a long line of George Jesse Turners, stretching all the way back to my great-great-grandfather. When I first started as a cameraman, John Sheppard asked me did I want the full version of my name on the credits. For a laugh I agreed, and a tradition was started. Only once in the last thirty-two years has someone mistakenly left out the middle bit. Within a minute my mother was on the phone to find out why.

Question One takes a little longer to answer, as programmes have many origins. They can be inspired by newspaper articles, a personal experience, letters from viewers, even an interesting conversation down at the pub. But they can also be borne out of someone's interests and obsessions – and their sheer determination to bring their specialist subject to a wider audience.

I've worked with many journalists and producers who are tenacious in the pursuit of a scoop. Their dedication ensured that, when there was a big story, we were often there to get the exclusive. We were the first to interview MI5 'Spycatcher' Peter Wright; the first to get inside the Maze Prison to film the IRA hunger strikers; and the first to unravel the business dealings of the architect John Poulson, and his network of corrupt councillors throughout the land. In later years it was our journalists who uncovered the shady arms deals involving Jonathan Aitken. The cabinet minister may have loudly denied them on oath – but he later went to jail for perjury.

Films like those took months of persistence, and usually created a big enough splash for others to follow. But there have been other programmes that tapped into issues and concerns before anyone else. They hit the screen just as the rest of the media was waking up to the story. Examples of great timing were our films on asbestosis in the seventies, and our investigations into the link between diet and heart disease a decade later. At the end of the nineties I was asked to work on a programme about rowdy passengers on aeroplanes. Although I took some convincing that it really was a story for us, I soon realized just how potentially serious drunkenness on an aircraft could be. The production team uncovered case after case where the safety of aeroplanes had been put in jeopardy because of aggressive behaviour by passengers. And they found it was much more widespread than the authorities were admitting.

Within a fortnight of that programme being shown, the newspapers were awash with stories about the frightening new trend of 'air rage'. An air stewardess was slashed with a broken vodka bottle by a drunken passenger. The rock group Oasis were arrested on a journey to Australia, a dozen Irish travellers were turfed off a flight to Jamaica and left in Florida to make their own way home. The government rushed in new rules making rowdiness on board a plane a criminal offence. While working on our programme I had filmed a sequence of flight crews being trained to deal with drunks on board. Suddenly every news bulletin I switched on was re-running those pictures to illustrate the growing problem.

There have been many other programmes that identified stories and issues just before they became huge. The producers and researchers would tell you they were merely 'keeping their ears to the ground' and doing their jobs properly. But sometimes it felt as if they were psychic.

ANARCHY IN THE UK

During the early eighties Britain started to read about a shocking new crime. Police forces up and down the country were coming across a young breed of thief who was targeting the old and defenceless. Even worse than taking their money, these new criminals were beating up their OAP victims and leaving them for dead.

So-called 'granny bashing' was a phenomenon of the inner cities – places where violent crime had always flourished, but where the elderly had usually been considered immune. To the tabloids, teenage muggers became public enemy number one. They called for boot camps, birchings and even a return to conscription. The Thatcher government made tough noises, too, promising 'short, sharp shocks' for violent young offenders.

As the moral outcry increased, our programme tried to discover what had led to the growing lawlessness. Steve Anderson, a researcher who lived on Merseyside, suggested making a film in Toxteth – the tough inner-city district that had long been home to the local black community. For generations it had also provided the dockers and factory workers for the busy southern banks of the Mersey. But by 1981 those docks had closed and whole industries had gone with them. Unemployment was edging 20 per cent. Among the black population it was twice as high.

Steve and the producer David Taylor spent a fortnight talking to the muggers and their victims. They portrayed an area where a whole generation was growing up without any hope of work. The programme showed how local youths had been alienated from society, no longer caring about its rules and conventions. It also revealed how the police had become mistrusted and resented after a series of disastrous clamp-downs. A local councillor who had witnessed the spread of poverty and decay over many years was asked if she had any optimism for the future. She gave this warning about Toxteth's new generation.

> Nobody wants them. They are excluded from society and they can't stand it. There is no work and yet the schools and the churches put work as the greatest virtue. And it is a mockery to say to young men 'work and you will reach Heaven'. There is no work, so they will say 'to Hell with you'.

Within days of that interview, Toxteth was in flames. In three nights of violence, gangs of youths challenged the authority of the police and the state. Petrol bombs were thrown, buildings burnt to the ground, and shops and offices looted. The police themselves were hopelessly ill-prepared, facing the mob with nothing more than their helmets and metal dustbin lids for protection. Throughout the seventy-two hours of rioting, more than 250 officers were injured. Order was restored only when Merseyside's Chief Constable approved the firing of CS gas – the first time it had ever been used on the UK mainland. Although there were copycat riots in several other large cities – and even small rural towns – Liverpool remained relatively quiet for the next three weeks. Then it erupted again, and I found myself in the thick of it.

Unusually, this wasn't a *World In Action* assignment. By late July the programme was going into its summer break, and I was due to start a holiday on the peaceful canals around Stratford-Upon-Avon. However, Granada's regional programmes were following the story closely and needed some experienced back-up. When the violence began again in earnest I was called in to help.

When I arrived in Liverpool, I left my car in the safest place I could find and made my way to Upper Parliament Street. This main thoroughfare marked the entrance to Toxteth and had become known locally as 'The Front Line'. Starting at the disused docks, it climbed uphill past the huge Anglican Cathedral and into the heart of the inner city. Along its path stood magnificent old Georgian mansions and terraces that had once housed the shipping merchants and cotton brokers of the nineteenth century. But now the buildings were decayed and split into seedy bedsits. They were overlooked by half-empty, vandalized tenements. And in their shadows stood the prostitutes and drug dealers for which the area had become notorious.

At the top end of the street was a patch of waste ground leading to some late 1960s deck-access flats. There I met a couple of Granada journalists who had become friendly with some of the locals. Whether these people were involved in the violence wasn't clear, but they were able to give remarkably accurate information about when and where trouble would start. The journalists went into one of the flats for a meeting with their contacts, leaving the sound recordist Ian Hills and me to get some general shots.

It was a hot summer evening and you could feel the tension in the air. Gangs of youths were milling around and armoured police cars cruised through the streets, attracting whistles and abuse. Reporters, photographers and other film crews were taking up positions on street corners, clearly expecting further trouble. Many of them looked nervous. In the earlier riots the media had been attacked when rumour spread that their film and photographs were being handed to the police. A BBC cameraman and sound recordist were beaten up while having all their gear stolen. The £15,000-worth of equipment was later found smashed up in the back seat of a burnt-out car.

Following the previous night's violence, the roads were littered with bricks, glass and rubble. Ian and I walked over to Lodge Lane, a nearby shopping street that had borne the brunt of the worst disturbances. It was amazing to see one store after another burnt out and trashed. Any glass front had been shattered – anything of value inside had been looted by youths. (One joke doing the rounds involved a teenage boy bringing home a new TV. When his dad asked him if he could also get hold of a new video, the boy replied: 'Do you think I'm made of bricks?')

On the way back to the flats we passed an old cinema and furniture warehouse that had both been set alight. Further along the street was the geriatric hospital from which the terrified elderly patients had been evacuated the night before. As we walked up the stairwell we concluded that Toxteth was in for another night of torchings. Stacked up against the wall was an ammunition dump – crates of Molotov cocktails ready for hurling at the police lines.

We had been waiting around on the landing for just a couple of minutes when we heard some other people coming up the stairs. Suddenly we were being confronted by half a dozen masked youths demanding our equipment. I tried to hold on to my camera but one of them managed to yank it from my grasp. I then saw Ian taking a hard punch in the face as he desperately clung on to his recording machine. As the blood began to pour from his nose, the gang ran. I helped him to his feet and went straight to the flat to tell the others what had happened. As soon as I did so, the locals hit the phones. Within a few minutes they told me they knew who the attackers were. Then, around half an hour later, the camera was returned, undamaged and ready to roll.

By 9 p.m. the disorganized roaming gangs had formed themselves into large noisy crowds on street corners. Most were in disguise, covering their faces with balaclavas, scarves and towels. As soon as they began throwing their petrol bombs the police sprang into action, driving armoured transit vans towards them to get them to disperse. In response, the vans were pelted with bricks and bottles, and soon they were being driven on to pavements and across wasteland to break up the mobs.

By this stage the filming had become highly dangerous. The vans were being driven so fast and recklessly that I was sure one of them would cause an accident. As well as the risk from the police side, there was a further hazard from the rioters. A number of them had broken into a car rental garage and were now doing handbrake turns in the vehicles they'd stolen. Another gang had smashed their way into a dairy depot to get to the milk floats. Then they jammed down the throttles and left them careering towards the lines of police. With mayhem developing all around me, I ran to a set of traffic lights next to a fire-scarred NatWest bank. They were surrounded by metal railings and I managed to wedge both myself and the camera in between. There, protected from the speeding traffic, I began recording Toxteth's descent into anarchy.

On the street in front of me, hundreds of rioters were now attacking the police. Their missiles included concrete slabs, bricks, car jacks and hammers. Burning barricades were being set up in the side roads that led into Upper Parliament Street. Hundreds of tyres had been looted from a nearby garage, and set alight. The cars stolen from the rental depot were now being overturned, with their petrol spilling out on to the tarmac and bursting into flames.

Many buildings were also ablaze, but the firemen who came to put them out felt the full fury of the mob. Under siege from stones and rocks, the crews were forced to pull out. Other people were being attacked, too. A taxi driver lost control of his cab and ploughed into a tree after a rock shattered his windscreen. And as the police led a baton charge near the entrance to a tenement block, one officer was felled by a TV set hurled from a landing.

At least the police were better equipped to handle the violence than they had been previously. Their plain helmets had been replaced by visors, and their uniforms were now flameproof. Gone were the dustbin lids. In their place were reinforced riot shields offering protection from the thousands of missiles. As their lines moved forward to break up the crowds the police banged their truncheons against their shields. But if the deafening noise was meant to intimidate the rioters, it only seemed to goad them into further violence. Every few minutes the lines would break as two or three officers pulled an injured colleague out of the fray and towards the safety of a waiting ambulance.

At around 11 p.m. it looked as if the whole street was ablaze, with the cathedral standing in silhouette against the flames. Suddenly a large section of the crowd began running from the middle of Upper Parliament Street towards wasteland nearby. Word had spread that someone had been seriously injured by one of the police vans. With the riot directly in front of me fizzling out, I extricated myself from behind the railings and followed the crowd. But when I got to the wasteland it was impossible to see what was going on. Hundreds of people were surrounding the ambulance and, as I tried to get through, I received a powerful kick in the leg. Once again, the rioters were turning their anger on the media. There were loud threats about what would happen to us if any film was handed to the police. One newspaper reporter was punched and kicked to the ground; several others were chased from the scene.

We soon heard that the injured man had been run over by a police personnel carrier that had driven across the wasteland to disperse one of the many stone-throwing gangs. The ambulance rushed him to hospital but he died from his injuries within a matter of hours. It later emerged that he was just twenty-two years old. Although initially assumed to be a rioter, he turned out to have no involvement in the disturbances. He was, in fact, disabled and had been on his way to visit his sister.

As the night gave way to dawn, the crowds began to disperse naturally and go home. That morning, throughout Britain, millions of people were preparing to take to the streets for a national celebration. It was 29 July – the day of Prince Charles's marriage to Lady Diana Spencer. On Toxteth's streets though, there were no celebrations. After another night of sustained rioting, there was merely smoke, rubble and devastation.

MAD COWS

Towards the end of the 1980s the government found itself in crisis over the way it policed our food safety. First there was the salmonella-in-eggs scare – a controversy that cost the health minister Edwina Currie her job, and led to the destruction of millions of hens. Then there was listeria – a disease few of us had heard of, but which was suddenly being found in all sorts of food including milk, cheese and pâté. When it struck in Britain, no one was prepared. By the time the outbreak was over, many people had fallen violently ill, and mothers had lost their unborn babies.

The year-long series of scares finally seemed to be subsiding when I was asked to work on a new programme about beef. Researcher Jacquie Hughes had been studying medical papers concerning a strange disease afflicting Britain's cattle herd. It lay dormant for years, then attacked their brains and made them demented. At the time we prepared to film, it was striking down around 200 cows a week, and some European countries were talking about banning the import of cattle from Britain. Until I read the brief I'd never heard of bovine spongiform encephalopathy, or BSE. By the time I'd finished I knew enough to be terrified.

BSE – or mad cow disease – was remarkably similar to a condition that affected sheep. That illness, scrapie, had been around for many years and nobody thought that it posed a risk to man, or any other animal. As farmers came under pressure to reduce costs they started feeding their cattle with the remnants of other dead animals, including sheep. The mixture was cheap and protein rich. As well as helping the cattle's growth it was also efficient – as none of the sheep's carcass need be wasted.

But as cows started to go mad the livestock industry realized its mistake. In a bid to cut corners and save money, farmers had interfered with nature. Vegetarian cows, which should be fed on grass, had been forced to consume the dead and diseased remnants of other beasts. Scrapie, for so long confined to sheep, had jumped species. Now that it was in the food chain, could it jump a second time?

Our first stop was Middlesbrough to meet a doctor who had written about the dangers of infected meat reaching our plates. He explained how some cows may have been slaughtered before they started to display the symptoms of the disease. Their brains and other internal organs could easily have been sent to food plants where they would be processed for human consumption. It was the first time I'd heard anyone from the world of science say they were avoiding certain foods. For the doctor, the risk of BSE jumping species to humans was real – he thought it was simply too dangerous to eat sausages, meat pies or burgers.

In Leicester we met an environmental health officer who warned that infection could easily spread around the slaughterhouse. By the start of 1990 the government had banned brains and spinal cord from the food chain. But, according to the health official, this protoction wasn't sufficient. During his interview he laid out a row of cattle entrails on the table in front of him:

> When you split down the carcass there will be bits of the central nervous system tissue that gets scattered over the rest of the meat, so how do we know we get rid of it all? It's impossible to remove it all. It's the job of my meat inspectors to make sure that none of the banned offal gets through, but there will certainly be some central nervous tissue left behind.

At 4 a.m. the following morning we began filming at an abattoir on the east side of Manchester. It was early February, cold and dark, as we saw the pens of cattle begin their short journey through to slaughter. Inside it was a hive of activity, with men in chainmail-like aprons rushing around. Several of them carried huge band-saws which they used to remove the cattle heads and split their bodies down the middle. Others had hoses and buckets of water to swill the blood-spattered floors and walls. The carcasses were hung up by their legs and sent to the long metal tables where the butchers chopped them up into sides and joints. They were then put back on the hooks and sent into the freezing chiller rooms to be collected later in the day.

The whole process looked speedy and efficient, but I couldn't help wondering just how much attention to detail there was. Sure, the heads and innards were cut off and sent down a special production line to be binned and destroyed. But how much of the debris was ending up on the 'good' meat, as the health official had told us? How did we know that all the animals we had seen weren't actually infected? Were some of them in distress because they were frightened, or was it because they were sick?

A vet whose job it was to inspect cattle at abattoirs believed many infected cows were being slaughtered and passed fit for human consumption. According to government figures, just eighty-seven cattle with BSE had been found at abattoirs in the last year. But he alone said he had intercepted around fifty. He thought the official figures were a massive underestimation.

Towards the end of filming, the programme's producer, Stephen Clarke, arranged an interview with the then Food Minister, David McLean. Like many other ministers afterwards he displayed a shocking complacency about the problem, and seemed more interested in attacking the people who were raising the alarm. When asked if there was any risk whatever to humans he was breathtakingly dismissive: 'There is a theoretical risk there – just as there is a risk that the sky could fall on our heads when we leave this room.'

But however much they tried to play down the fears, BSE was a story that simply wouldn't go away. A few weeks after transmission European governments imposed a ban on live cattle from Britain aged more than six months. As more doctors and scientists went public with their worries the Agriculture Secretary John Gummer arranged a photo call where he tried to give his daughter a beefburger. It was a huge own goal, attracting wide-spread press criticism and giving much wider publicity to the problems. By that stage the meat industry had become incredibly sensitive about the story and it was proving impossible for TV crews to get inside slaughterhouses. The shots we got in Manchester had become like gold-dust – used repeatedly by the news bulletins to illustrate the dangers of cross infection in the abattoir.

Of course we now know that all the ministerial complacency was a terrible mistake. While the MPs and officials gave their assurances about safety, BSE was quietly seeping into the human food chain, potentially putting millions of us at risk. In 1995 *World In Action* journalists Kate Middleton and Isabel Tang took up the story again. They uncovered the case

Above: Dressing the part, with Afghanistan's Mujahedin fighters, 1989.

Left: Seven years later, and the Taliban are in control. With Mark Atkinson, Sandy Gall and Mike Lewis, Kabul, 1996.

Above: Simon Berthon (centre), Alan Bale and I listening to radio reports as we sail into Lebanon in 1982.

Right and below: The Israeli shells that greeted us. © Alan Bale

Above: Devastation
after the Mexican
earthquake, 1986.

Above right: Dan
Eldon, shortly before
his death, aged twenty-
two.
*Reproduced with kind
permission of the Eldon
family*

Right: One of Dan's
haunting photographs
from Somalia's civil
war.
*Reproduced with kind
permission of the Eldon
family*

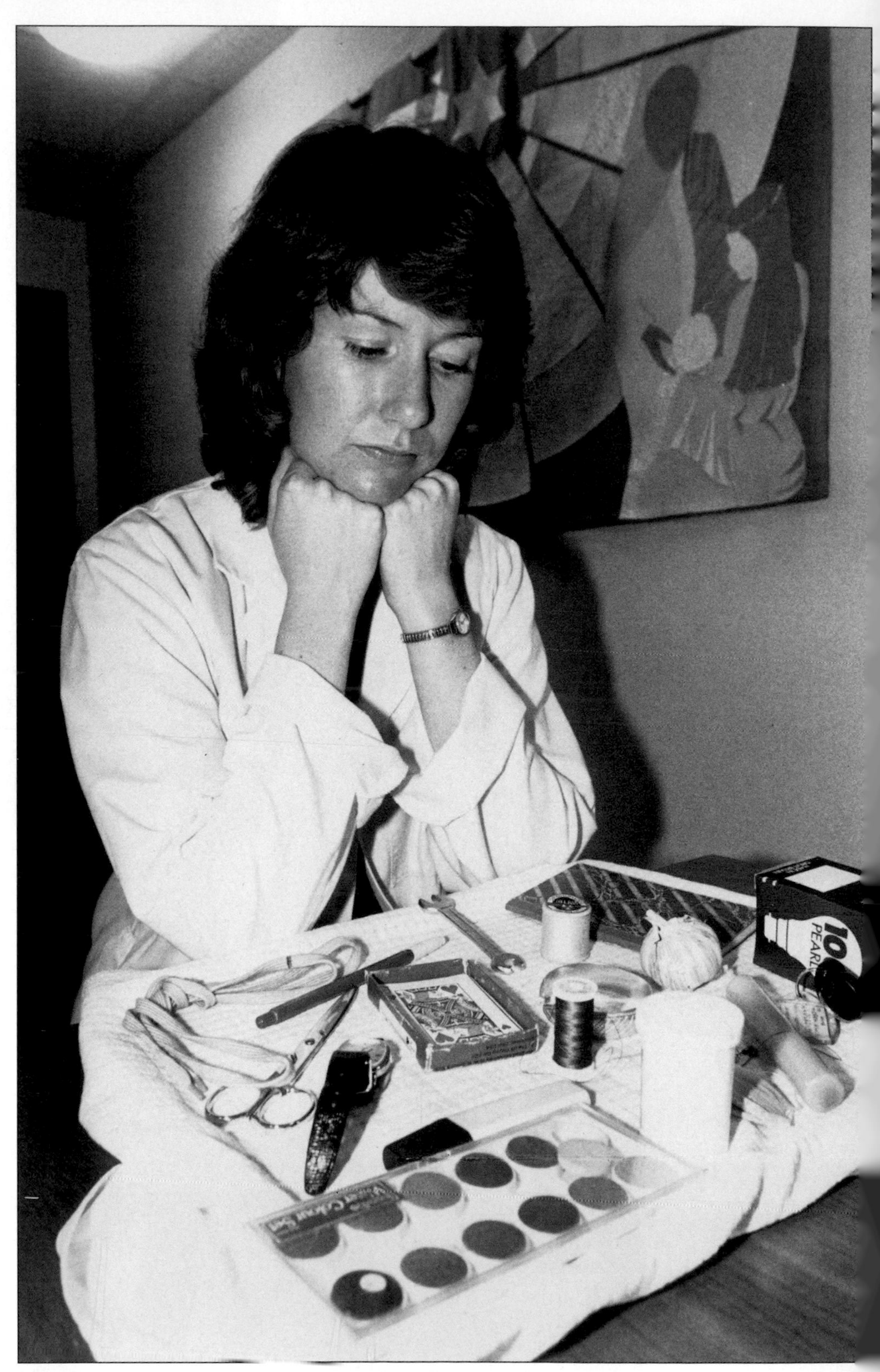

Junior doctor Katherine Hignett undergoes a memory test during a 72-hour shift.

Coronation Street actress Julie Goodyear visits the village that quit.

Anwar Ditta pleading for the return of her children from Pakistan in 1981.

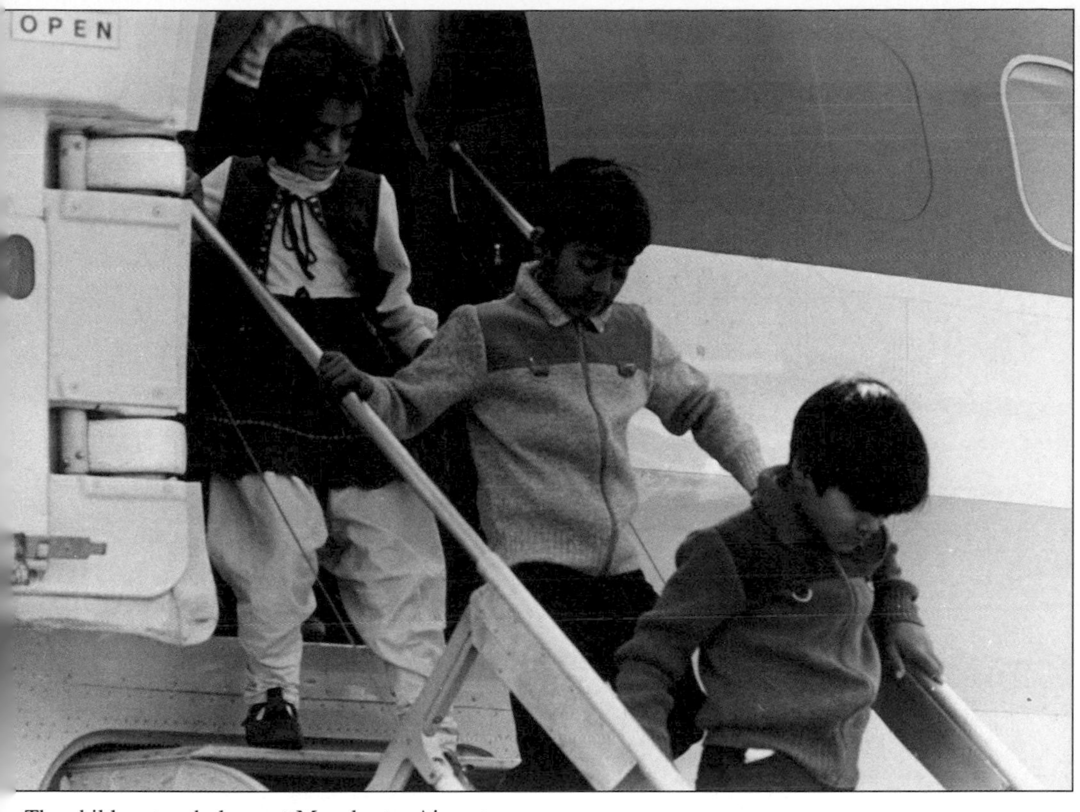

The children touch down at Manchester Airport.

Together at last.

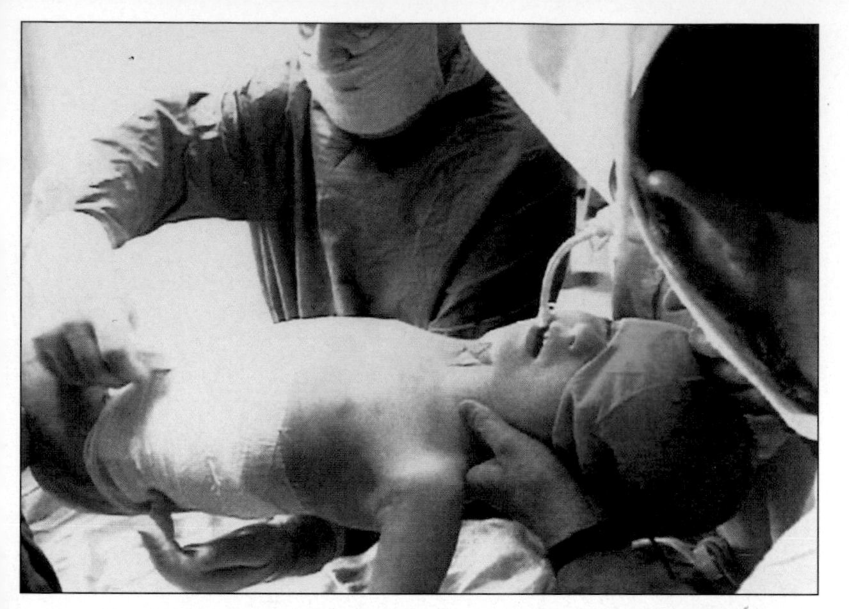

A surgeon operates to save the life of a Chernobyl victim in 1993.

Nina Rogerson revisits her home town following the nuclear disaster.

Some of the children who didn't survive.

of Stephen Churchill, a nineteen-year-old, who had died from Creutzfeldt-Jakob disease. Until his last year he'd been a fighting fit teenager with ambitions to go into the RAF. Then his brain was ravaged by the illness, causing him to die a lingering and horrible death.

After Stephen's death, doctors discovered that his form of CJD was different to the type that usually kills fifty people in Britain every year. His disease was a new variant – directly related to the infected beef that got into the food chain in the eighties and early nineties. Stephen was the first human casualty of BSE. By the time the government finally admitted a probable link, in March 1996, there had been another nine victims. At the time of writing, twenty-seven others have died, and no one knows how many more will follow.

LA LAW

The rise of the camcorder has provided TV viewers with some great entertainment moments, but it has also revolutionized news coverage. Watch any bulletin these days and you're likely to see home video footage of fires, car crashes, even bomb blasts. Such material was still relatively rare a decade ago. But then, in March 1991, a motorist shot eighty-one seconds of tape that would dominate news programmes throughout America and the world. Not since the famous footage of President Kennedy's assassination did a home movie create such an impact.

The tape showed four policemen stopping a car on the streets of Los Angeles. Within seconds of the driver getting out they began to beat him, while eleven other officers looked on. The police later claimed that the motorist, a black man named Rodney King, had led them on a high-speed chase and then resisted arrest. What millions of viewers saw was a defenceless man falling to the ground unconscious, while the armed officers continued to kick and club him.

A year after the televised assault, relations between the police and LA's ethnic population were at an all-time low. The four officers were standing trial, and King was suing the force for $56 million (one million for each blow). Meanwhile the police might have had appalling publicity over their aggressive methods, but they had no intention of changing the way they kept order on the streets. In their eyes they were in the middle of a war zone, keeping inner-city crime, violence and drugs away from the comfortable suburbs. Nearly all LA's police officers were white; the city itself was 60 per cent black and Hispanic.

I flew over LA at night by helicopter, with the millions of city lights stretching out for endless miles. It was a beautiful and mesmerizing sight, but it hid the brutal reality of life at ground level. There, on the streets, I was due to film with the men and women of the city's toughest precinct, Newton. They had agreed that we could follow them for three nights, seeing the problems they faced and listening to their solutions. Although they had already allowed various American crews 'along for a ride', they were willing to give us unprecedented access to their operations. They were particularly keen to demonstrate their 'pro-active' philosophy, which meant going out and looking for trouble, rather than waiting for it to happen.

Newton itself lies in the heart of South Central LA, an area notorious for poverty, drugs and violence. Gangs are a common feature, with around 100,000 youths claiming allegiance to one or other of the street tribes. Feuds between them are continuous and violent. During the early nineties, some 700 gang members – or 'homeboys' – were being shot and murdered every year.

Our guides to this urban jungle were Sergeants Mike Chamberlain and John Paige, both in their forties and each well used to the dangers of patrolling South Central. When approached by our producer Debbie Christie, they agreed to be followed but only on three strict conditions: we must never get out of the car without being told, we must never get in their way, and we must never expect them to wait while I got my camera ready. Although we rode with the men separately and on different nights, their questions to us were very similar. They both wanted to know how their policing methods were viewed by people back in the UK. And they were both fascinated to hear that most British police officers didn't carry guns as routine. (Actually, nearly all US cops are amazed at this. As one Miami detective once asked us: 'What the hell do they stop the bad guys with? Harsh words?')

Our first night with Mike was to prove unforgettable. We'd been driving around for a couple of hours when he got a radio message about a possible shooting at a house in the centre of Newton. When we arrived we found that two drunks had had a fight in the street, and that one had fled into a white bungalow with a gun. Mike questioned a number of witnesses and called for reinforcements while he tried to coax the man out. He was believed to be a Mexican, so Tannoy messages were shouted in Spanish.

When the man failed to emerge from behind the barricades, police cars began to flood the streets, and armed SWAT teams surrounded the bungalow. We followed Mike as he supervised the evacuation of all the nearby properties, warning people that shots might soon be fired from inside the house. Within the space of a few minutes, a low-life street brawl had turned into an armed siege with highly trained police marksmen taking up their positions. I was getting some great shots of the unfolding drama, but couldn't help worrying about my own safety should the drunk in the house open fire. But, as it turned out, I was equally in danger from the other side. One of the newly arrived officers didn't know there was a film crew present. When he saw me creeping forward to crouch beside one of the marksmen, he pulled his gun on me. Luckily, our local driver, Les, moved in quickly and explained who I was.

Meanwhile, as the sirens blared and helicopters hovered, other cameras started to appear. Since the well-publicized police brutality incident, LA had become home to a new breed of amateur news gatherers, all hoping to get more valuable footage. One neighbour with a camcorder told us: 'This goes on every day and night around here – we go to bed with the sound of gunfire. I may be able to do another Rodney King video – maybe I'll make a buck.'

In the end the video man got action, but no brutality. The siege ended four hours later when the SWAT team fired in tear gas, forcing the gunman to come out.

By that time, Mike had dealt with more serious incidents. The first involved a young Hispanic man who'd been gunned down at a roadside. At the scene it was chaos, with police and paramedics trying to make sense of what had happened. The victim, who was still alive, refused to talk. In the middle of the road, there was an abandoned yellow Honda car with its windscreen smashed. After questioning some witnesses, one of Mike's colleagues concluded that the man had become the victim of a deadly new craze among LA's gangs – the drive-by shooting. According to his information, the wounded man had been standing on a pavement when two men went past in a station wagon. They drew their guns, fired four rounds and hit him in the leg.

I moved in to get close-ups of the victim being stretchered into the ambulance when Mike's radio crackled into life again: there had been another shooting two blocks away. He headed back to his car with me following, jumped inside and sped off. When we arrived at 48th Street – the supposed scene of the gunfire – there was more confusion. Police cars, ambulances and fire engines were driving around, all getting conflicting reports from their control rooms. Nobody knew where the victim was. The only clue was a large pool of blood slowly spreading out across the middle of the road.

We seemed to have been driving around in circles for about ten minutes when I spotted a car that had crashed down a side street. As I looked closer, I saw a door wedged open and what appeared to be a pair of legs sticking out. 'Isn't that a body over there?' I asked Mike. Sure enough, inside the vehicle was a huge man sprawled across the driver and passenger seats. He was naked except for a pair of shorts, and blood was streaming down his torso and legs. I went round to the driver's side and got shots of his face, which was contorted with pain. Mike put his head inside and managed to ask him one or two questions, but the victim soon blacked out. It later emerged he was a homeboy who'd got involved in a gun battle with other gang members. The two cars had driven side by side with the occupants shooting at one another. Finally, a bullet had gone through his door and into his back, causing him to crash. A few hours after I filmed him he was dead.

The casual, everyday violence among the gangs was truly frightening. Katy Jones, the programme's researcher, had spent weeks getting us access to some of the most feared in South Central. Members included 'Shadow' a nineteen-year-old drug dealer who made around $800 a night selling crack and cocaine. His Hispanic gang – The 18th Street – was involved in a vicious turf war with rival drug dealers from other neighbourhoods. As he drove us around, he was asked how he protected himself from the other gangs. Without hesitating he reached into his glove compartment and pulled out a .45 pistol which he claimed to use at least three times a week.

Another infamous Hispanic gang called White Fence counted girls in its ranks. Among these were 'Curly', a fourteen-year-old who had left a relatively comfortable home and family to live with other gang members. She showed us graffiti that warned her and her friends that they would soon be shot by rival groups. She described dodging bullets fired from passing cars as 'kind of fun'. And, giving us a run-down of a typical Saturday night on the streets, she spoke of 'fighting, spray painting, murders and getting into drugs'.

Her best friend was known as 'Baby Loca'. Apart from being shot at herself, she had pulled a gun on a rival gang member, injuring him with a bullet. Asked how she felt about what she had done, the sixteen-year-old girl replied: 'Nothing, I guess. I think because I was on drugs, you know, really into drugs, I was all sprung, messed up, and it didn't mean nothing to me. I didn't care.'

Riding around with the police, it was clear that they regarded those gang members as the lowest form of life. The Crash Unit – to which John Paige belonged – was set up specifically to target them. It didn't wait for trouble to develop, but tried to stop it happening in the first place. The theory was that if gang members were on the street then sooner or later they would commit crimes. According to Paige, there was only one solution. 'Our technique is to arrest them for anything that we can get them on, just to get them off the street . . . take 'em off the streets, remove them from society, put them in prison, put them on the moon. Whatever it takes to get rid of them.'

He admitted that officers needed to be aggressive to join the Crash Unit. And that taking on the gangs was exciting for his men.

> They go out there and actively pursue their job. They go out looking for a gang, they go out looking for people having fights and carrying out shootings and stabbings. They know the area and they get excited about what they're doing. Oh, and they love getting guns off people – to them that's the biggest thrill of all.

The Unit may have got results, but it did nothing to improve relations with the wider ethnic population. One in four officers had received formal complaints about excessive force. In the previous year the Los Angeles Police Department had paid out $11 million to the victims of alleged brutality.

On the streets though, the controversial 'pro-active' policy continued. We filmed the Unit driving through high crime neighbourhoods, shining spotlights into houses and using its stop and search powers at the slightest of excuses. At one point the officers heard Spanish music inside a house, then went inside to break up a party. There'd been no reports of trouble, and no complaints from local residents. But, because the police thought there might be gang members inside, they hauled the revellers out and made them kneel in front of a wall with their hands behind their back.

Later the police helicopter shone its powerful beam down on a car suspected of driving erratically. Within minutes the car had been stopped by a patrol vehicle and surrounded by twelve armed officers. The young driver and his three friends faced an hour of accusations – firstly about stealing the car, then about drugs, and finally about drinking. Officers turned the vehicle inside out looking for weapons. Desperate for an arrest, they then started to question one of the passengers about a gold watch he was wearing. Eventually the police had to admit that there had been no crime. The youngsters were allowed to go, with a policewoman complaining that they were now 'free to commit more crimes'.

In our three nights on patrol we had gained more than enough material to give a true picture of life in the crime-ridden areas of LA. We were able to show the genuine difficulties and dangers that the cops faced, but also the consequences of their zero-tolerance approach. It was clear they were having success against the gangs, but they were creating many enemies in the process. Our programme, transmitted on 13 April 1992, ended with the words of Clay Jacke, a black lawyer, and himself a former policeman:

> We have an invading army coming into the black community who do not, as a matter of fact, understand the econ-

> omy, the mores, the people they are dealing with. And so, since they don't understand the people, they have a short fuse in dealing with them . . . Because the police department is in the crucible of our social structure they bring things to an edge more often than is felt by the diversity of our citizenship. We could have a racial conflict here involving the several minorities that has never been heard of in the whole history of this city.

Sixteen days later a largely white jury acquitted the four policemen who had been captured on home video beating the motorist Rodney King. For the next forty-eight hours the world watched as Los Angeles was engulfed in the most serious rioting America had ever seen. Stores, offices and government buildings were stormed and looted; white drivers were pulled from their cars and beaten; police stations were attacked by mobs.

South Central was set ablaze, with the smoke from 150 fires causing the re-routing of flights due into Los Angeles Airport. As the rioting spread from the ghettoes to the wealthy suburbs, the National Guard was ordered in and curfews imposed. The simmering feud between the police and LA's ethnic population had finally erupted into war. By the time the violence came to an end, at least fifty people were dead.

DIANA'S LEGACY

There are many famous images of Princess Diana, but some of the most enduring are those of her meeting the land-mine victims of Africa. Her visit to Angola, just seven months before she died, confirmed her status as the world's leading goodwill ambassador. It also brought unprecedented attention to the international trade in land-mines, and the appalling suffering it caused. As I watched those TV pictures of her tour of the Red Cross clinics, I was struck with an overwhelming sense of déjà vu. I'd been to those same towns, seen the same aid workers, perhaps even filmed the same victims. And as she came face to face with children minus their arms and legs, I knew exactly the sense of outrage she must have felt.

Angola lies on the south-west coast of Africa, between the Congo and Namibia. By rights it should be a wealthy place with its natural abundance of gold, diamonds and oil. But in reality it is one of the world's poorest nations. Its economy lies in ruins due to a quarter century of almost constant civil war.

The country gained its independence from Portugal in 1975. The government that took over was the communist MPLA, backed by the Soviet Union and Cuba. But from the start it was bitterly opposed by the anti-Marxist guerrilla group UNITA, which was supported by South Africa and America.

It was 1981 when I first visited. At that time South Africa had occupied Namibia, and was using it as a base to attack Angolan government positions over the border. Up in the central highlands, where UNITA was strongest, we filmed with the refugees from the fighting. Thousands had lost their homes and land and were starving. But among the familiar scenes of sunken eyes and swollen tummies, there was a new sight: row upon row of people with missing limbs.

UNITA, it appeared, was fond of land-mines. They were devices that were designed to maim opponents and not to kill. From the cynical military point of view this was useful, as a cripple is more of a drain on the enemy's medical resources than someone who's dead. But, filming in the camps, it was clear that there were no medical resources to speak of, at least for civilians. The effects of UNITA's land-mines were indiscriminate, and these were their innocent victims.

When I returned thirteen years later, the war between the government and the rebels was still raging. But by then both sides were using land-mines. In a country of nine million people there were estimated to be just as many anti-personnel devices lying around. And, in the main hospitals, doctors had performed around 20,000 amputations.

Travelling with us this time was Simon Coaton, a tough ex-paratrooper who had served in Northern Ireland and the Falklands. He had also been to the Gulf War, where he had seen a colleague blown to pieces by a land-mine. Now a civilian, he was working for the Mines Advisory Group. The British-based charity had been set up to help clear land-mines from war-torn countries, but it was also spearheading the campaign to ban their manufacture and sale.

The programme's producer, David Leigh, aimed to show how British companies were profiting from this trade. He persuaded the Angolan army to show us some of the mines they had captured from the rebel forces. Filming them in a line, I could see that some had been manufactured in the USA, while others had originated from China, Italy, France and South Africa. But also in the collection was a mine known as the Mark 7, a highly effective weapon designed to blow up tanks. Then there was the HB876 which explodes when tilted. And a third anti-personnel device which promised not to kill, but to 'immobilize'. All three had been used to terrorize not only enemy forces, but innocent civilians. They had each wrecked lives and caused injury and suffering. And every one of them had been made in Britain.

Although the UK didn't officially export these weapons to Angola we did sell them to other countries, such as Saudi Arabia. At the time, we were the second largest arms exporter in the world. And, trading in secret, our companies were supplying land-mines to armies around the globe. According to Simon, the trade didn't end once the devices left British shores. They found their way on to the world arms markets, to be resold and supplied to oppressive regimes. Or, in the case of Angola, to a rebel army.

In the capital, Luanda, we joined Simon on a visit to the main hospital. On some of the wards there were up to thirty youngsters, mostly in their teens, who had been injured by mines. What first struck me there was the almost complete silence. Usually, wherever I film children, they play to the camera, waving, smiling, asking me if they can look down the eyepiece. But here, the youngsters appeared dazed and confused. It was easy to see why. Some had lost one or both legs, others a hand or an arm: one child had lost both eyes as well as a limb. The stories of how they had stepped on the devices were heartbreaking. A doctor told us of a girl who had gone into the fields to collect food because she and her family were hungry. The mine had been covered with crops and soil, making it invisible. She had no idea of the danger until it exploded, taking off her leg.

Out in Luanda's teeming streets there were other amputees who had left hospital and who were trying to make a living. I would often see them on street corners holding fistfuls of the near-worthless local currency, offering to exchange it for Western dollars. Some operated around the hotels where they might get the chance of doing some trade with a visiting businessman or tourist. You had to admire their spirit, but they were a desperate sight. Standing one-legged, they were thin, bedraggled, and old before their time. To me it looked as if their lives were over before they had really begun.

But it was inland where the crisis was at its worst. Here, cities had been captured by the rebel forces and others were under siege. We arrived in one town, Malange, as it was being shelled by UNITA. All the roads surrounding it had been mined, and many of its people were starving. In one clinic we saw a little baby girl called Tunisia whose mother had stepped on a mine while desperately trying to harvest food. She was seriously injured but had returned home to breastfeed her baby. She made it, but later died from her injuries. When Tunisia was discovered three days later, she was still clinging to her mother's body.

Simon was keen to gather evidence of the extent of the land-mine hazard on the roads leading out from the besieged towns to the countryside. At one point I got out of the car to film a row of tanks that were lying in ruins at the roadside. I moved in close but he warned me to go no further. It might have been a long time since the tanks had been blown up, and the land surrounding them was now thick with vegetation. A mine could easily be concealed underneath. I carried on filming from a distance, but soon got a painful reminder of another African hazard: I was bitten by a mosquito.

Later in the day we were with an army patrol on a road leading to a deserted village in enemy territory. Craters in the ground were evidence of earlier land-mine ambushes against government forces. I climbed on to an old dilapidated building to get some shots of the terrain when suddenly we heard a loud explosion followed by shouting. Although our immediate reaction was to go into the bush to find out what had happened, Simon and our army minder told us to hold back. Both were convinced that we'd heard the sound of a land-mine going off, and both were confident that others would be lying around.

A few minutes later a soldier emerged from the undergrowth. He confirmed that a mine had exploded injuring several members of his patrol. His own legs had been hit by shrapnel and were bleeding. But it seemed he was the one in best shape to come out and organize some help. Immediately our patrol swung into action, putting together makeshift stretchers from bamboo and old uniforms. They went into the bush and emerged minutes later carrying a succession of the injured. Several of them were in a bad way, bleeding heavily. One soldier was a particularly gruesome sight with deep lacerations to his face and legs. As they bundled him into an armoured personnel carrier I walked across to get a shot of the military vehicle driving away. Once it had, I took the camera off my shoulder and looked down to the ground: I was standing in a pool of his blood.

Towards the end of the shoot we went to another town, around five hundred miles inland. Here, there were no trained surgeons, so the four local doctors had taught themselves how to perform basic amputations. Over the last six months they had removed limbs from 112 people – many of them teenagers and children. There was the eighteen-year-old who had stepped on a mine while out walking with her two friends. And the twelve-year-old boy who had been riding on a tractor when it drove across a device laid in the fields. Surveying the human wreckage, Simon explained why his organization wanted to get land-mines outlawed internationally, in the same way as chemical weapons and nerve gas. 'All these people are civilians who are trying to live. They're trying to fetch food, trying to fetch water. Anti-personnel mines are designed to injure and maim and not to kill. It's totally inhumane. You only have to walk through these hospitals to see that.'

It had been a gruelling project, and one that had brought me face to face with some of the worst suffering I had seen for many years. But aside from the human images, I had another reason to remember it. Just three days after I arrived in England I got a call from the office, asking me to go back to Africa on another story. I had felt under the weather since I got home, and when the time came to go to Manchester Airport again, my wife Jackie had to help me shuffle through the departure lounge. I was booked on a flight to Durban in South Africa where we were making a programme about mercury poisoning. Throughout the journey I was desperately tired and lethargic. I had a temperature along with an excruciating headache, and, by the time we touched down, I could barely summon the energy to hail a cab.

After a welcome night's sleep I met up with the producer, Sarah Manwaring-White, and my assistant Keith Staniforth. We began shooting a sequence near to a factory that was producing the mercury, but I quickly realized that I couldn't hold the camera still. My hands were shaking and I seemed to have no control over the twitching in my arms. Later I set up for an interview but couldn't bear to look through the lens because of a searing pain in my eyes. By mid-afternoon my shakes had become worse. I was shivering and breaking out in severe sweats. What vestige of energy I had left had gone. But most debilitating of all was the headache. My brain was pulsating and I felt it was about to burst out of my skull.

Sarah called off the shoot and persuaded me to see a doctor. Keith drove me to the casualty unit at Durban's main hospital. A short time later I was being examined by a doctor who fired a series of questions about where I'd been recently. When I told him about the Angola trip he organized a blood test, with the results quickly confirming his suspicions. I was suffering from a lethal form of cerebral malaria. The mosquito that had bitten me two weeks earlier was carrying a parasite that had invaded my liver, then broken out into my bloodstream. By the time I was diagnosed my red cells were infected, obstructing the blood vessels in my brain. Another few days without treatment and I would have died.

I spent a week in the hospital recovering, with the doctors giving me hefty doses of quinine. The symptoms went gradually, but the terrible headaches didn't start to ease for a good three days. In all, I lost twenty pounds in weight. It transpired that I'd been taking the wrong anti-malarial drugs when I was in Angola. The rest of the team had gone to a different clinic and been prescribed the correct pills. Lying in a bed 10,000 miles from home it would have been easy to feel sorry for myself. But by that stage I had been travelling the world for twenty-seven years, and this was the first time I had been struck down with a serious illness. Apart from doctors' orders to stay off the booze for the next six months, I'd been lucky.

Not so the people of Angola. It was three years after our programme that the Princess of Wales first visited them and drew the attention of the world in the most dramatic way. Within weeks of her death the international community finally agreed to put an end to the trade. But in the intervening period many more had become victims of the land-mines. Today, even with an international ban in place, Angola's innocent civilians remain at risk from the millions of devices scattered throughout their land.

CHAPTER 6
LOOK AT IT ANOTHER WAY

When he built the Granada studios the company's founder Sidney Bernstein laid down a golden rule: on every office wall there should hang a portrait of the legendary nineteenth-century circus owner, Phineas T. Barnum. The reason for this, Sidney explained, was that all programme makers – whatever their field – needed a constant reminder that they worked in showbusiness.

No one disputes that dramas, sitcoms and game shows should be entertaining, but introducing 'showbusiness' into current affairs has always been more tricky. The stories we cover are often serious, and sometimes harrowing. Producers who try to inject some popular appeal get accused of trivializing the issues. Even today there are critics who believe current affairs should consist of dry analysis and debate among politicians and experts. They dismiss any attempt to make the format more entertaining as 'dumbing down'. Thankfully, I've worked with many producers who think otherwise. They've shown that the words 'serious' and 'popular' can go hand in hand. And time and again they've brought big audiences to important subjects, simply by using their imagination.

The entertaining twist – or 'spin' – was pioneered by *World In Action*'s original editor Tim Hewatt. In one of his first editions he wanted to raise awareness of the number of deaths from bronchitis. Any traditional programme maker would have filmed a doctor sitting behind a desk reciting a number of statistics. But Tim rightly denounced that sort of approach as 'boring'. So he hired a crane and mounted it above a terraced street in Salford. Using actors dressed as pallbearers, his opening shot showed scores of coffins emerging, one by one, from each of the houses. As the black-suited actors carried them through the smog-filled streets, a solitary church bell rang out. Then the narrator gave the facts: 'There is a disease which in Britain causes more death and pain and misery than in any other country in the world. The name of that disease is bronchitis. Last year it killed 39,148 people.'

Such arresting images aside, the early programmes found other ways to capture the viewers' attention. As an Australian, Tim Hewatt was fascinated by Britain's class system and keen to explore how deep-seated it had become. The result was an edition called *Seven-Up* which profiled a number of primary school children talking about their lives, hopes, ambitions and expectations. It was so effective in pointing up the class divisions that, every seven years since, Granada has returned to the programme's subjects to find out how their lives have progressed. For the last three decades I've filmed them recounting their triumphs and disasters, marriages and divorces, births and bereavements. And while the lives of some of them have taken unexpected turns, it is apparent that for many their future was predetermined by their past.

Throughout those decades we managed to popularize many more issues. These have included unemployment – with a Tory MP living on the dole for a week – and the inequalities of the benefits system – with TV host Nicholas Parsons presenting a spoof game show called *Spongers*. When Britain prepared for its referendum on joining the EEC, we set up a special debate at the Oxford Union. When the whole country was in uproar over the poll tax, we profiled the people who had found perfectly legal ways to avoid paying it. And when beggars first appeared on our streets we sent an undercover reporter to live among London's homeless for a month. Carrying a secret camera he was able to portray the raw brutality and loneliness of 'cardboard city' as never before.

All these programmes tackled important subjects that the average viewer would normally avoid. But a touch of creativity and lateral thought attracted unusually large audiences. Mr Bernstein would have been pleased at the imagination that went into them. And I'm sure even old Barnum would have approved of some of the other stunts we pulled.

THE VILLAGE THAT QUIT

High up in Derbyshire sits the tiny village of Longnor. It's one of the oldest market towns in England, popular with walkers and anglers who fish in the upper reaches of the rivers Dove and Manifold. It's also home to some of the most spectacular scenery in the Peak District. In the middle of winter though, this beautiful countryside spot can become isolated by swirling mists and heavy snowfalls. Cut off from the outside world there's little for the locals to do but watch TV, visit the three local pubs . . . and smoke.

At least, that's what used to happen back in 1971. But then a *World In Action* team made the short trek from Manchester and spent a month persuading Longnor's 320 adults to take part in a unique televised experiment. For one week they would be bombarded with health messages. They would see educational films and slide shows. They would be visited by doctors, celebrities and even hypnotists. All the attention would be directed with one single aim in mind – to get the entire village to give up cigarettes.

The programme had been commissioned by the then executive producer Jeremy Wallington. He was aware of a new report from the Royal College of Physicians that was about to blame smoking for the huge rates of lung cancer in Britain. The first study linking the two had actually been published in 1964, but while it had hit tobacco's popularity hard, the dip in sales was short-lived. It had become clear that people wouldn't give up permanently just because of one day's bad publicity. Nicotine is a highly addictive drug, and smokers needed constant reminders of why it was bad for them.

Jeremy asked producer Mike Ryan to find a town that would take part. He then spent time looking through the parish registers of England trying to identify a place with the right number of residents. When Longnor was finally selected, Mike dispatched his researchers Brian Blake, Claudia Milne and John Slater to the Peaks to get the locals to sign up to the idea. Their persuasive skills were obviously strong – by the time they'd finished, 100 of the 110 village smokers had agreed to become guinea pigs.

Brian, who was a forty-a-day man himself, had an ace up his sleeve when dealing with some of the more hardened smokers. Each night, he rounded up more volunteers in the village pubs by promising to give up the habit, too. Impressed that he was prepared to share their pain, even the old domino players in the Horseshoe Inn came on board. However, Isaac Thomson, part-time church bell-ringer and village gravedigger, remained reluctant. He was seventy-two and said he simply enjoyed his fags too much. And if people were going to stop experiencing early deaths, then trade down at the cemetery would suffer.

Finally, a date was set for the week-long experiment to start. We set up base in the Crew and Harpur pub with Mike laying down a strict rule for the production team. As we would be living in a non-smoking village, no lighting up was allowed among the Granada staff. Brian had already agreed to quit, but now Claudia and Mike himself also had to give up. Back in Manchester our chain-smoking production manager Tom Gill offered them all moral support. For the first time in his adult life he promised to break his eighty-a-day habit.

As a non-smoker myself, I could simply concentrate on getting the pictures while enjoying the carnival atmosphere. It kicked off at 11 a.m. on Sunday 10 January, when Longnor's brass band wound its way through the country lanes proclaiming the start of non-smoking week. Down in the main square there were posters and banners. Local dignitaries gave speeches, while some of the villagers made a bonfire of their fag packets. 'Wicked' Will Thompson, the local poet, turned up to entertain the crowds with one of his truly awful rhymes:

If everyone packed up smoking
If only for a week or two
People could be in better health
Well I think so, do you?

The press were out in force too. The experiment had caught the imagination of Fleet Street, and that morning they got a great photo opportunity when the *Coronation Street* stars Julie Goodyear and Peter Adamson arrived to lend their support. While it was all welcome publicity for the programme, one or two of the newspapers almost threw a spanner in the works. Determined to get a different story, they tried to bribe a couple of residents so as to get a shot of them taking a furtive puff. Luckily the locals were having none of it. They told the photographers to get lost and even warned Brian which ones to look out for.

Down at the village hall, Longnor's smokers crowded in for a talk by a doctor from the Christie Cancer Hospital in Manchester. Across the road at the local clinic, others were subjecting themselves to tests on breathing machines that showed their diminished lung capacity. Over at the sweet-shops and tobacconists, the owners were beginning to count their losses. Before we'd arrived they were selling 17,000 cigarettes every week. Now trade was down to a trickle, as only those passing through the village called in to pick up their packets of twenty.

By the end of the first day, eighty-nine of the 100 volunteers had stuck firm to their promise and left the cigarettes alone. The first to weaken had reached for a puff at five past eleven, after waking up with a hangover and forgetting all about the experiment. When he realized what he'd done he stubbed out the cigarette and didn't touch another one all week.

When willpower started to wilt we invited village smokers to spend a day watching a constant stream of anti-smoking propaganda. A health expert had collected TV and cinema advertisements from around the world underlining the message that smoking killed. Commercials from health-conscious Scandinavian countries were the most effective. One showed ashtrays made of human skulls, and another included cigarette packets in the shape of coffins.

If the propaganda failed we unleashed our secret weapon – the seventy-year-old hypnotist Henry Blythe. I filmed him sending several of the most hardened smokers into a trance while reciting his familiar mantra: 'Your whole body is so heavy . . . you simply do not want to smoke . . . you have finished with smoking . . . never . . . ever . . . ever . . . let your hands touch tobacco again.'

As the smokers collapsed into his arms, he clicked his fingers, counted from one to five and told them to wake up. Some of his subjects were amazed at the effect he had on them, happily promising never to smoke again. It all looked very impressive until we asked local grocer Ken Dunn whether Henry's act had had the desired effect on him. Ken, who readily admitted he was the village addict, complained that it had all been a waste of time. He then went back to work, spending the rest of the day smoking thirty cigarettes – and ten cigars.

But by the end of the experiment he was in a minority. Of the 100 smokers, seventy-four stopped completely for the full week. Even the twenty-six people who failed all cut down – some from forty cigarettes a day to five. On the last day there was another celebration, with the band bringing no-smoking week to an end. Many in the crowd said that they'd never touch another cigarette. Then the actor Peter Adamson, who had also managed to give up, gave them all a final pep talk. 'I'm in awe and admiration for all those of you who have stopped and stayed stopped. You've cracked it for a week, and if you can do it for a week you can do it for another day. Just do it for the next day, just for one day at a time.'

It was another two decades before I returned to the village. By then the hazards of smoking were much more widely accepted, and its impact on the nation's health was plain for everyone to see. According to the government's Health Education Authority tobacco was responsible for one in six of all deaths. Smoking was killing twelve people an hour, 300 people a day. As for the cost to the National Health Service, more than 9,000 hospital beds were occupied by people suffering from tobacco-related diseases. Yet one in three British adults still smoked and – among young women – cigarette consumption was actually rising. It seemed that all the health messages of the previous twenty years had done little to stem the craving for tobacco. But was the national addiction shared in Longnor?

Brian, who by then was the programme's senior producer, wanted to find out. In January 1992 – exactly twenty-one years after our first programme – we once again drove down those isolated country roads and into the mist-covered village. The first surprise was just how little things had changed. Sure, there was a little more entertainment on offer – the odd restaurant and even a strip-o-gram down at the social club. But otherwise things looked exactly the same. People were still drinking in the Cheshire Cheese, and the Crew and

Harpur, while Saturday-night dominoes was still a feature of the Horseshoe Inn. In a village where few outsiders come to settle, the most popular surnames were still Mellor and Thompson. And while a few of the locals had moved away, nearly all those interviewed back in 1971 were still around.

The second surprise was the gravedigger. Isaac Thompson was by then ninety-three years old. He had retired from the cemetery, but he was still enjoying his fags. Not surprisingly he held to the view that smoking did no harm, and he was determined to carry on puffing until the end. But as we asked around we found others who had taken part in our experiment and had managed to steer clear of cigarettes ever since. They included local councillor Peter Francis and his wife. When we left the village in 1971 they counted up how much they had saved, and realized they would be significantly better off if they each quit their sixty-a-day habit. Then there was June Inglefield. She had tried to pack it in several times, but it was only our experiment that had finally given her the will to succeed. Watching a tape of the old programme, she relived the excitement and atmosphere that had been generated.

> I think that crusade spirit really helped. Knowing that there were so many people around who were all suffering withdrawal symptoms made it easier for me to give up. I've never smoked another cigarette from that day, and I don't think I ever will do.

It was hard to gauge just how many other unqualified success stories there were. Our best guess was that about a dozen people had quit for good, while many others had smoked less or only intermittently. As for the production team, Mike managed to kick the habit but Brian started lighting up again about nine months after the experiment finished. Meanwhile, back at base, Tom Gill became a convert to the health cause.

He never touched another cigarette in his life, and anyone caught smoking in his office was chucked out.

A STATISTIC, A REMINDER

Unemployment was the great challenge. It was the issue that dominated the British political scene for more than twenty years, and the one that probably touched the lives of our viewers more than any other. But how do you find a fresh angle on a story that runs for so long? Where are the new facts and figures? What do you have to say that is genuinely different?

Looking back I'm glad to say that our more creative producers didn't let the audience down. They consistently found radical ways to cover the subject, thereby ensuring that it stayed on the agenda. Some programmes were more off-beat than others, but all of them underlined the huge waste – both in financial and in human terms – that mass unemployment represented.

The most famous of these editions was, of course, the MP on the dole mentioned earlier. The member in question was Matthew Parris, then a thrusting young Tory who had gone on record criticizing what he claimed were high levels of benefits to the jobless. After agreeing to become 'unemployed' in Newcastle for a week, his view changed considerably. He accepted that £26 was not enough for a young man to live on, and he returned to Westminster with some uncomfortable home truths for his Conservative colleagues.

But there were equally entertaining programmes. There was *On Yer Bike*, following a group of jobless men from Middlesbrough who had taken Norman Tebbitt's advice and left home to look for work in the affluent south-east. Unfortunately the search led them to High Wycombe where it was virtually impossible for them to afford a place to live.

Then there was *The Job*, which followed a group of hopeful applicants going in search of one of the only full-time posts available in Manchester that week – a road sweeper with the City Council. And then there was the programme that turned the coverage of the early nineties recession on its head, by profiling those who were successful. In *Recession – That'll Do Nicely* we spent time with debt collectors, liquidators, and pawnbrokers, for whom business had never been better. The message of the programme was clear: if the likes of them were doing well, things must be bad.

Unemployment was a curse affecting many middle-aged workers whose factories had closed and who had little chance of finding another job. But even worse was the large number of young people who faced a bleak future the moment they left school. In 1981 we found a new way of examining youth unemployment, by profiling the then up-and-coming reggae band UB40. All eight members hailed from Birmingham, the centre of Britain's industrial heartland. But after a series of huge plant closures the West Midlands had become an economic blackspot, holding out few prospects for teenagers coming on to the jobs market.

The band were no strangers to enforced leisure time – they had even named themselves after the code at the top of the unemployment form. As part of the film, a couple of members had agreed to go to a school in Walsall to talk to the kids about getting into the music industry. When we got there we found the teachers actually giving a lesson on filling in dole forms. In that same week the local careers offices had just 100 vacancies for the 15,000 school leavers searching for work.

The band members themselves had refused to sit back and wallow in self-pity. They had decided to channel their anger and energy into their music. I followed the saxophonist Brian Travers on a tour around south Birmingham's multi-racial district – the same neighbourhood where he had until recently cashed his unemployment cheques and dreamed of stardom. While he and his fellow band members didn't see themselves as spokesmen for the unemployed, he felt they had a duty to raise awareness of their problems:

> UB40 is a result of us having absolutely nothing and no prospects of anything. But now we've got a chance to speak publicly. We've put ourselves on a platform, so rather than say inconsequential things, we'd rather sing about things that we feel are relevant.

On a December night in Birmingham thousands of unemployed youngsters gathered for a free concert by the band. In 1969, when I filmed the Rolling Stones playing their famous open air set in Hyde Park, the young audience was full of hope for the future. But on that night, standing among the crowd in the cold and draughty Bingley Hall, I could sense only pessimism. The biggest cheer was reserved for 'One In Ten' – the song in which vocalist Ali Campbell described life as one of the faceless army of unemployed

I am the one in ten
A number on a list
I am the one in ten
Even though I don't exist
Nobody knows me
But I'm always there
A statistic, a reminder
Of a world that doesn't care

For Ali and his band, the memory of the dole queue was still fresh. But within just a couple of years they had become one of the world's biggest selling groups, with massive success on both sides of the Atlantic. For millions of others though, unemployment didn't go away, and neither did the misery it caused.

Three years after the UB40 programme I was on a train taking my son Richard back to Southport following a football match at Anfield. I'd bought a copy of that evening's *Liverpool Echo*, and soon became fascinated by one of the inside-page articles. It was about a street where virtually all the adult males were out of work. To supplement their meagre DSS benefits, they were relying on the local black economy.

The following Monday I passed the cutting to *World In Action*'s editor Ray Fitzwalter. He was equally interested in the story and sent a couple of researchers out to look into it further. Soon afterwards they came back with a tale that none of us could quite believe. In Birkenhead, just a forty-minute drive from where I grew up, people were making a living by scavenging on a rubbish tip.

We went to the old shipbuilding town in the summer of 1984. By then the yards that had once employed 17,000 men were on the brink of collapse. Cammell Laird, where the *Ark Royal* was launched, provided work for fewer than 2,000 people. In the lifeless docks the rusting cranes stood idle. On the surrounding industrial estates, factories and warehouses were boarded up. In Birkenhead's north end, prospects were particularly bleak with six out of seven school leavers failing to find work. The fathers of many of them once thought they had secure jobs in the shipyards and factories. But now they worked in a twilight world that was both dangerous and degrading.

It was in the north end that we met Micky and Dot, a couple who had married when they were young. Micky had worked all his life in ship repair, winning promotion to chargehand and leading a team of riggers. But when he was made redundant at thirty he began drinking heavily. Soon he was getting into debt and having frequent rows with his wife. Then, when his redundancy money ran out, he turned to crime to pay for his beer and bills. The arguments at home became worse and Dot decided to divorce him. Micky got into trouble with the police and finally found himself in jail.

But when we arrived to film, Micky and Dot were getting married again. He had cut out the drinking, turned away from crime and regained some of his old self-respect. During the evening wedding reception in the local pub he explained how his life had changed. It all stemmed from a meeting with a friend who invited him to the tip where he searched for cast-off clothes and furniture:

> I was only there for about half an hour and I came out. I couldn't take it. You know, you've got to wait by a skip and dive in if you see anything. It just wasn't me. But then gradually I went over and over there again and I just got used to it.
>
> Now it's helped me pull myself together. I just wake up in the morning about 8.30 and go over there, come home about twelve and have something to eat. I go back out there, come home at six, then sit in and watch the telly. The way I look at it, I've just been out and done eight hours work. It's just like a job to me. The only trouble is I don't get paid for it.

The following day we went to Bidston Moss tip to see Micky at work. We found a twenty-acre municipal dump rising like a mountain between Birkenhead docks and the M53 motorway. Every few minutes the dumper trucks delivered skips loaded with the rubbish from around 100,000 households. As the bin-bags cascaded down swarms of seagulls would descend looking for scraps to eat. But just as frenzied as the birds were the people. There were dozens of them – men, women, children as young as seven – all clambering into the mounds of egg shells, potato peelings, discarded hamburger cartons and soiled babies' nappies. They were searching desperately for something to use, wear and – above all – sell.

To watch this scene was to witness the true meaning of the survival of the fittest. Micky and his fellow 'rooters' took no prisoners; whoever got their hands on something first took it home. They seized on anything that looked as if it could be fixed. Old TV sets were grabbed immediately, along with broken furniture and bikes without wheels. Copper and scrap were stuffed into holdalls. Old mattresses and torn blankets were slung on top of supermarket trolleys and babies' pushchairs. One out of work painter and decorator found half-tins of gloss that he could use for jobs on the side. Another man got his hands on a beat-up old fruit machine that still contained some tokens. He wedged it open to get the coins which were later to be sold in Birkenhead's pubs and gambling arcades.

Public health officials had warned about the dangers of injury, and disease spread by rats. But the rooters themselves were more concerned with the law. They feared their benefits would be stopped if the Department of Social Security knew they were selling the things they found. As a result, many of them refused to speak to us. And when they covered their faces with scarves it wasn't to mask the foul smell of rubbish; they were simply scared of being identified.

We stayed in Birkenhead for a week, seeing at first hand how long-term unemployment had bred poverty and despair. Among the most pitiful sights was the elderly man who had worked all his life – now reduced to sorting through bags of bacon rind and rancid dog food to find an old pair of shoes to wear. Then, under the moonlight, gangs of jobless teenagers leaning against cemetery headstones to smoke heroin from tin foil. But the most awful scenes were on the tip as those desperate rooters ploughed through other people's rubbish. One moment in particular made me think that Britain was heading towards Third World status. Slithering through the filth, and with all dignity gone, was a man hunting for food.

On The Scrapheap may not have had the entertainment value of those earlier unemployment programmes. But, by finding a vivid image and compelling human testimonies, the production team had managed to make an old issue appear fresh. Modern-day unemployment and poverty became a story again, with the Birkenhead tip its symbol. Within just a few weeks of our programme, documentary crews were arriving from America, Europe and Japan.

YOUR LIFE IN TIRED HANDS

Hospital shoots have been a recurring feature of my career. Waiting rooms, operating theatres, geriatric wards, intensive care units: you name it, I've been there. The nation's health, and the state of the NHS, throw up so many stories that we could have spent an entire series covering them. Some years, it felt as if we did.

Although most hospital programmes have blended together in my mind, one or two still stand out. Back in the early 1970s we set out to portray a day in the life of an accident and emergency unit on Merseyside. During a chaotic twenty-four hours, patients were admitted with industrial injuries, dog bites and domestic wounds. Among the drunks and drug users, one woman needed her stomach pumping out. Another man required emergency treatment after pushing lighted matches into his own skin. In the early hours of Sunday morning, a youth came in with gashes to his head and face – the result of a drunken bottle fight. Within an hour his attacker had also appeared at the reception, displaying the same sort of injuries. The nurses stitched and bandaged them both. By the time we left they were lying in adjoining beds, putting the world to rights and apologizing to each other.

Although *The Blood And Guts Shift* was a simple access film, it proved to be the forerunner of many other fly-on-the-wall documentaries and series. From *Jimmy's* to *Children's*

Hospital to *Special Babies*, television has tapped into the human dramas that take place every day of the week inside our major hospitals. But while nearly all of these have concentrated on the patients, very few have looked at the problems of the people looking after them.

In 1987 we aimed to do just that. The idea came from producer Debbie Christie who had just started going out with a junior hospital doctor, and who was amazed to find out the number of hours he and his friends were working. Researching the subject further she discovered that the scandal was well known within the NHS. A few years earlier, a parliamentary report had called the shift patterns 'indefensible' and had warned of the risk to doctors' health – along with their patients' safety. But despite the lack of improvement in their working conditions, few were prepared to complain openly. Consultants were the kings in NHS hospitals. And if juniors wanted to stay on the right side of them, they did as they were told.

To illustrate the hazards of the crazy shift patterns, we were to follow three junior doctors through a seventy-eight-hour weekend shift. Access was agreed with Furness General in Barrow – a hospital serving a major slice of Cumbria. Admission figures showed it was busy, so we were confident there would be plenty of action sequences. But although the doctors would no doubt look increasingly tired as the weekend went on, how could we quantify their exhaustion? After making a few calls, Debbie came up with Jahved Bhatti.

Jahved was a Leeds University psychologist and an expert in the effects of sleep deprivation. He agreed to devise a number of simple mental tests that could be given to each of the doctors at various intervals through their shifts. The night before filming began he arrived at our hotel with his bag of tricks. They included a magnetic board with seven tiny lights spread out in a semicircle. To test reaction times, the subject would have to touch one of the lights as soon as it illuminated. Then there was the box of twenty household objects to be laid out in front of the doctors and memorized like the prizes on the *Generation Game* conveyor belt. His third experiment didn't involve any props. To test their mental agility, he would simply give the doctors a list of numbers and ask them to recite them back. In reverse order.

The shift began at 9 a.m. on Friday. The hospital had laid on a special room where we could leave our gear and wait for the inevitable action to begin. It was also in there that Jahved could conduct his experiments in front of our cameras. The three doctors we were following were all young women. Rachel, Katherine and Joyce had recently qualified from medical school and were now beginning the long arduous training periods to become either consultants or GPs. They were a cheerful bunch but they admitted to finding the hours tough. A couple of weeks earlier, one of them had worked continuously for 104 hours.

All three passed the first tests with flying colours. The psychologist was impressed with their reaction times, and said their powers of memory and their ability to process information were stronger than average. As the day wore on we could see how vital those mental reserves were. In A&E, Rachel dealt with a series of admissions ranging from minor injuries to road accident victims. Joyce, working on the gynaecology wards, was called on to deal with labour problems and births. Over in the Special Baby Care Unit, Katherine was constantly in demand from nurses and anxious parents.

Our hotel was on the main road out of Barrow, near to the ruins of Furness Abbey. The filming schedule had been drawn up in such a way that we could go back and grab a few hours' sleep shortly after midnight. But every eight hours we had to go back, both to catch up with what the doctors were doing, and to film the latest wave of tests. By Saturday afternoon their performance had started to deteriorate. All of them were slower to react to the magnetic light-board and Katherine in particular was having greater difficulty with the numbers sequence. Jahved studied her results and said they were what he'd expect from someone who'd taken a sleeping pill.

By the early hours of Sunday morning the decline was even more marked. Rachel, who by then had been on constant call for forty-two hours, performed the worst. Her reaction times had slowed further, she couldn't remember most of the household objects, and then failed to recite any of the number sequences correctly. The psychologist said the results were deeply worrying and that the doctor was showing the signs of exhaustion. But then, just minutes later, she was called to an emergency. A man had been admitted with acute chest pains and she had to make an instant diagnosis, along with life-or-death decisions about the drugs to administer. Luckily, she chose correctly. But if I had any doubts about the wisdom of long hours, the frightening evidence was right in front of me.

A few minutes after the emergency admission Katherine agreed to a short interview inside her room. It was little bigger than a broom cupboard and I had difficulty fitting in the camera and lights. I can still picture her now, sitting on the bed at 4 a.m., almost in tears as she described her frustration and anger. 'I honestly wonder why I'm doing this. I'm chronically tired and I feel like I'm beginning to lose touch with real life . . . I feel like I'm sacrificing too much just for a job.'

By the time they reached the end of their seventy-eight hours all the doctors were failing badly on the tests. According to the psychologist, Katherine's performance was similar to someone who'd been on major tranquillizers. Joyce, who had started off with the best results, had shown the steepest decline. From remembering all the household objects she could now only memorize half. Jahved reckoned that sort of mental decline usually happened over a period of decades.

The Barrow experiment proved for the first time on TV that long hours were damaging to the people we trust to look after us in hospital. Viewers were outraged and the Department of Health received many letters of complaint. But just as powerful as the tests had been the interviews with families who had lost loved ones as a result of junior doctors' mistakes. They included the parents of baby Gemma Jones, who had died after a massive overdose of antibiotics. The doctor who wrote the prescription had been working continuously for eighteen hours and was unable to think straight. Remarkably, Gemma's mum and dad had forgiven her. According to the baby's father Brian, the blame lay with the ridiculous hours she had to work.

> We all make mistakes at work – for most of us that means costing our company just a few pounds. But doctors have people's lives in their hands, and a system that forces them to work these sort of hours is wrong. It's the system that is allowing these mistakes to happen and causing deaths.

Several newspapers featured stories about little Gemma afterwards, and the publicity undoubtedly helped the junior doctors' union in their campaign for a civilized working week. Their progress may have been slow, but at least the situation has improved in the last decade. According to the government, junior hospital doctors now work an average of fifty-six hours a week.

CHAPTER 7
THAT'S WHAT I CALL A RESULT

It would be nice to think that our programmes changed the world. That wars ended, torture finished and greedy multinationals stopped exploiting their workers. Unfortunately, things like that don't happen because of a single television programme. We may help raise public awareness of certain issues, but too often those same problems just carry on – or become worse. It's amazing to think that back in 1973 we were all making programmes denouncing the government for allowing the jobless total to reach one million. And how many times have we exposed underfunding of the health service, only to see waiting lists grow?

But on another level television can make a real difference, as a number of current affairs series have demonstrated. Corrupt politicians have been jailed, rogue firms put out of business, and dangerous products made safe. Had it not been for some tireless TV campaigning, many innocent people might still be behind bars. There's no sweeter feeling than when you see your own efforts help bring about such a change for the better. Although that change may take a while, sometimes it can be almost instant.

At the end of the 1980s diarrhoea was one of the Third World's biggest child killers. Each year four million infants were dying from the dehydration caused by the illness. What was so frustrating for medical workers was that many of those deaths were preventable. A simple mixture of sugar and salt, mixed with clean water – oral rehydration solution – had been shown to restore a sick child's body fluids and bring him back to full health.

Out in the wilds of western Kenya, I watched ORS work its miracle on a four-year-old boy called Vincent. When his mother brought him into the village clinic he was displaying the classic signs of dehydration – sunken eyes, dry mouth, listlessness. His skin was shrivelled. When the doctor pinched his arm, then let go, the lump of flesh stayed upright. Another couple of days in this condition and Vincent would lapse into unconsciousness.

The doctor showed his mother how to mix a sachet of ORS and feed the solution to her son, using a spoon. During the course of the day I filmed his progress. First his head stopped drooping and he became more alert. An hour later he was put on the scales and he had gained weight. By the end of the morning his eyes looked normal and he was well enough to play with a toy. After six hours the doctor performed the 'pinch test' and the skin went back to its proper position. By that time Vincent, who had been dying, was out of danger. The cost of his treatment was just six pence.

Unfortunately, the same treatment wasn't getting through to many others. The aid workers distributing ORS found themselves in competition with the huge multinational pharmaceutical firms who were marketing their own highly profitable products. These drugs were heavily advertised and promoted as sophisticated western remedies. Drug company representatives also encouraged local doctors to prescribe them by showering them with gifts. But the medicines and tablets were expensive, sometimes costing poor African families the equivalent of a week's wage. Even worse, they didn't work.

We looked at two commonly prescribed drugs that were not only useless, but potentially dangerous. One of them –

loperamide – was not allowed to be given to children under the age of four in the UK, because of the risk of damage to the central nervous system. In Kenya, the same manufacturers recommended it for babies as young as twelve months. The second drug – an antibiotic called neomycin – had been linked with liver damage and deafness. While many developed countries had banned it, the makers saw no problem in selling it to the Africans. Inside a pharmacy in Kisumu, near the border with Uganda, the chemist showed me his well-stocked shelves with neomycin prominently displayed. According to him it was one of his most popular products.

But Kenya's biggest selling anti-diarrhoea treatment was an over-the-counter medicine called ADM. When we filmed at Kisumu's run-down clinic, many of the desperately ill children had been taking it for days. As a result of heavy advertising campaigns, their parents thought it was the best cure available. But, day after day, the children were deteriorating because they were missing the one thing they really needed – rehydration.

ADM was made by the British company, Wellcome, which boasted that the mixture contained a special ingredient known as Diarex. But when we had it analysed we discovered that Diarex was in fact pectin, a thickening agent commonly found in jams and marmalades. Along with kaolin – another ineffective treatment for diarrhoea – and some flavouring, that was the sum total of the supposed remedy. The mothers we met had spent all they could to get hold of the bright blue bottles but, in reality, they had wasted their money.

Back in Britain, medical experts came on the programme to denounce ADM as completely inappropriate for Third World children with diarrhoea. The instructions on the packet – which made no mention of the need for rehydration – were also described as 'woefully inadequate'. Within a couple of days Wellcome announced that it was revising that packaging information. But as the week went on, the company received protests from viewers who were outraged at what they had seen. The production team behind the programme were just starting to consider a follow-up when Wellcome made a fresh announcement: it was withdrawing ADM from sale in Kenya.

Such real results are immensely satisfying for everyone involved. They make you forget all the hassles that surround the filming process, and they remind everyone that – for all the criticism it receives – television can be a real force for good. I'm privileged to have been a small part of that force – and proud to have witnessed some of the benefits.

A MOTHER'S CRUSADE

Public speaking is an art form that few people master. Those who do often wind up in politics, grabbing the attention with powerful speeches from the platform. Great orators make their listeners think. They can alter opinions and even inspire their audience to go out and take action. But if they're rare in public life, they're even more scarce among the general population.

Anwar Ditta was an exception. By day she was an ordinary working mum, sewing NHS pillow cases at her home in Rochdale. By night she took to public platforms across the north of England, speaking with a passion and intensity that often moved her listeners to tears. For Anwar had a cause for which she was prepared to fight to the death. It was to be reunited with the three children she had left four thousand miles away in Pakistan. It was six years since she'd seen her eldest daughter and two young sons, aged nine and eleven. Now the Home Office refused to believe she was their mother.

I met Anwar in 1981 as she told her story to an audience of trade union activists and students. Standing at the front of a chilly Liverpool University hall, this diminutive twenty-eight-year-old had them spellbound as she explained why her children should be allowed into Britain. She told how she herself had been born here, only visiting Pakistan as a teenager, where she met her future husband, Shuja. While living there she had married and become pregnant with her eldest son Kamran. Two years later came another boy Imran, and then, in 1973 daughter Saima.

In 1975 Anwar returned to Britain, hoping to find a job and buy a home. When she and Shuja had found a place to settle they would apply for their children to join them. But then the nightmare began, as immigration officials demanded definitive proof that the children were really theirs. Unable to provide it, the couple found themselves accused of trying to cheat the system. The Home Office refused to believe that Anwar had ever even been to Pakistan, let alone given birth there. Officials claimed the children actually belonged to Shuja's sister, and had no right of entry into Britain.

Anwar's anger and frustration were palpable. She had provided immigration officials with documents supporting her claim to be the mother. But, for them it wasn't enough:

> I'd like to ask you how you would prove you are the parents of your children. What would you do that I haven't done? You tell me what I should do, and I will do it to prove that I'm the mother of those three children.

She spoke of her youngest daughter who had been born in Britain but had never seen her sister and brothers. Her voice cracked and tears streamed down her cheeks as she recounted her conversations with the little girl:

> My child who was born here is going to be five on the 6th of April. She says, 'Why can't my brothers and sister be here, why can't they sleep with me, why can't we go out together?' She says, 'Mummy, why don't they come here?'

> She asks me when I go on meetings, 'Mummy, are we going to get my brothers and sister?' and I say, hopefully, yes. And I'm not giving up that hope, because the Home Office can't prove I'm telling lies.

Sitting among the audience was Granada researcher Jane Leighton. She had followed Anwar's campaign while working for our local news programme, filming her addressing a series of other public meetings, including a Labour Party fringe assembly. She had also interviewed Anwar's MP, the Liberal Cyril Smith, who told her: 'It's either the worst injustice I've ever seen, or she's the best actress north of London.'

But Jane had little doubt that Anwar was telling the truth. She brought the story to the attention of *World In Action*'s editor Ray Fitzwalter, who then passed it on to one of our strongest investigative producers, Ian McBride. Together, Ian and Jane set out to prove Anwar's case to the immigration officials. But it wasn't going to be easy. In the words of one former Home Office minister, they would need to turn up 'sensational new evidence'.

The quest for that evidence took us, inevitably, to Pakistan. Our first stop was in Lahore where the children were now living with their grandmother. When we got to the house we were all struck by the warm and loving atmosphere. Apart from the grandmother, there were various aunts, uncles and cousins, paying visits and helping to provide a happy and secure home. The three children themselves were not only clean and well-fed, but dressed in the latest Marks & Spencer clothes sent from England by Anwar. They were receiving a good education at the local school and each appeared to be happy and content.

But their grandmother Mushtaq knew that their proper place was with Anwar. That evening, as the children played cricket on the waste ground outside, she told us how she was getting old and finding it increasingly difficult to care for them. Her own daughter was about to marry and depart from the house, leaving her to cope on her own. Despite monthly cheques arriving from England, it was becoming more difficult to manage financially.

Ian and Jane needed to spend several more days in Lahore, tracking down witnesses who could help verify Anwar's story. As they pursued their research, sound recordist Phil Taylor and I decided to spend an hour getting some shots capturing the everyday life and culture. The city itself is a typical teeming Pakistani sprawl – and filming there presents typical Pakistani problems. Set up a camera on a busy street and you will have a crowd around you within seconds. Carry on for longer than a minute and you'll have a mini riot.

In order to get the sequences we wanted, we decided to hire a truck complete with a military-style canvas draped over the back. This enabled me to get out the tripod and film with the camera peeking out of a small gap as we parked on a street corner. Usually it worked for about two minutes before someone spotted me. Then there would be the familiar rush of passers-by shouting, waving and pulling at the canvas, making any further shots impossible. So as soon as we were rumbled, we drove off to another part of town, only for me to be spotted again. By the end of the day I had the shots I wanted – but it took six hours instead of one.

Meawnhile Ian and Jane were making better progress. They had found a cousin of Anwar who backed up her story that she had come to Pakistan as a child: she knew, because she had made the journey with her. Then they had taken Anwar's official Pakistani Identity Card to a government registration office, where an official had declared it genuine. As this card contained her thumbprint, the programme had proof that Anwar had actually lived in the country.

The next step was to verify that she had also married there. Anwar and Shuja had given us a marriage document naming the Muslim priest – or Imam – who was supposed to have officiated at the ceremony back in 1968. While in Lahore, Ian discovered he was not only alive, but still practising. When we tracked him down to a mosque on the north side of the city, we found a wonderful old character in white flowing robes. As well as wearing a permanent smile, the Imam also had a full-time companion: a goat that he insisted went everywhere with him.

The old priest took us to a ramshackle wooden building where births, marriages and deaths are registered. Using his influence, he persuaded the government officials to open up the vaults and get out the past records that could be cross-checked against Anwar's certificate. After several minutes poring through the torn, yellowing and dog-eared pages, the Imam found what he was looking for: an entry recording the marriage of Anwar and Shuja, and – next to it – his own signature. He had indeed performed the ceremony.

Over the next few days we gathered further evidence, travelling from Lahore, to Jhellum and to Karachi. Interviewees included a railway worker who had shared a house with Anwar and her husband in the early seventies. Then there was the midwife who claimed to have delivered Anwar's daughter, Saima. In all, Ian and Jane had turned up fourteen witnesses to testify that Anwar had not only lived in Pakistan, but that she'd also married and had three children there. We flew five of them to Islamabad to swear their statements on oath before the British vice-consul. The Imam was so keen to help he even agreed to the airline's order to leave his goat behind.

But despite sworn affidavits the witnesses could always be lying. Only independent scientific evidence would finally convince Britain's Home Office that Anwar was telling the truth. In order to gather it, Ian had arranged for a British doctor to fly to Islamabad to collect blood samples from the three children. After filming his arrival at the airport, we both drove directly to the city's Intercontinental Hotel. There the doctor, John Sachs, set out his array of test tubes and freezer cabinets in which the samples would be stored. As well as taking samples from the children, he was also to take blood from Shuja's sister – who the Home Office had claimed was the real mother.

It was a tense time in the hotel room as the doctor conducted his tests. He worked quietly and clinically, inserting a needle into the arm of each of the children before storing the samples away. All three were quite frightened by what was happening and at one point the eldest boy, Kamran, began to cry. But Dr Sachs wouldn't allow himself to be distracted. If his tests were to be performed correctly, the samples needed to be taken, stored and analysed with as little delay as possible. Two hours later he was back on a plane, bound for Heathrow.

It was another week before we arrived at his lab inside the London Hospital. By then he had concluded his investigation, supervised by an accredited scientific tester from the Home Office. The first results were definitive: Shuja's sister couldn't have been the mother of the three children we had met. Then, after analysing both red and white cells, the hospital came up with the clearest result its scientists had ever seen. According to the professor in charge, it was 99.99% certain the children belonged to Anwar.

Armed with this conclusive proof we drove back to Rochdale. The last time we visited the Lowry-like landscape of mills, chimneys and cobbled streets, we had found Anwar in frustration and despair. But now we were back with the news that she so desperately needed. And, as she studied the scientific results, she knew she was within sight of winning her battle: 'It's not a surprise to us. It will be a surprise to the Home Office, because they are our kids and we wouldn't have gone through all this if they were not ours. And I hope the Home Office will now allow them back without further delay.'

The programme went out on 17 March 1981, and that same

evening the Home Office said it would reconsider the case. Within a fortnight of transmission, its review was complete: the minister, Timothy Raison, announced that the children would be allowed into Britain.

Anwar's case was a triumph for her personally, but also a victory for the series. We had taken up a cause on behalf of an ordinary member of the public whose life was being ruined by the full force of the state. Had we not invested the time – and the money – to fight for her she might never have been reunited with the children she loved so much. *These Are My Children* deservedly won the Royal Television Society award for Best Programme that year. As Ian went up to collect the award, he took Anwar with him.

THE FORGOTTEN CHILDREN

Around 60,000 people once lived in Pripyat in the northern part of Ukraine. Then, on 27 April 1986, a thousand buses arrived and took the entire population away. Today it remains a ghost town with empty homes, deserted shops and disused offices. On a freezing March morning in 1993 I became one of the few people to venture back inside Pripyat since its evacuation. I climbed the stairwell of a nine-storey apartment block and set up my camera on the snow-covered roof. Stretching out in front of me were the scores of abandoned homes and flats, the rusting cars and weed-covered playgrounds. And there in the middle distance, casting a giant shadow, was the cause of this scene of desolation: the nuclear power plant, Chernobyl.

Pripyat was where most of Chernobyl's workers lived before scientists botched a safety test and accidentally blew up a reactor. The authorities didn't tell the people the full scale of what had happened at the plant for another twenty-four hours. By that time lethal radioactive chemicals had escaped from the reactor's core and scattered themselves all over Europe. But the six miles surrounding Chernobyl had borne the brunt of the radiation poisoning. Today, it is still the most contaminated area of land in the world.

My visit was almost seven years after the disaster. By then the old Soviet Union had fallen apart and the Ukraine had gained its independence. The fledgling country was only eighteen months old but it was already facing an economic crisis. There was massive inflation and unemployment. The local money was virtually worthless and the complete lack of foreign currency meant imports were unaffordable. For doctors treating the thousands of Chernobyl victims, this was a catastrophe. In their care were adults with cancer, children with leukaemia and babies born with terrible deformities. But with the economy on the point of collapse, the most basic medicines were no longer available. Denied treatment, their patients were dying.

I arrived with the producer Brian Blake and a tall, striking woman called Nina Rogerson. Although her home was in Bolton, she had been born and raised in Ukraine's second largest city, Chernigov, which lies forty miles east of Chernobyl. She still had many relatives in Chernigov and had recently learned that her great-niece had become seriously ill. Like many other children in the city, six-year-old Anya was a victim of Chernobyl. Since the disaster struck, around 50,000 of them had suffered from blood disorders, severe stomach complaints and tumours.

Brian had decided to make Nina the focus of our programme – a woman who had become so appalled by the conditions back in her home country that she was raising money to help relieve the suffering. A few months previously she had organized the transport of two lorry loads of medical aid to be transported from England. On board were the most basic of supplies, like vitamins, bandages and syringes. They were bound for Chernigov's children's hospital where many of the young victims, like Anya, were being treated.

When we reached the hospital ourselves we found that the wards, designed for 300 patients, were home to double that number. For the next couple of hours I filmed the terrible living legacy of the disaster. It included nine-year-old Yura, who was suffering from thyroid cancer. His doctors were desperate to put him on a course of chemotherapy, but they couldn't afford the special chemical compounds that were necessary. There was little Katia who had been born prematurely, mentally handicapped, and with both legs paralysed. Now, at four, she wanted to walk but the hospital didn't have enough money for the stabilizing equipment. And there was Natasha, whose father helped clean up after Chernobyl. When she was born, two years later, her body was deformed and she had kidney cancer.

Down in the operating theatre I set up to film an operation on Yana, another cancer victim. There, the enormity of the hospital's problems struck me hardest. To me, it was like filming in a museum, with strange old surgical instruments and dilapidated fittings. The bandages looked as if they had been used dozens of times over – some actually appeared to be brown. And here the staff were attempting to remove a kidney tumour and save the life of the four-year-old girl. I looked at Yana and hoped she'd make it. But in those cold and dimly-lit surroundings, I was doubtful. The surgeon told us: 'We have problems with bandages, sutures and surgical equipment. We don't have enough scalpels. Everything is old and keeps breaking down. We don't have enough for courses of chemotherapy. Other drugs just aren't available at all.'

Away from the hospital we showed how the people of Chernigov were trying to live normally, despite the high incidence of illness and the disastrous economy. Clearly, it had been a beautiful city with the River Desna running through the centre, the fabulous old Russian Orthodox churches and surrounding forests. But post-Chernobyl it just appeared drab and sad. Over in the city's cemetery there was a particularly poignant sight. In one corner were the graves of the men who had helped clear up the radioactive debris at the reactor. Next to them were those of the children who also died after the accident. And, on the headstones, the hauntingly innocent faces of these young victims had been etched into the marble.

Amazingly the source of all these problems was still functioning. Although Chernobyl's Reactor No. 4 had been sealed, the rest of the plant continued to work. There had been more serious safety problems in recent years, but the government simply couldn't afford to shut it down. While we were there, it was still providing Ukraine with a third of its electricity.

The authorities had given us permission to film inside the plant and it was on the way there that we stopped at Pripyat. Our government 'minder' told me I had half an hour to get the shots I wanted. He warned me that if I was climbing the stairs of apartment blocks I mustn't touch the walls or railings in case they were contaminated. Later, as I got some low shots among the weeds on a deserted football pitch, he ordered me to get back in the vehicle. He was worried that we were disturbing the soil and kicking up radioactive dust that we would all breathe in.

It was only a mile from Pripyat to Chernobyl, but on the way the scenery became even more bleak. There was no living vegetation to speak of. The roadside was lined with tall, thin trees that looked as if they'd been fashioned from charcoal. I jumped out to get some shots and had the feeling they would crumble and fall if I touched them.

As we arrived at Chernobyl itself, I wound down the car window to get some exterior images. The rows of concrete buildings were spread out behind a wire fence, and the complex was dominated by a large red and white tower. A guide pointed to the exploded reactor on the far side, then took us indoors for a tour of the rest of the site. As in nuclear power plants everywhere, there were the white-coated workers and black-and-yellow radiation signs. But here, better than anywhere else, the staff knew the real dangers of working in such an environment. Even a senior safety engineer was worried about the continuing hazards it posed. He told us there had been two fires in the previous twelve months.

Throughout our time in Ukraine we had been struck by how little food was available. Even our hotel dining room could stretch only to bread, jam and tea in the morning. But, as so often happens in poor countries, the people were determined to demonstrate their hospitality. On our last day, the whole twenty-four hours seemed to consist of eating, as first the hospital, then the Mayor of Chernigov, and finally Nina's family all laid on vast banquets for us. There was more food than I've seen before or since, and – despite feeling honoured – we were more than a little embarrassed at what they had done for us. In reality, these were a people who could barely afford to feed themselves and their own families.

After Brian had edited his programme I asked him to check on the progress of Yana, the little girl who had undergone surgery in that awful operating theatre. To my surprise, and delight, he found that the operation had worked and she was recovering. Today, following the removal of her tumour, she remains clear of cancer and is living a normal life.

But even better news was to come. When the programme was shown, Nina was inundated with letters offering money and support. Among those who contacted her was Richard Robinson, a City businessman who was so moved by the film that he wanted to join her in her fund-raising efforts. A short time afterwards Brian met up with Richard and Nina and the three agreed to set up a charitable trust fund called The Forgotten Children of Chernobyl. Six years on, around £5 million has been raised, with the trustees making several trips a year to Chernigov carrying medical supplies. Best of all, the money has enabled them to build an up-to-date rehabilitation centre in the city. And, as I write, almost 2,000 children have been treated successfully.

THE BIRMINGHAM SIX

I've filmed the aftermath of many an explosion, but it wasn't until I saw a bomb actually go off that I fully appreciated its powers of destruction. The moment of detonation is deafening. Glass and rubble fly with awesome force. Surrounding buildings shake and, even standing several hundred yards away, you can be knocked off your feet. Seeing the impact at first hand makes you realize that there's only one aim behind a bomb, and that's to kill. Its effects are indiscriminate, and there's no such thing as a safe explosion.

My own experience was in Northern Ireland a year or so after the Troubles broke out. I was having lunch in the restaurant of Belfast's Europa Hotel when a member of staff rushed in to say the IRA had telephoned a warning. Although it could well have been a hoax, neither I nor any of my fellow diners were taking any chances. At the time the Europa was known as the most bombed hotel in the world. Nice as the food was, the restaurant emptied within seconds.

Outside on the pavement a policeman confirmed that it wasn't a hoax. A device had been discovered in a first floor toilet block, and it was too late to send in a bomb-disposal unit. The road was sealed off and surrounding buildings were evacuated. I was ushered to the end of the street, about 250 yards away. I crouched behind a wall, pointed the camera and waited for the inevitable to happen. Forty minutes later it did. The blast tore through the lower floors and devastated the reception. Concrete and glass were hurled skyward while the ground underneath us trembled. When the smoke cleared I could see twisted metal scaffolding jutting out of the hotel walls. In the car park our vehicle lay crushed underneath tons of plate glass that had fallen from the floors above.

While they may have been shocking to visitors like me, those relatively small scale bombings were an everyday feature of Northern Ireland life in the early seventies. The people had become used to the warnings and the evacuations. Even the media, which had given saturation coverage to Ulster, was devoting less and less space to the continuing violence. The IRA leadership knew this and were determined to bomb their way back into the headlines. In 1973 they began a terrorist campaign on the British mainland in which twenty-nine people died. Then, a year later, came the biggest outrage of all.

On 21 November 1974, a bomb went off in a crowded pub in the centre of Birmingham. Two minutes later, at 8.20 p.m., thirty tons of gelignite ripped through a second bar. By the time the emergency crews had got the victims out, the Birmingham pub bombings were already going down as the biggest terrorist atrocity in modern British history. In all, twenty-one people lost their lives; another 162 were seriously injured.

Within hours of the explosions five men were arrested as they boarded a Belfast-bound ferry from the port of Heysham, in Lancashire. A sixth man, who had waved them off on the train from Birmingham, was also taken into custody. It later emerged that the men on the ferry were on their way to the funeral of a dead IRA member. Following a number of forensic tests, a scientist claimed he was 99 per cent certain that some of them had been handling explosives. All six were then charged with planting the bombs and, in August 1975, they were given twenty-one life sentences each. At that moment the 'Birmingham Six' became known as Britain's biggest mass murderers.

It was another nine years before *World In Action* took up their cause. The Labour MP Chris Mullin was a friend of the programme's editor Ray Fitzwalter, and persuaded him to look at the men's claims of innocence. An investigative team, led by producer Ian McBride, spent eight months examining the evidence against them. They studied their backgrounds and supposed links with terrorist organizations; they investigated claims that police officers had beaten their confessions out of them; and – most crucially – they tested the reliability of the damning forensic evidence.

I met up with Ian at the home of one of the prisoners, Richard McIlkenny. We were there for an interview with his wife Kate who had campaigned tirelessly for the men's release for almost a decade. Ian asked her why her husband was on his way to the funeral of an IRA man. It turned out that the terrorist – James McDade – was a distant relative of hers, and had grown up in the same small Belfast neighbourhood as her husband and the other prisoners. In their eyes, McDade wasn't a terrorist, he was a childhood friend. They were going to his funeral to pay their respects and show support for his family.

After we had packed up the gear, Ian and I went for a cup of tea at a local café. He asked me what I thought of the interview and I said I couldn't believe Kate's husband was really a terrorist. By then I had spent time in many Irish Republican homes and I had become used to the tell-tale signs of IRA support. But in her house there was nothing: no Celtic crosses, plaques, murals: not even a copy of Sinn Fein's newspaper *An Phoblacht*. To me, it looked a perfectly normal home in a Birmingham suburb.

This first impression was strengthened when we interviewed a man named George Lynch who had been Sinn Fein's organizer in the West Midlands in the mid-seventies. He was adamant that the six men behind bars hadn't been active in the Irish Republican movement during that period. They may have sung the odd sentimental Republican song at closing time, and maybe they bought a raffle ticket to raise money for

Irish prisoners, but as far as he knew, their political involvement went no further. In his words they were 'public house Republicans'.

Lynch's testimony was useful, but Ian needed more conclusive evidence that the six were not connected to terrorism. This was to come as a result of work by Eamon O'Connor, a young researcher from Belfast who had recently joined the programme team. Along with Chris, he spent many hours meeting senior figures within the Provisional IRA. The organization spent weeks debating whether to take part in the programme, but finally they agreed. An interview was arranged with the legendary Provo leader, Joe Cahill.

To British intelligence, Cahill is known as 'The Bald Eagle' – a short, squat man who's spent a lifetime fighting for the IRA cause. In the 1940s he received a life sentence for murdering an RUC officer – escaping hanging only when a terrorist colleague admitted actually pulling the trigger. When the modern-day Troubles erupted he re-emerged as one of the organizers of the Provisionals' Belfast Brigade, eventually becoming its leader. He's been involved in shootings, bombings and gun-running. And – to many young Republicans – he remains the IRA's elder statesman.

Ian arranged to meet him in Dublin's plush Shelbourne Hotel. Although we expected him to arrive incognito he strode into the lobby, making no attempt to conceal his identity, and swapping pleasantries with the staff who clearly recognized him. At his side was another notorious IRA man, Seamus Twomey, who had gained a reputation for ruthlessness even by Provo standards. It was he who brought the car bomb to Northern Ireland back in the early seventies. And, as a key figure in the Belfast Brigade, he was suspected of planning 'Bloody Friday' – a series of horrific explosions that killed nine people in the city one July afternoon in 1972.

Up in the hotel room, Ian questioned Cahill about the Birmingham bombs. For the first time, he admitted they were the work of IRA members, but he rejected claims that the men in prison were involved. Further, the six had never even been part of his organization. As a leading light in the Provisionals he undoubtedly knew who had – and who had not – been in the ranks. But he had another reason for being so definite:

> Their whole attitude . . . certainly their attitude in the courts. During their whole trial they denounced the IRA. They denounced bombings. They denounced shootings. They denounced violence. That is not the action of IRA men. IRA men are dedicated people who are fighting for a cause. They believe in that cause and they'll not deny it.

We were just about to wrap up the interview when there was a loud bang on the wall. Eamon ran to the door to find an Italian hotel concierge in a state of panic: a waitress had told him who we were interviewing and he was now complaining that we had brought the IRA into the building. Eamon spent several minutes trying to calm him down, explaining that no one had any guns and the hotel wouldn't be identified when the programme went on air. Cahill, who seemed to find the whole thing highly amusing, asked him if he could bring back some fruit. The man stormed off, still unhappy, and threatening to bring his manager. As he got into the lift we could hear him muttering: 'I may be a waiter, and I may be foreign, but I'm not f***ing stupid!' Meanwhile Twomey, who had been against the interview taking place, sat unsmiling behind his trademark shades. It felt like time to leave.

With hard information that the men did not belong to the IRA, the team set about demolishing some of the so-called 'confessions' that the six had made in the days after their arrest. Central to this was evidence that they had been beaten and tortured by officers while in custody. Ian had made several visits to Gartree maximum security prison in

Leicestershire where one of the six, Paddy Hill, was serving his sentence. Although he himself had never made a confession, he gave a graphic account of the treatment he and the others had received after they were taken from Heysham to Morecambe police station. Ian smuggled out a tape recording of Paddy's voice:

> I was kicked, punched and battered all around the room. I was dragged around the room by the hair. I had lighted cigarettes placed against my eyelids, although not touching the skin but very close so I could feel the heat. I was told that I would be blinded.
>
> I had cigarettes put on my legs, they stood on my ankles, at times I was made to sit on the chair, and when I sat on the chair I was hit from behind and knocked off it.
>
> I could hear the others screaming as well. I've no doubt they also heard me. I knew they were all getting the same sort of treatment.

He said that on the way back from Morecambe to Birmingham the men were assaulted again. One officer attacked him with a gun: 'He put the gun in my mouth. He pulled the trigger and he took the gun out of my mouth and he said to the other one, "This bastard must have a charmed life – we must have a dud bullet." In all he pulled the trigger three times.'

Four of the other prisoners – John Walker, Hugh Callaghan, Gerard Hunter and Billy Power – had all since given statements alleging brutality at the hands of the police. Kate McIlkenny told us how her husband displayed the visible signs of a severe beating – black eyes, bloody ears, a gash on his chin and a bruised and swollen nose. The police had always claimed those injuries were the result of a beating by prison officers after the six were remanded in custody by the courts. But when still photographs of the men – taken a few days after arrest – were shown to an eminent pathologist, he concluded that the injuries must have been sustained while in police cells. The basis for their conviction was beginning to look extremely shaky.

The clincher, though, was still to come. As the programme investigation progressed, researcher Charles Tremayne began to look into the reliability of the forensic evidence. His inquiries centred on the so-called Griess Test – the method by which scientists were able to conclude that some of the prisoners had been handling explosives. The test involved coating the suspects' hands with ether, taking swabs and putting the drops into a dish. If the samples turned pink within ten seconds, the result was positive.

But as he spoke to experts, Charles found more and more people who considered the test to be unreliable. Some even suggested that innocent substances could give the same positive result as nitroglycerine. These included the varnishes and polishes that are commonly found on furniture in bars and railway carriages. There was the chemical coating found on postcards and cigarette packets. And, most interestingly of all, the nitrocellulose found on the surface of playing cards.

Ian thought it was time to reconstruct the events of 21 November 1974, when five of the supposed bombers took the night train from Birmingham to Heysham. British Rail supplied a carriage commonly in use at that time, and let us film on a disused track at Manchester's Victoria station. Together with a larger-than-normal crew, I set about trying to recreate the scene from a decade before. Firstly, we smeared the windows with glycerine to simulate the rain that had been falling that night. Secondly, we hoisted the carriage on to sleepers and got a couple of stagehands to jump up and down to make it rock. Lastly, I dug out an old cylinder that I hadn't used since working on a drama production some sixteen years earlier. It was covered in mirrors, and had a handle enabling an assistant to rotate it. When a light was flashed on to the drum, the mirrors reflected the beams through the carriage window. Setting up my camera inside, I could see this gave me exactly what I wanted – the impression of lights flashing past a moving train.

While I had fun with my real-life train set, Ian directed the five actors to go through the routine that had been described by the men in their statements. While their 150-mile journey up to the Lancashire coast had been uneventful, each had always claimed they helped to pass the time by playing card games. After filming the actors lounging on the polished leatherette seats and taking out their cigarettes, we got each of them to shuffle and deal a well-worn old pack.

The reconstruction sequence was to work brilliantly in the edited programme. A few days earlier Ian and Charles had conducted their own tests on the reliability of the forensic evidence. These proved conclusively that handling wholly innocent substances like cards and cigarette packets could trigger positive results in the Griess Test. When their own lab experiment was intercut with the reconstruction, the conclusion was obvious. Roy Jenkins, Home Secretary at the time of the bombings, gave his reaction:

> The new evidence which I have seen would be sufficient to create in my mind what's sometimes called a lurking doubt as to whether the convictions in these cases were safe. My own belief is that terrorists must be put inside and must be kept permanently inside. But, in the interests of justice, a new trial should take place for the Birmingham pub bombers as soon as possible.

Unfortunately that didn't happen. Instead we got hysterical press coverage in which the programme was denounced for giving comfort to the IRA and insulting the memories of those who died in the Birmingham bombings. Ian, who had taken relatives of one of the prisoners for an Indian meal during the research, was accused of 'wining and dining terrorists' families'. One tabloid leader column said we belonged in the dock along with the IRA.

It was to Granada's eternal credit, though, that the programme was allowed to continue to campaign for the release of the six, even after their appeal was turned down in 1987. *World In Action* made three more programmes questioning their convictions, gradually convincing more and more people that they were unsafe. Then, in 1990, came the drama-documentary *Who Bombed Birmingham?* which portrayed the battle to prove the men's innocence, and ended with the names of the real bombers being displayed on screen. In this dramatized version Ian was played by the actor Martin Shaw, while John Hurt took on the role of Chris Mullin. The glossy Hollywood-style production standards introduced the story to millions more viewers, and gave the campaign a new lift. Just a year later it would reach its climax.

By the beginning of 1991 more doubt had been cast on the convictions. A former policeman had come forward to say that he had witnessed the men being beaten. Our allegations about the weakness of the forensics had been vindicated. And the evidence of the detective in charge of the pub bombings case had been discredited. People were also much more willing to believe that the police could make mistakes or falsify claims against suspects. There had been a series of high profile miscarriages of justice, culminating in the quashing of the conviction against the Guildford Four – another group wrongly jailed for IRA explosions.

On Thursday 14 March the six men imprisoned for the Birmingham bombings were brought before the secure court on the upper floor of London's Old Bailey. There was huge expectation in the air: the police had cleared the street outside, crowds had begun to gather, and press photographers and TV news crews from around the world had descended. I had got there early and manoeuvred myself into pole position – dead centre of the press pack, wedged behind a temporary pedestrian barricade. While no one could be sure how the judges' decision would go, there was something of a carnival atmosphere. One Sky News cameraman had even brought along a pint of Guinness with a shamrock carved into the creamy head.

At around 3 p.m. the front door of the court swung open and Ian ran out wearing his trademark full-length Burberry mac. Cradled between his shoulder and ear was one of those huge first-generation mobile phones, which he'd hired to keep in touch with Ray Fitzwalter back at base. I later found out that he'd actually been talking to Hugh Callaghan's wife, Eileen, who simply couldn't bear to be in court for fear of the appeal failing.

But this time it hadn't. As Ian put the phone back in its holder he ran towards me giving the thumbs up: the Birmingham Six had finally been released after more than sixteen years in jail. A few minutes later the men themselves emerged into the mid-afternoon sunshine, walking towards me and the other cameramen, acknowledging the wild cheers from the crowd. Around them were their lawyers and families, some completely overcome with the emotion of the moment. The men themselves wore broad grins, but as they got nearer I could sense there was anger mixed with the joy. Paddy Hill, in particular, looked agitated, darting from friend to relative, towards the crowd and away again. Who knows what was going through his mind? There he was, wanting to celebrate his new freedom but – at the same time – frustrated and bitter about his lost years behind bars.

Following the initial chaotic scenes, the men were whisked away to a secluded religious retreat in North London. After spending an hour or so with their families they agreed to be taken to a secret location for a series of exclusive interviews with us. Ian, Charles and Eamon had come up with the code-

Sicily's 'walking corpse', Leoluca Orlando, 1993.

LA's (white) cops and their (black) suspects shortly before the city's worst ever race riot in 1992

The Birmingham Six celebrate their freedom in March 1991, along with Labour MP Chris Mullin (centre) who campaigned for their release. © Popperfoto

Toxteth 1981, and a hopelessly ill-equipped police force comes under attack. © Mercury Press Agency

The Six, pictured after their arrest, and bearing the scars of their beatings.

The men tell their story on TV, sixteen years later.

Left: Crew member Keith Staniforth retrieves my oil-sodden boot from Kuwait's desert sands.

Right: Darkness at noon: Keith, sound recordist Dave Hollingworth and me, Kuwait, 1991.

Below right: When the heat becomes too much.

Below: Capping one of the wells sabotaged by Saddam's troops.

Above left: Refusing to smile for thc camera – the corrupt architect John Poulson arrives at court in 1973.

Below left: Olympic gymnast Olga Korbutt (foreground) with John Sheppard, and her trainer, 1974.

Above right: The people of Vilcabamba give us their secrets of a long life.

Right: Ecuadorian farmer Gabrielle Sanchez, who claimed to be 130 years old.

Above and left: Fighting for their rainforest and their whole way of life – the Penan people of Sarawak, 1991.

word 'Bristol', and went round attaching special Bristol badges to all those who would be allowed to come. The idea was to stop newspaper interlopers trying to get in and take shots of the men being interviewed.

In the event the press followed us anyway, sending motorcycle dispatch riders to tail our vehicles out to Monkey Island near Maidenhead. However, the location provided perfect security, just as we'd planned. Set in the middle of the Thames, the island's one and only hotel is separated from the mainland by a single drawbridge, where we had placed security guards. Some photographers planned to swim across; others made frantic attempts to charter a boat. But, for the next twenty-four hours we had the Birmingham Six to ourselves. It was here that they would tell their own story in their own words.

And what a story it was! From the moment of their arrest British justice had failed them. They had been wrongly identified as suspects, treated brutally by the police and prison guards, formally accused as the result of faulty science, and then ignored by a complacent judicial system. In the time they had been in prison they had missed family weddings and funerals. They had missed watching their sons and daughters growing up, and the birth of grandchildren. Yet at that moment there was little sign of bitterness. I filmed them walking in the gardens, smelling the flowers, looking at the sky and enjoying the scenery. One of the six, John Walker, later told us how it felt to be free again:

> When we went to the hotel last night I put my arm around my youngest baby, and me and her went for a walk. My youngest baby – eighteen years old!
>
> We just went for a walk, walked round the corner, and two ducks were there and they quacked – I nearly died. And there was a river and trees in there, the atmosphere was fantastic. Oh it was great, it really was great.

Paddy Hill, too, was savouring those simple pleasures the rest of us take for granted:

> The first thing I heard this morning was my mother's voice, talking to my grandchildren. It felt really strange but something to be looking forward to.
>
> After a little while I was in another room in bed, with my son in the bed beside me – and I got out of the bed and went to look at him.
>
> I just can't find the words to describe just seeing my family together after all this time. It's out of this world.

All the others described similar feelings. Listening to them talk it was often hard for us to hold back the tears. Ian, who did all the interviews, ended up drained both physically and emotionally. Charles, who had been asked to edit a special sixty-minute edition, worked through Saturday and Sunday nights to get it ready. At 8.30 p.m. on the Monday, the programme we had all dreamed of for so long was finally transmitted. It was, for me, our finest hour.

CHAPTER 8
RESTORING MY FAITH

It would have been easy to become cynical about human nature. Most stories have brought me face to face with people I would rather avoid, and throughout the years my own personal rogues' gallery has continued to expand. It includes dictators, torturers and terrorists. There are more than a few corrupt politicians and profit-before-principle businessmen. Plus a hefty sprinkling of con artists, thugs and thieves.

But where there are villains, there are always heroes. A programme about famine caused by Third World warlords will bring you face to face with aid workers who've given up comfortable western living to look after the impoverished. I've met doctors saving lives while their hospitals are shelled. And – back in Britain – ordinary parents who've taken on drug dealers to clean up their estates.

South Africa produced more than its fair share of political gangsters, but it also had Nelson Mandela. I shot an interview with him in 1992, not long after his release from prison and before he finished his incredible journey from Robben Island jail to the South African presidency – finally marking the end of apartheid for ever. The filming at ANC headquarters began at 6 a.m. with myself and the rest of the crew extending embarrassed apologies about the ridiculously early start. 'No problem,' he said. 'I've been used to getting up early for the last twenty-seven years.'

This was a man who was an inspiration to human rights activists around the world. He had suffered the loss of his freedom to fight an evil regime, and now he was on the road to the ultimate prize. But my lasting memory was his humility. How many other world leaders would help a film crew carry their lighting equipment to the lift when their interview was over?

Good and evil also co-existed in the Philippines. In the sixties it was one of the most developed and prosperous countries in south-east Asia. By the mid-eighties it was debt-ridden and among the poorest. The reason was its President. Ferdinand Marcos was a corrupt tyrant who had held on to power by declaring martial law and imprisoning his opponents. As his country went downhill he used foreign loans and government funds for his own family's personal gain. So, while the people of Manila lived in slums and on the vast municipal rubbish tip known as 'Smokey Mountain', their President decorated his lavish palaces. As malnourished Filipino children went barefoot, his wife Imelda amassed 12,000 pairs of shoes.

I went there in 1986 to meet the woman who would finally help get rid of that criminal regime. Corazón Aquino was the widow of one of Marcos' chief political opponents, who had been assassinated three years earlier. We sat in a garden at her home in the suburbs of Manila the week before 54 million Filipinos went to the polls in an election the Americans had forced Marcos to hold. The death of her husband Ninoy had turned this ordinary, religious, middle-class woman into a political crusader. She was now the leader of the opposition, and risked assassination herself. Asked why she was carrying on his work, she was clear: 'God has a plan for all of us, and I have come to accept my husband's death as part of that plan. I see now why it had to be so, if only to awaken the Filipino people from their apathy and indifference.'

Seven days later the Philippines did awaken. Cory was

voted in on a huge wave of so-called 'people power'. The Marcos era was over.

Meeting Corazón Aquino and Nelson Mandela were both memorable experiences. But over the years I've come across many others who have moved and inspired me. There are those who've endured suffering with amazing dignity, and those who've overcome persecution. Some have turned terrible disadvantage into opportunity, and others have shown fantastic courage to help their fellow men. They may not have achieved fame and power, but they rank among my own personal heroes.

KEVIN DONNELLON

In 1957 a group of German scientists marketed a new tranquillizer that was amazingly effective without producing any apparent side effects. It sparked huge excitement in the medical world. Here was a pill that could be taken by anyone suffering from the full array of symptoms linked to anxiety and stress. You couldn't overdose, and even a child who accidentally swallowed a batch of tablets would be safe. By 1960 the makers were actively playing on this safety aspect. A typical advertisement showed a child taking bottles from a bathroom cabinet. The text read:

This Child's Life May Depend
On The Safety Of Distaval

> Consider the possible outcome in a case such as this – had the bottle contained a conventional barbiturate. Year by year, the barbiturates claim a mounting toll of childhood victims. Yet it is simple enough to prescribe a sedative and hypnotic which is both highly effective . . . and

> outstandingly safe. Distaval has been prescribed for nearly three years in this country . . . but there is no case on record in which even gross overdosage with Distaval has had actively harmful results. Put your mind at rest. Depend on the safety of Distaval.

Distaval was only the brand name. The name of the active ingredient was thalidomide.

During the summer of 1961 Agnes Donnellon was pregnant with her fifth child, and suffering continual morning sickness. She went to see her doctor who told her it would clear up soon, but in the meantime she should try Distaval which would help her sleep. Neither the mother nor the doctor had received any warning that taking the drug during pregnancy could have devastating consequences. Over the following few days she took five tablets.

Later that year Agnes gave birth to her son, Kevin. For two days she wasn't allowed to see him. Then when she did, she collapsed. Her little boy was terribly deformed, with three fingers protruding from his left shoulder, and two more from his right. He had no legs. At the same time a new report was being published linking the growing number of birth deformities like Kevin's with Distaval. On 28 November 1961 – the very same day Kevin was born – the drug was withdrawn from chemists' shelves.

Kevin was eleven when I met him for the first time. Although the thalidomide scandal was well known by then, it was difficult to report the issue because of legal wranglings between the parents and the drug's manufacturers, Distillers. The *Sunday Times*, which had taken up the victims' cause, had even been prevented by the Attorney General from running an article critical of the compensation payouts. Producer Alan Segal came up with the solution as to how we could tackle the story without running into our own legal problems. We would focus entirely on the lasting day-to-day effects of thalidomide on both a child and his parents. The way to do it would be to film twenty-four hours in their life.

Kevin's family lived in a small bungalow in Litherland, just north of Liverpool. Although his parents had put Kevin's settlement money into a Trust – to be held and invested until he was eighteen – Agnes had spent all of her own £2,000 payout adapting the home to his needs. Central heating had been fitted inside, and there was a ramp leading up the steps to the front door.

When I went inside to meet Kevin I knew this was a subject that had to be treated sensitively. In physical terms he was little more than a torso with a head. He had on a pair of short trousers that his mum had sewn up at the bottom to prevent him getting friction burns as he shuffled around on the carpet (with amazing speed, as a matter of fact). The trousers had patches sewn on as a result of the continuous rubbing against the surface. These, too, would wear out after a couple of days. Every week his parents would buy him a new pair.

Despite his problems he was lively and cheeky, with a great sense of humour. For the first sequence we followed him to the bathroom to show how his family got him ready for the day ahead. As his sister Elizabeth went to brush his teeth, Kevin grabbed the toothbrush between two of his little fingers and had a go himself. He turned and gave me a wonderful smile as I filmed him.

An hour or so later we followed him to school. A taxi, funded by the local authority, called at the house to pick him up. Propped up in the back seat, he had to travel with an attendant who stopped him from falling and banging his head against the door each time the cab went round a corner.

At school it was obvious that Kevin was also very bright and able to hold his own in the classroom, eagerly answering questions about history and the industrial revolution. His classmates loved him, and he had no trouble mixing and making friends. Outside, though, it was a different story. Disability was still a taboo in the early seventies and, according to Agnes, many people didn't want to see it or talk about it.

> I think the problem's getting worse, because when he was a baby you could wrap him up in a shawl and that was it. But he's getting bigger, he goes out a lot and we take him on holiday with us, where of course you meet the public.
>
> Their reactions are so different. Some people are shocked, some are sad, some get sentimental, but you also get people who just don't want to look at him. They turn away, they don't want to know. One person actually shuddered when she saw him, she actually shuddered.

Later in the day we saw Kevin being fitted with artificial limbs. Although these had provided a new lease of life for many thousands of amputees, they were largely useless for thalidomide children. The protruding stumps of feet made it almost impossible to get limbs to fit properly. Despite many hours of practice, Kevin suffered a series of falls, cuts and bruises.

We finished the film with Agnes fretting over what the future would hold for her son – a boy who would need constant care, even after she and her husband were no longer able to provide it. On his own, he would always be helpless. Someone would have to be around constantly to wash him, dress him, lift him, cut up his food, comb his hair. She saw little prospect of him finding paid work when he reached manhood, and marriage appeared to be an impossibility. To help him through life with such catastrophic physical deformities Distillers had agreed to pay him just £22,000.

A Day In The Life Of Kevin Donnellon was an immensely powerful and moving film. For the first time on TV the story of the thalidomide scandal was stripped to its bare essentials – a child whose life had been blighted for ever, and a family struggling to cope every day of their lives. It was so popular that there were calls for it to be repeated. In the weeks and months afterwards there were constant letters and phone calls inquiring about Kevin and how he was doing. But it wasn't until nearly nine years later that *World In Action* returned to film an update.

By 1981 Kevin was at further education college taking his A levels. He had matured into an intelligent nineteen-year-old, looking forward to higher qualifications. He had a wide circle of friends and, while his physical problems were the same, he'd emerged from his difficult teenage years with his sense of humour intact. 'I don't really get depressed a lot. I mean we can have a laugh and joke about my handicap especially with the other kids at school. When we talk about what we want to do when we leave, I'll say I want to be a shorthand typist!'

Five years after that interview I met Kevin again, quite by accident, while filming demonstrations against America's military presence in Britain. President Ronald Reagan had just used British bases to help him bomb Libya, and peace protestors had targeted US depots throughout the country. Covering one demo at Burtonwood near Warrington, I saw a familiar figure grappling with a hacksaw blade, trying to open up the perimeter fence. He was then arrested and carted away by a group of Cheshire's finest.

For Kevin, political activism was clearly beckoning. In the years since then, he's joined Arthur Scargill's Socialist Labour Party. He's also become a leading light in a group called the Disabled People's Direct Action Network, protesting against organizations that practise discrimination, and – on one memorable occasion – throwing paint at No. 10 Downing Street when it looked likely that Tony Blair might cut disability benefits. He has even stood for election to his local council on a Socialist Labour ticket, coming within just twenty votes of the Conservative candidate.

Kevin has also made the best of his personal life. Despite his mum's worries, he has managed to hold down a job – as a welfare rights worker in the Merseyside borough of Sefton. As I write, he's back at college studying for a degree in Applied Social Sciences: when he gets it, he hopes to become a lecturer. He has a flat of his own, complete with a home-help who visits each morning, plus a specially adapted car that he can drive himself.

Most poignantly he has also joined the fight against the re-emergence of thalidomide as a medical drug. Incredible as it may sound, it is being used again throughout the Third World to treat a range of illnesses, including leprosy. And, tragically, in South America, some women have taken it while pregnant, unaware that it can cross the placenta. Almost forty years after the first thalidomide babies, a new generation has been born. For Kevin it's astonishing that this should have been allowed to happen again:

> I saw some pictures of a little kid in a remote village in Brazil. He had no arms and legs and he was shuffling about on his bottom. I just thought 'that's me'. There were tears in my eyes.
>
> Until that moment I thought we were a unique race. I thought that once we all died off that would be the end of it. But now I know there's a whole new bunch coming after us.

Kevin may not be part of a unique race, but as an individual he's a one-off. A born fighter who's always done his utmost to live normally despite the cruel hand that fate dealt him. No one can ever say his life is easy but he remains determined to live it to the full.

LEOLUCA ORLANDO

In Francis Ford Coppola's classic film *The Godfather*, the Marlon Brando character takes his name from Corleone, a small town in Sicily. The movie portrays it as a bloodthirsty place ruled by the Mob: in reality that's only 99 per cent true.

In 1993 I found myself in this cradle of organized crime following a man determined to break the influence of the real godfathers for ever. To the police he was known officially as 'a man in danger'. The ordinary Sicilians – well used to seeing what happens when you upset the Mafia – had a more blunt name for him: 'The Walking Corpse'.

Leoluca Orlando was the mayor of Sicily's capital, Palermo. He was an idealistic young lawyer whose evidence had helped to jail a series of Mafia bosses in the mid-eighties. He then went further, rooting out corrupt councillors on the Mafia's payroll, and preventing businesses with Mob links from getting council contracts. The leaders of the Cosa Nostra were outraged and put him under sentence of death. But he refused to be intimidated and his clean-up campaign grew even stronger. By the early nineties he'd formed his own party, La Rete (The Network), which aimed to bring together all the businesses, civic organizations and honest politicians opposed to organized crime. From that moment he was taking on the Mafia across the whole of Italy.

We set out to make a profile of Orlando (Leo, as we came to know him), examining both his campaign and the massive security that surrounded him. I had already seen the sort of protection given to terrorist targets in Britain, particularly the former Northern Ireland Secretary Merlyn Rees when he was under threat from the IRA. But, within just a few hours of arriving in Rome, it was clear that Leo's security arrangements were on a different plane altogether.

For twenty-four hours a day he was surrounded by armed

bodyguards. He was driven round in armour-plated cars designed to withstand bomb blasts. His hand-picked personal staff didn't use phones for fear of being tapped. They changed his diary and travel arrangements constantly, and at last-minute notice. Each night Leo himself slept in a different bed, often inside military barracks. Although he was married with two young daughters he hardly ever saw his wife and children. A devout Roman Catholic, he couldn't even go to Mass without the church being searched for explosive devices.

As a documentary character Leo was terrific; as a subject to film he was a nightmare.

The security staff who surrounded him were understandably paranoid about his safety, and about strangers. Even the most limited access to him would have been impossible without the help of an Italian journalist called Cecilia Todeschini who had strong contacts inside Leo's inner political circle. She told us why his bodyguards were now ultra-suspicious. Just a few months previously, two of his anti-Mafia friends had been blown up and killed. Both were judges. In the second slaying, a bomb was placed by the roadside as the judge was being driven through Sicily. He died, along with his wife and eight bodyguards. Since then, there had been two foiled attempts on Leo's own life, plus endless threats. However, the murder of his allies made him only more determined. He was seized by an idea. And that idea was to destroy the Mafia.

After filming him on the campaign trail in Rome and Calabria, Cecilia sent a message to our producer, Dorothy Byrne: Leo would give us an interview. It would take place at a hotel in Modena where he'd be arriving shortly after midnight. It was pitch black and silent when we got there, and the town was enveloped in an eerie mist. Inside, the bodyguards stood in a line leading along the corridor to Leo's room. Although they had been told to let us through, they looked tense and confused at the arrival of a group of foreigners they didn't know and couldn't trust. All of them were brandishing machine guns.

Leo greeted us inside the small room that, for tonight, would be his home. He hadn't been back to his real home in Palermo for months. He'd even been warned against carrying photographs of his family to help protect their identities from any Mafia hitmen who might succeed in catching up with him. The interview went on until around 2 a.m., with Leo painting a vivid picture of loneliness:

> I put in a secret place the photos of my past years when we lived as a normal family. It is a way to defend their security. We are not able to walk in the gardens together, not able to go to a restaurant together, not able to say 'Let's go to buy the newspapers this morning.' But they understand me. They love me, and that is the worst of it for me. It would be more easy for me if they would not love me.

There was very little sleep for any of us that night. At 6 a.m. we were up and on the road, driving the fifteen miles to the airport to catch a scheduled flight. Leo was booked on it too, bound for a particularly dangerous public meeting in another notorious Mafia stronghold, Naples. As usual, the plan would be for him to board last, flanked by his armed guards. Dorothy wanted a sequence of him arriving on the tarmac in his bulletproof Fiat, followed by shots of him climbing the steps to the plane, then doing his paperwork during the flight. I took my seat by the window and set up the camera. Sure enough, the plane was full by the time the Fiat came into view. But as I looked through the lens, it began to dawn on me that something was wrong. The car with the police escort was heading for the steps – but not those attached to our plane. At the last moment his guards had decided to change the arrangements again. We were stuck on a flight to Naples; Leo was off to Rome.

In fact, Leo did turn up in Naples later on in the day. His

advisors had altered his travel plans because they had heard about a possible ambush. We filmed him on a walkabout in Castellamare di Stabia, birthplace of Al Capone. It was a scene of wonderful Italian chaos and confusion – horns blaring, drivers shouting, people pushing and arguing with each other in the street. His guards were obviously nervous, as were the police. But this was Leo in his element, greeting the people and spreading his message. And it was clear to see that the people held him in respect. His party was new, but it had just won twelve seats in Parliament. Leo himself had polled the second highest number of votes in the whole of Italy.

But while his anti-crime and corruption message was gaining popularity on the mainland, his main aim was to win the hearts and minds of the people back in Sicily. The day after his Naples trip we boarded a plane again, this time bound for Palermo, then on to Corleone. Leo himself knew the risk he was taking going there.

> To say no to the Mafia in Corleone is more difficult than anywhere else. Because in Corleone the Mafia is not an idea, the Mafia is not a tale, the Mafia is not a film. Here it has a face. It is the face of people working near the place where you work, and the face of people living in the same building.

Corleone itself nests in the hills amid breathtaking Sicilian countryside. Students of organized crime will tell you that it was in this beautiful rural setting that the Mafia was born around two hundred years ago. Criminal families set themselves apart from the rest of society. Their business was to make money and take care of themselves, without the hindrance of laws or taxes. There were crime families throughout Sicily but the Corleonese were known as the most audacious – as well as the most feared. Their brutality became legendary. Only the bravest of the brave would risk offending them, let alone threaten their power.

But here was Leo doing just that. His 'lion's den' was a public hall that had been searched for bombs throughout the day. We got there a couple of hours before he arrived and wondered whether any of the locals would dare to show. Earlier in the week a man named Salvatore 'Toto' Riina – supreme godfather of the Mafia – had been arrested after more than twenty years on the run. Talk of a revenge attack on the visiting politician was rife, and many people must have suspected that there would be violence at the meeting.

Gradually though, as the appointed time grew near, people did start to arrive – men and women, young and old. Everyone was frisked before Leo walked in. More armed bodyguards surrounded the hall. Finally he appeared, moved to the microphone and began to talk. I studied the faces of the audience as he made his speech and I couldn't help but wonder about their own backgrounds. Had they lost relatives in the bloody vendettas? Did they have family members or neighbours who were part of the Mafia? Were they themselves 'connected'?

The older men with weather-beaten farmers' faces were particularly fascinating. I could see in their eyes their amazement, even their disbelief, that this lone man had come to their town to challenge its most feared force. They must have thought he was mad. But Leo wasn't holding back:

> It's wonderful to be in Corleone because it shows there's light amid the darkness. Just think how much better Corleone would be, how much better the tormented, beautiful city of Palermo would be if it were not for the violence that has blighted peoples' lives, shattered their dreams and made everything else seem unimportant.
>
> Just being here is a great victory, because it means there is a great will to go ahead. They have tried everything to stop us. They will try to stop us. But they will never succeed.

When his speech ended, the applause was warm rather than enthusiastic. Perhaps the audience were too close to the organized crime network he condemned. Or maybe they were too frightened to be seen supporting its worst sworn enemy too enthusiastically. But for Leo the night had been a triumph. He headed back to Rome on a high, while his bodyguards felt only relief.

Six years after that meeting Leo is, thankfully, still alive. The Mafia hitmen have failed to get him. His fight to bring back morality into Italian public life has brought him further political rewards. He's been elected to the European Parliament and in 1997 he was once again voted in as mayor of Palermo with a huge majority. But his personal success is nothing compared to the advances that have been made against the Mafia in Sicily. While still influential, its power has been eroded due to a string of arrests and prosecutions of the Mob's leading lights. Leo's long campaign is bearing fruit.

In his interview with us Leo had no doubt about the importance of breaking the Mafia's grip. 'What is at risk in Italy is democracy. Because a democracy in which to walk on the street can be dangerous for a politician is a democracy in crisis. If I win, if democracy wins, then millions of people will be safe.'

At the moment he is winning. For his sake, I hope he stays one step ahead.

THE KUWAITI FIREFIGHTERS

One of the great regrets of my career is not covering the Gulf War. By 1991, when Operation Desert Storm got underway, the whole relationship between the military and the media had changed. Gone were the days when the forces had to deal only with a couple of national news broadcasters and the odd documentary unit. We had reached the age of multi-channels, instant satellite feeds and open-ended live coverage. America and its allies, including Britain, had their press plate full with the three main US networks, CNN, the BBC, ITN, Sky, plus any number of European news channels. For a weekly current affairs series like us, it was virtually impossible to get access to the front. In TV terms this was a war for the news bulletins only.

Of course we did try to come up with our own fresh angles. We made programmes about the British forces in Germany who were preparing to deploy in the desert. There was another edition about the propaganda war, and how the hostilities were being reported and sometimes distorted in the newspapers. Then I was sent to Tel Aviv to show how the Israelis were reacting to the Scud missiles Saddam Hussein was firing into their country in revenge for the Allied bombing of Baghdad. Against its natural instinct Israel didn't retaliate. If it had, who knows how many Arab countries would have joined the war on Saddam's side.

The programmes were OK, but we all felt we were just providing coverage at the margins while the news teams delivered the real stories. However, we did hit the bull's-eye later in the year. It was a programme that provided me with the best images I've ever captured on film. And one that brought me face to face with some of the bravest men I've ever met.

It was October. Desert Storm had finished eight months earlier, but Saddam's legacy in Kuwait was causing continuing horrific problems. As his soldiers had retreated in the last days of the ground war, they had set hundreds of Kuwaiti oil wells and crude storage facilities alight. It was an unprecedented act of sabotage that exposed millions of innocent people to tons of air pollutants, plus a cocktail of smoke, gases and harmful chemicals. The war may have been over but, with the wells still blazing, Saddam continued to torment the country he had invaded.

Like everyone else, I had seen the news pictures of the burning wells and could only wonder at the cost in environmental, as well as financial, terms. But viewing that footage it was obvious that the news simply couldn't do justice to this story. These were images that deserved longer than two minutes on a late-night bulletin.

Producer Debbie Christie agreed. Over lunch with the then editor, Nick Hayes, she suggested a film profiling the men who were at that moment trying to put out the fires. He was enthusiastic and gave her a couple of days to try to negotiate access with one of the companies that had been employed by the Kuwaiti government. At first it didn't look good. The big companies had given some very limited access to a few news crews and weren't interested in having a film unit follow them around for days on end. They were also worried about disclosing commercially sensitive information. All the companies were trying out new and experimental techniques, and none was keen on letting its rivals know what it was doing.

Finally, though, Debbie got a break. She heard of a Canadian company called Safety Boss who were relatively new to the industry and viewed as outsiders. They had no fancy new equipment or special techniques – in fact their gear was no better than that used by an average firefighter back in Britain. But despite this low-tech approach the company was achieving real results, and outperforming most of its rivals. So far its teams had extinguished 175 of the 700 burning wells. A call was put in to their head press officer over in Canada who gave approval for us to film with them in Kuwait. At the same time our researcher John Williams got agreement to film with the Royal Ordnance teams who were busy clearing the desert of Iraqi mines and unexploded Allied bombs. This was more than enough information for Nick. The project was commissioned and Debbie flew out with a title and a transmission date already agreed. The programme would be broadcast on 28 October; it would be called *The Most Dangerous Job In The World*.

Dave Hollingworth, Keith Staniforth and I set off a couple of days later. It was very late at night when we arrived at the hotel in Kuwait City, but there was to be little sleep: Debbie and John told us we had to be up and out by 4 a.m. The city was about thirty miles from the scene of the fires. When we woke up it was hot, smoggy and the air smelled of carbon. But, as Debbie later pointed out, it was better than Birmingham in the rush hour.

Although we could see smoke and the odd shot of flame in the distance, we had no real sense of what we were going into until we registered our names at the Safety Boss headquarters and set off in convoy for the oilfields an hour later. Then, at around 6 a.m., we went from bright morning sunshine to pitch darkness. The only light was provided by the flames that leapt skyward. The sound, the power and the heat were awesome.

No wonder the space satellites had little trouble taking pictures of the burning oilfields. Some of the well heads we passed had flames that were shooting 200 feet into the sky. The plumes of smoke reached 16,000 feet, causing black rain to fall on parts of Iran and Saudi Arabia. In some cases the Iraqis had exploded well heads but failed to set the oil ablaze. That meant the equivalent of 40,000 barrels of crude gushing into the air every single day. Back on the ground, that crude formed massive oil lakes, four feet deep, and growing wider every hour. The desert sand was totally black.

The firefighters were organized into teams who would tackle individual well-head fires. The leader of the team we would follow was Cal Vallete, a twenty-seven-year-old Canadian. He was quiet, intense and an expert at his job. It was thanks to people like him that Safety Boss was emerging as the élite of the world's firefighters. They moved faster, took more risks and cut more corners. Red Adair may have been a legend but these were the young turks who were busy making their own reputations for the future. Meanwhile the team's paramedic looked on, anxious that some of them failed to wear their breathing masks, and others got too close to the intense heat for too long without a break.

Before letting us film him, Cal made sure we had no illusions about the dangers of our new environment. No one had died on his own team, but six people had been killed in the oilfields since the clean-up operation had got underway. Another twenty-five had been permanently injured, while scores more had received hospital treatment for burns and heat exhaustion. We were issued with protective clothing and boots and told in no uncertain terms how close we could get, and how unpredictable things could be. I understood what he was saying, but in truth I wasn't really listening. I was like a kid in a toyshop, unable to believe the visual treats that were spread out in front of me as far as the eye could see. I couldn't put the camera down as I spotted fabulous image after fabulous image. Cal was obviously worried that my enthusiasm was going to land me in trouble. His fears weren't eased when I squatted down to get a low shot, only to lose my boot in oil-soaked sand when I lifted my leg. Keith found a shovel from somewhere and dug it out of the slimy earth. I squelched around for the rest of the day having learned a lesson – this was treacherous territory, and you simply had to take the safety warnings seriously.

The first phase of Cal's task was to extinguish a burning oil lake that surrounded a well. Bulldozers brought in tons of fresh sand to smother the flames in an operation called 'landscaping'. This was highly dangerous for the bulldozer drivers because even the fresh sand could catch fire as the oil bubbled from the ground. To give them some protection, another member of the crew held a safety hose ready to douse them if their cab ignited.

With this part completed successfully, the crew then

prepared to put out the plume itself. As I couldn't follow them as closely as I would have liked, I used telephoto lenses to capture the skill and strength that were now needed. In an incredible operation Cal and his team pumped thousands of gallons of water into the base of the flames. The first water jet hit the flame with such force that it severed it from the well head. The second forced the flame upward where, denied of its fuel, it finally fizzled out.

At around £2,000 a week each, Cal and his crew were being paid well. But when you saw the process up close you realized they were worth every penny. And they weren't just doing it for the money. As experienced oilmen they knew the scale of this environmental catastrophe, and many of them were prepared to risk their lives to bring it to an end.

As for us, we were completely exhausted after our first day in the blazing fields. The only few minutes of rest came when we went back to our own crew vehicle for a lunchtime sandwich. In the complete darkness of noon we got out our food and cans of Fanta and Sprite. Within seconds, we were attacked by the largest swarm of flies I've ever seen in my life. Whatever effect the oil fires were having on human health, they didn't seem to be troubling the insect world.

Throughout the afternoon the noise was deafening, the heat stifling. You could not only smell the oil, you could taste it too. It filled the air like a fine mist and got up the nostrils and into the back of the throat. Looking at us as we drove back to Kuwait City that night, anyone would think we'd been dipped in it. Our boots and overalls were black with oil and sand, and we had to lay down newspapers to stop the oil getting everywhere. Back at the hotel I stripped off my protective clothing and got ready for a bath. Then I caught myself in the mirror: an entirely white body with a little black face.

Another day, another 4 a.m. start. We were to meet up with Cal again as he and his team revisited the well to plug the flow of oil, then – finally – cut off the head and cap it. Although the first phase went smoothly, the second would be the most tense and risky. Cal's colleague Rob Frizell was chosen as the man to cross the still smouldering oil lake, go up to the well head and cut it off. His equipment was a thermal lance that gave off sparks. If any of these touched the deck they could cause the entire oil lake to re-ignite. His suit had been covered with a fire retardant, and he wore a cotton balaclava that gave him exactly five seconds' protection from the flames. My protection was my legs – if we were engulfed in flames I would just have to run for it.

As Rob moved in, Cal stood guard with a hose. Then the nightmare came true. A spark hit the oily sand and within seconds the lake erupted again. Cal rushed in and began dousing us with the hose. Debbie – audible on the film soundtrack – was screaming at us to get out. The heat was searing and the fumes overpowering. But high on adrenalin, Rob, Cal and I escaped the flames and scrambled to safety.

While this made a great sequence for us, it was disastrous for Cal and his team. They were already under pressure to move on to the next burning well. Now they had to spend several hours landscaping the lake surrounding this one. But, true to form, they went about it efficiently, and by the next morning they were ready to go in again with the lance. This time the operation was successful. A well that had been gushing five million dollars' worth of oil every hour was now capped.

As the firefighters tackled the wells, the Royal Ordnance teams were clearing the area of its lethal collection of bombs and land-mines. Russ Bedford was a Scotsman who'd given up civilian life in Glasgow and now toured the oilfields in his Range Rover each day as a bomb disposal officer. In one memorable interview sequence I was able to shoot him behind the wheel of the vehicle. Ahead of him were plumes of smoke. In the rear view and wing mirrors were the reflections of flames shooting to the sky. As he spoke of his own first impressions, you had the feeling that the whole earth was on fire: 'This is like a scene from Dante's Inferno. The oil, smoke, the fire and the blackness are indescribable. Nothing could have prepared me for coming into this environment.'

Steve Kerwin was a former London pub manager who had been lured to the oilfields with a tax-free salary of £60,000 a year. But, money aside, his work was if anything more treacherous than the firefighters'. Two of his team had lost their legs. Just days before we filmed, six Egyptian bomb disposal officers were killed in an explosion.

We spent a couple of days with Russ and Steve as they helped assemble a mass of unexploded bombs, mines, guns and other weaponry. These were brought together on a site the size of a football pitch about a mile from Kuwait City. At a prearranged time all that military hardware was going to be exploded high into the desert sky. There was a huge irony in all this. The bombs had been dropped by Allied warplanes, paid for by British and American taxpayers. Now those same taxpayers were footing the bill for the same bombs to go up in smoke. Still, this was the only way the area could be made safe; the only way innocent children could be protected from losing their limbs in the years ahead.

I couldn't get close enough to film the actual explosion with my own camera, but I had taken along a little Arriflex which I was able to place near the scene. I inserted a connecting cable and ran the wire back about a quarter of a mile to the point where Steve was about to set off the detonation. At the same time he was laying his own cable – known in the trade as the 'exploding washing line'. After that was completed, he detonated. At that moment the earth shook and we were left with a deafening ringing in our ears. I couldn't be sure that my little Arriflex had done the job, but later – back in Manchester – I was able to watch the spectacular moment of explosion.

In fact quite a lot of people took an interest in our unedited film once we were back at base. Word had spread around the building that we had brought back some extraordinary images. Ensconced in the cutting room late at night, Debbie would suddenly find that complete strangers were 'just passing by'. Film editors working on prestige dramas would wander down the corridor and pop their heads in 'just to say hello'. But although we were all pleased with ourselves we knew who the real heroes of this story were. And while we were going home to our nice safe beds they remained on the front line, putting their lives at risk to bring one of the world's largest ever environmental disasters to a close.

Not that Cal ever saw himself as a hero. After the programme was broadcast, Debbie sent him a VHS cassette. A few weeks later he rang her to say thanks: 'You know, it's funny. When you watch it back here in Canada with your folks, I suppose it does all look a bit scary.'

I could have told him that at the time.

CHAPTER 9
DISAPPEARING WORLDS

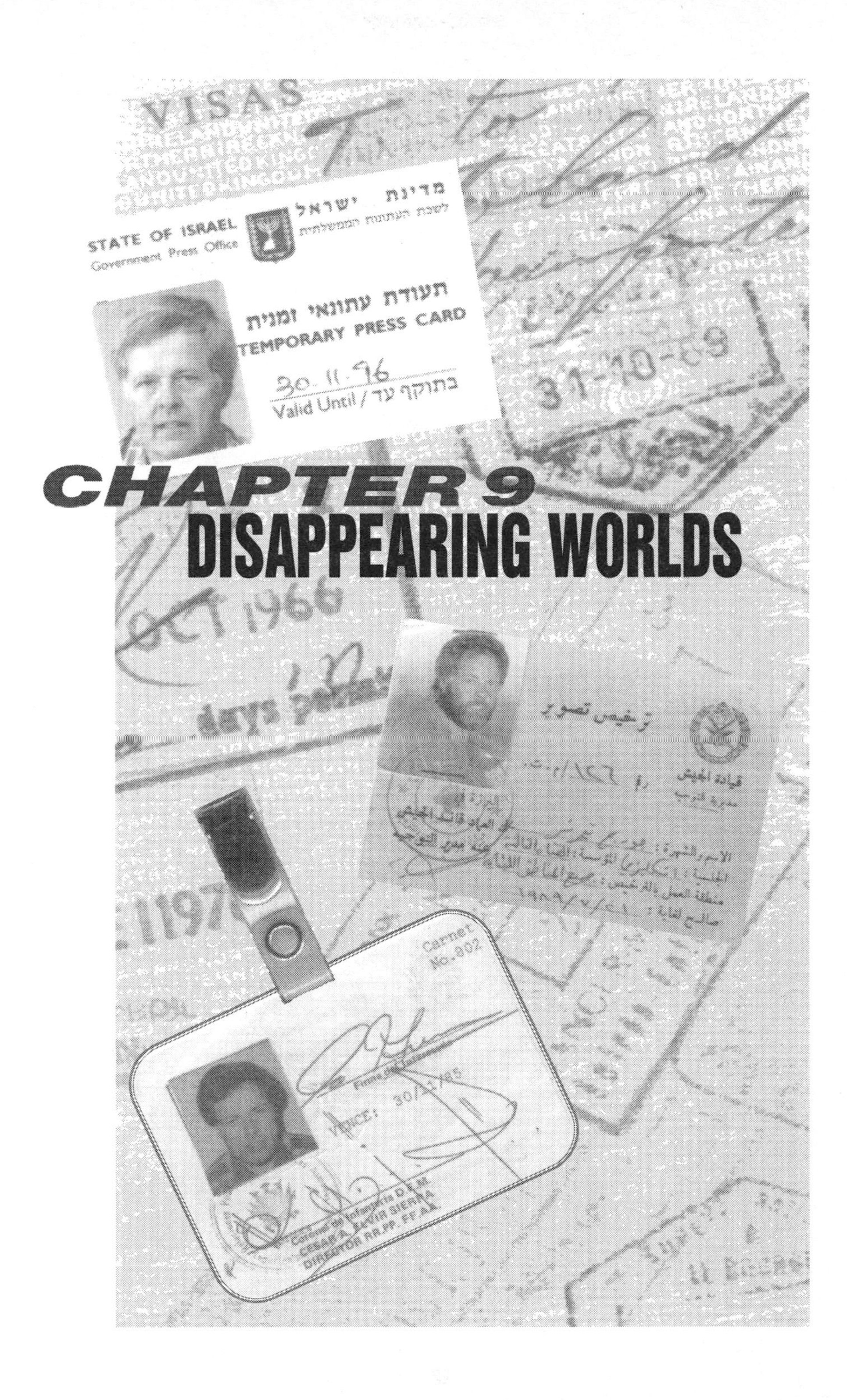

At the last count, I'd been to ninety countries and all five continents. There've been deserts and jungles, equatorial heat and arctic blizzards. I've visited every time zone, and – after all the jabs – my backside now resembles a pin-cushion. Travelling can be tough but after a while it gets in your blood. I can think of many producers who've given up a life on the road to climb the management ladder, only to pine for that out-of-the-blue phone call telling them to get to the airport that night. As for me, a full week at home is a luxury. Anything longer than a fortnight and my feet get itchy.

One of the greatest pleasures is returning to places after long intervals, and finding things just as I left them. Whenever I'm in Hong Kong I retrace my steps from my first visit in 1969, taking the Star Ferry across Kowloon Bay and soaking up the atmosphere in the magnificent Peninsular Hotel. In Jerusalem I know I'm assured of tremendous Arab hospitality at the American Colony. And no trip to New York is complete without antipasti and lasagne at Bernito's restaurant in Little Italy.

Inevitably, though, other old haunts do change; sometimes entire countries. A few of the places I've visited now bear no relation to what they once were, and their people's way of life has altered beyond all recognition. Perhaps one day I'll go back. But I'm sure to feel like a stranger all over again.

THE OLD COUNTRY

If you're planning a tour of the world's remotest spots, you could start with Vilcabamba – the 'sacred valley' of Ecuador – 9,000 feet up in the Andes. For many years anthropologists, doctors and scientists have made the trek to this ancient paradise, nestling on the equator. By a freak of nature it remains in constant sunshine, despite being surrounded by darkened and cloudy mountains. At the top of the valley there's thick forest, while the lower reaches give way to a quilted patchwork of sugar cane fields, fruit orchards and cattle pastures. But it's not the idyllic scenery the visitors go to study: it's the people. They want to know why they live longer than anyone else in the world.

In 1973 I joined another group trying to discover the secrets of eternal youth. We were led by producer Gavin McFadyen, who had just read a magazine article about the valley and its amazing record on ageing. He thought it would make one of those off-beat, timeless *World In Action*s that we kept on standby to transmit – just in case one of the more controversial editions was pulled by the lawyers. Alan Bale and I were finishing the programme about the Chilean coup when we were told to travel on to Ecuador. We met Gavin in the capital, Quito, where we chartered a small twin-engined plane from an army general. He flew us to a landing strip near the valley and, from there, we boarded a pick-up truck to take us along the last few miles of dirt road.

The village we arrived at had been built at the beginning of the nineteenth century. It looked as if it hadn't altered since. In the centre of the square was a large Roman Catholic church, surrounded by rows of two-storey buildings. Tucked away in the corner was a rickety old hotel that would be our base for the next few days. Once we had unpacked Gavin took us out to film some street interviews in which passers by were asked their age and their secrets of a long life. One old man told us he was 101, another ninety-one. Two women said they were aged ninety and 100. The reasons for their longevity were wide and varied. Some claimed it was the constant sunshine, others the fruit-rich diet. Many believed hard work and clean living were the recipe for a ripe old age. A few said it might be the pure mountain air and the minerals found in the local water supply.

We heard about one man further up the valley who still farmed his mountainside plot at the age of 130. His fields were around 10,000 feet above sea level, so to reach him we needed to go on horseback. Gavin was delighted. A giant of a man, with huge long legs, he obviously saw himself as a John Wayne figure in the saddle. I, on the other hand, hate anything without an engine and a brake. By the time we reached the old farmer my thighs were in agony, while Alan was nursing bruised legs and damaged ribs, having been thrown off. To add insult to injury, the farmer had finished his day's work and was now making his way back home.

He told us we should meet him at his house at the bottom of the mountain and walked off, displaying the biggest set of calf muscles I've ever seen. Some scientists had speculated that the legs of the mountain people were so strong that the muscles actually provided their bodies with a second heartbeat. As they contracted they pumped the blood, so each step they took helped the real heart. Whether this was the secret of long life or not, old Gabrielle Sanchez was as fit as a fiddle. He went home on foot while we – 100 years his junior – had to rely on the horses again.

The journey back down was, if anything, even more difficult. The terrain was rough and painful, and when Gavin decided to show off his riding skills and break into a gallop, my horse followed suit. I was already clinging on for life when it came to a stream and decided to jump. Somehow I managed to hold on – but I'll never know how the camera, tripod and rolls of film stayed safe.

Later, Gabrielle told us he worked seven days a week. To get to his plot, he woke at dawn and walked a mile up the mountain. Only when it was dusk did he come down. He told us he didn't drink, but liked to smoke as often as he could afford. Apart from a little rheumatism he had no health problems whatsoever. He agreed that hard work, clean air and fresh water all helped keep him fit and agile. But he had another recipe for living long, that none of us fancied: 'My secret is to peel and eat donkey meat. It's the best safeguard against illness.'

Back down in the village we met 103-year-old Mrs Quezada, who ran the local bakery. She worked ten hours a day and spent the rest of the time looking after her extended family. She told us about a distant relative who was in his twenties when she was just a little girl. A few hours later we tracked him down, eating and enjoying the company of some of his ninety-eight grandchildren. Miguel Carpio had fathered his last child at the age of eighty, and had worked all his life herding cattle – a job that involved walking fifteen miles a day up and down the mountainsides. Two years earlier he'd finally retired – aged 125.

The Andes is a place of breathtaking sunrises. One Sunday we got up around 5 a.m. to drive into the mountains and film the dawn breaking. It was a riot of colour, with the peaks of copper mountains becoming visible through the clouds, and their long shadows stretching for miles down the valleys. On the way back, our lungs filled with unsullied air, we decided to sample another of the possible reasons for long life. Down on one of the farms was Vilcabamba's only factory. It took tons of sugar cane from the fields, crushed the plants into juice, poured it into vats . . . and made it into rum. We had been told that many of the old men in the valley drank three or four cups of this local brew every day. But just seconds after I took a sip, my mouth felt as if it was on fire. I was then told it was 110% proof – half as strong again as Scotch whisky.

Despite living in what's supposed to be the healthiest spot on the planet, I had started to feel ill. Perhaps my body was just too used to pollution and processed food. Perhaps I needed a good dose of fluoride in the water, or maybe I'd just eaten too much of the local fruit. Whatever it was, I was beginning to recognise the tell-tale signs of Third World Tummy. Later that morning we headed back to the village square to film the mass at the Catholic church. I was wandering around getting close-up shots of these fantastic weather-beaten old faces in the congregation when the dysentery finally kicked in. I really shouldn't have crouched.

After a quick change of trousers, I was whisked off to the village doctor. While Gavin took the camera to film the ritual slaughter of a pig, I was getting an injection in my backside and a medical instruction to drink plenty of Coca-Cola. I was in terrible pain for a couple of hours, but then both measures seemed to work. Later the same day, I felt fit enough to head back to the church.

Vilcabamba is so important to scientists because documentary proof of the people's ages exists. Other societies may have laid claims to longevity but there are rarely any birth certificates to back them up. In devoutly Catholic Ecuador, however, babies are baptized, and those christening records are kept by the priests. Father Bravo, who conducted the services in the village, had agreed to help us decipher the names on the worm-eaten records down in the church cellars. He was able to find faded entries for Gabrielle Sanchez, Miguel Carpio and Mrs Quezada. There was also a record of Petronal Pineda – another woman we interviewed – proving she really was 110. The parish register showed many other entries of people who had died in the valley after living to great ages. Most remarkable of all was a recently departed man called Jose Toledo. According to the records, he was 140.

Scientists have never been able to agree on the real reason for these amazing life-spans. Of all the theories, the healthy low fat diet and the trace elements in the local water are the most common. But while we were there we found another possible factor – the almost complete absence of stress. The people may have been poor, but they lived in a peaceful, tranquil valley with none of the pressures the rest of us associate with modern living. A survey by Ecuadorian doctors found none of the stress-related illnesses that kill off so many people in the West. There were no heart attacks, no ulcers, and no apparent mental illness.

The vast majority of people were visibly content with their way of life. As for crime, there simply was none. When we spoke to Vilcabamba's two policemen they confirmed that no law-breaking ever took place in the valley. When pressed, however, one of them did admit that he'd had to take a woman into custody a few weeks earlier. Her crime? 'It was for being unpleasant. She slandered one woman, then another. I had to arrest her for saying bad things about people.'

But, if physical isolation really was a reason for the people's longevity, Vilcabamba's amazing life-expectancy record was about to be threatened. On our last day we again went high into the mountains where I was able to place my camera and film the area surrounding the valley. There, along with the tobacco fields, the two rivers and the flowing corn was . . . a building site. A new road had reached the valley, and it would soon snake its way right through to our time-warped village. The government had decided to open Vilcabamba to the outside world, and – more particularly – to its wealthy tourists.

Twenty-five years on I'm able to log on to the internet where – among 516 web pages for Vilcabamba – I can read the official guide. It boasts a dozen hotels offering not just beds for the night, but massage, reflexology, steam baths and saunas. Restaurants and cafés are advertised, along with popular activities such as walking, hiking, horse-trekking and mountain-biking. And, written above a spectacular aerial photo of the Sacred Valley, is the tempting holiday slogan: 'Vilcabamba: Where Years Are Added To Your Life – And Life Is Added To Your Years'.

The tourist industry has certainly taken off. But at what price?

WALLS COME TUMBLING DOWN

In the early 1970s a group of Granada programme-makers came up with a new TV format called the drama-documentary. Although these programmes used actors to portray real people, their purpose was not to sensationalize, or fictionalize, the truth. For years, Western current affairs crews had been barred from filming in the communist countries of Eastern Europe. The new format was simply an inventive way of getting around the censorship, and alerting British viewers to the grim reality of life behind the Iron Curtain.

There was the odd exception to the blanket ban on overt filming. In 1973 Granada gained permission to make a profile of Olga Korbutt, the seventeen-year-old Russian gymnast who had just won three gold medals, and the hearts of the world's TV viewers, at the Munich Olympics. For five weeks, we were allowed to follow her from her training camp in Moscow, to her home in Grodno near the Polish border. The only snag was that we had to be accompanied at all times by a crew from the official *Novosti* Press Agency. I may have been free to film inside Olga's home and the gymnasium, but any exterior shots had to be recorded by our state-approved cameraman, Boris. The authorities were so paranoid about us catching sight of everyday life that they arranged for nearly all of our travelling to take place under night-time darkness.

Despite the security arrangements we did gradually get a flavour of life under communist rule. Although the people were friendly, their lives were hard. Incomes were low and shortages in the shops were common. Walking around Moscow was like being transported back to 1950s Britain. Everything was grey and drab, old cars spewed out polluting fumes, the antique phone system usually didn't work.

Half-way through the shoot we saw the greatest contrast between East and West. Olga had been performing at a sports festival in Frankfurt and, on her way home, had to pass through the divided city of Berlin to catch her flight. Travelling by coach, we left the bright lights, skyscrapers and illuminated advertising hoardings of West Berlin behind. A minute later we approached a huge sign announcing 'You are now leaving the Western Allied Zone'. Grim-faced guards inspected our papers at the checkpoint, our surroundings suddenly became austere, and the passers-by dressed shabbily. In the streets the traffic consisted almost entirely of Trabants, the ugly little cars that ran on two-stroke fuel and struggled to hit 50 mph. This was East Germany – and about as pretty as it got.

Because of the difficulties in filming behind the Iron Curtain, other projects were rare. The next time I went was in 1982, a year after Poland had introduced martial law in an attempt to crush the trade union, Solidarity. Producer Mike Beckham had arranged for us to enter the country by ferry via the Swedish port of Malmö. We boarded as ordinary tourists but, hidden inside the panels of our hired Volvo, were the camera, lights and sound equipment.

Filming in secret over the next fortnight we saw full well how the Polish people were suffering under the iron hand of

General Jaruzelski. The economy was on the point of collapse, with everything from clothes to food to cigarettes the subject of rationing. Even soap was in desperately short supply, with each family limited to one bar every two months. We visited Warsaw and Cracow, meeting the steelworkers, dockers and Catholic priests who were heading the underground resistance to communist rule. But, despite Solidarity's massive popular support, the government appeared in complete control of events. Demonstrations were put down ruthlessly, strike organizers were thrown in jail, the phones of ordinary citizens were bugged routinely by the all-powerful secret police.

How different things looked in the Eastern Bloc seven years later. By then Mikhail Gorbachev had come to power in the USSR, introducing *glasnost* and *perestroika*, and helping set off a chain of events that would finally finish the Cold War. One by one, Moscow's puppet governments began to fall: the Solidarity leaders took over the reins of power in Poland, Bulgaria's politburo was kicked out and Hungary flung open its borders to Austria. Once that happened the end really was in sight. Suddenly thousands of East Germans were flooding into Czechoslovakia on their way to Hungary and – finally – a new life in the West. On 9 November 1989, the biggest symbol of communist oppression was removed: the Berlin Wall came down.

I was in Czechoslovakia the night it fell. Pro-democracy demonstrations had been taking place in the capital, Prague, for weeks. However, the Czechs – who had seen their 1968 uprising crushed by Russian tanks – could not quite believe that communism was on the point of collapse. Even when news of the momentous events in Berlin came through, the atmosphere was muted. However, within a fortnight of us leaving, the Czechs too were celebrating revolution. Alexander Dubček, the exiled leader of the 1968 protests, came back to address the ecstatic crowds in Wenceslas

Square. Václav Havel, the jailed dissident playwright, took over the running of the country.

But even though the Warsaw Pact governments were crumbling, there was one country where no one expected revolution. Under President Nicolae Ceauşescu, Romania was the most hard-line Stalinist state of all. In power since 1965, he had installed his family members into key government positions, enriched himself at the country's expense, and employed a hated and feared secret police – the Securitate – to crush anyone who voiced opposition to his rule. Just over a week after the Berlin Wall came down, Ceauşescu assured his supporters that communism in Romania was under no threat. While their neighbours began tasting democracy, Romanians voted their dictator in for another five years.

But, blinded by power and surrounded by sycophants, Ceauşescu had completely misjudged the mood of his people. Shortly before Christmas there was an uprising in the city of Timişoara. After troops and Securitate officers fired on the protestors – killing an estimated 100 people – the President came on to the balcony of the Central Committee building in Bucharest to address the crowds. Such a mass audience – heavily infiltrated by Securitate officers – could always be relied upon to show its obedience and undying devotion to Ceauşescu. But this time was different. When one small section of the crowd began chanting 'Timişoara', confusion and panic set in. As Ceauşescu tried to address the throng, booing could be heard, then anti-government slogans. With live TV cameras on him, the dictator – who up until that moment had been all-powerful – was clearly at a loss. His guards led him away. By the next day he and his wife were climbing into a helicopter to flee as the crowds began storming the building.

I arrived in Romania two weeks after the Christmas revolution. By then Ceauşescu and his wife Elena had been deposed and executed by firing squad, their bullet-ridden bodies left slumped against a wall and videoed for all the world to see. However, there were stories that the National Salvation Front – the group that had taken over the running of the country – was led by some of the main players in the old regime. Were they really going to deliver ordinary Romanians from the nightmare of dictatorship, or could the people expect more of the same?

Unable to fly directly to Bucharest, sound recordist Phil Taylor and I jumped on a plane to Belgrade in the former Yugoslavia. We hired a twelve-seater Citroën and set off on a marathon journey that would take us into Romania, over mountains and through driving rain and snow. Already on the way we discovered that our map contained road details only as far as the border. Once we were across, we were on our own.

By a mixture of luck and a natural sense of direction we arrived in the Romanian capital around midnight after twelve hours continuous driving. Amazingly, the first time we stopped to ask for directions to the hotel, we discovered that we were just half a mile away. Minutes later we met up with Steve Boulton, the producer, and the researcher, Andrew Jennings, who had both arrived a week earlier.

They had arranged for us to film in Focşani, an industrial town that Ceauşescu had described as a 'workers' paradise'. In reality it was an urban nightmare: hundreds upon hundreds of identical five-storey apartment blocks, badly built and painted concentration-camp grey. On the streets hungry women, old before their time, queued for what few supplies the shops had in stock. As we remained snug in our overcoats and quilted anoraks, the people here wrapped themselves in blankets and towels to protect against the sub-zero temperatures. On one street corner an old man held some portable scales, hoping to make some money by weighing the passers-by.

We visited a family whose electricity had been cut off because they couldn't afford to pay the bill. The grandmother rocked herself in a chair to try to keep warm while some of the children huddled around a candle and a paraffin heater, obviously suffering from colds and bad chests. The father explained that, under Ceauşescu, birth control and abortions were forbidden unless couples had already produced five children. Large families were compulsory, even though parents couldn't afford to support them. When we finished filming the sequence at their home Steve gave them some money. Temporarily, at least, they were able to stave off the winter cold.

We had been warned that food was in short supply in Romania, so, before setting off, we had packed fruit cake and packets of Cup-a-Soup. These were to prove a godsend while staying at Focşani's hotel – an establishment that was able to offer only a local stew (actually little more than potatoes boiled in stock) and plates of chips topped with melted cheese. The scarcity of food was remarkable as the town itself lay in the country's most fertile region. Under Ceauşescu's rule though, the whole harvest was taken by the government and exported for hard currency. Meanwhile the people who worked the land went hungry. One woman told us how she was jailed for seven months for stealing crops to feed her children.

Such desperate conditions were in sharp contrast to the lifestyle enjoyed by communist party officials. The First Secretary in Focşani was a woman who had designed herself a lavish mansion in the centre of town. Her offices contained stained glass windows celebrating the workers' struggle against capitalism – but the workers themselves would have been arrested and jailed if they had dared to venture inside.

In fact, she was so keen to distance herself from the ordinary people that when her granddaughter was due to be born at the local hospital, she ordered all other mothers and children to be cleared from the ward. When we toured the hospital we saw just how obscene that instruction was. There, in the premature baby unit, newborns were sharing incubators; in the maternity wing's recovery room, mothers were sleeping two to a bed.

Depressingly, many of the other officials who had presided over this state of affairs were indeed now playing major roles in the National Salvation Front. Local author Liviu Stoicu, who had served a jail sentence for writing a book critical of Ceauşescu, was the leader of the NSF in Focşani. He told us it was impossible to make things work without the former communist apparatchiks. They might have been responsible for putting Ceauşescu's evil policies into practice, but they were the only people around who knew how to manage an economy and administer the public services.

Even former members of the secret police were seeking positions in the new administration, and those who might have expected punishment from the new leaders appeared to have got away with it. On the last day of the shoot Andrew tracked down Colonel Sambra, one-time head of the Focşani Securitate. Banging on the door of his flat, in an apartment block reserved for the communist élite, Andrew challenged him to come out and answer questions about his brutal past. But he refused to budge, shouting at us from behind the closed door to leave him alone and accusing us of trying to put him in an early grave.

We left Romania unsure of what direction the country was taking. The people were clearly relieved that their hated President had gone but there was confusion about the future. The last time we filmed a meeting of Focşani's National Salvation Front, its leader Liviu Stoicu suddenly quit, accusing former government officials of seeking only to look after themselves, and claiming that nothing in the country had changed.

Fortunately, that pessimism turned out to be misplaced. Despite the questionable make-up of the National Salvation Front, it did start to tear apart the country's repressive communist structure. Political parties reappeared quickly and many of the human rights abuses associated with the old regime stopped. By 1996 Romania was a genuine multi-party democracy with free and fair elections, plus a growing economy. There could be no greater contrast to the twenty-four years of fear under Nicolae Ceauşescu.

A WALK THROUGH THE RAINFOREST

Perhaps it was the hole in the ozone layer and the links with skin cancer. Or the fear that global warming would soon put our seaside towns under water. Whatever the cause, somewhere around the late 1980s the people of Britain began to care for their environment. Anyone who doubted the seriousness of that concern had only to look at the 1989 Euro-elections. In that year two million people cast their traditional political allegiance aside – and voted for the Green Party.

It was only natural that we should reflect viewers' worries about the deteriorating state of the planet. For many years we had exposed governments and multinationals for the way they treated their citizens and exploited their workers. But suddenly we were making programmes on their environmental record: how they were polluting our rivers, adulterating our food and causing acid rain. The age of the 'ethical consumer' had arrived. People were prepared to leave products on the shelves if they thought the manufacturers were harming the world around them.

Green issues didn't stop at home. The news bulletins told us about greenhouse gases that would lead to permanent climate change. They showed the once-flowing rivers that had dried up as deserts ate into fertile land. And they revealed how thousands of animal species were in danger of extinction.

One of the most poignant stories concerned the devastation of the world's rainforests. The recurring TV image was of a mass of trees and vegetation laid waste, with long thin plumes of smoke heading skyward. It was to become a symbol of man's disregard for his planet, and it was to spur many environmental campaigners into action.

The tropical rainforests have been called the world's natural medicine cabinet. They support the richest and most complicated eco-systems on earth, with thousands of species of trees, plants, birds, animals and insects. Their vegetation has provided the source for most of our life-saving drugs. The trees and the plants store carbon dioxide in their roots, stems and leaves. And, by filtering out the harmful gas, they effectively make our air fit to breathe. But despite all these benefits, much of the rainforests have been wiped out, never to return. What areas that do remain are under serious threat.

Sarawak is one of them. It forms the northern tip of Borneo, the world's third largest island. Controlled by the government of Malaysia, four fifths of the state is covered in jungle. It's also home to the Penan, one of the last remaining nomadic tribes of the rainforest. I went there in 1992 as that gentle and timid people were making a last-ditch attempt to save their forest – and their entire way of life – from the giant logging companies of Japan and Korea. The Far East corporations had moved in to tear down the trees, to provide their own countries with timber for the building industry. As they advanced inland, the Penan were setting up blockades to keep them at bay. But what chance did a primitive tribe stand against the mighty lorries and chainsaws?

We wanted to find out, but the Malaysian government refused us permission to film. Logging was earning them millions of dollars' worth of export revenue, and they had allowed and encouraged the deforestation to take place. They were also sensitive to criticism and didn't want the effects of their policy to be shown to the outside world. When his application was turned down, producer Don Jordan decided he was going in anyway. I would travel with him carrying just a miniature home video camera.

Don's researcher Brian Eades teamed up with the sound recordist Phil Taylor to form a second crew. The four of us caught a flight to the tiny kingdom of Brunei – and from there we drove across the border to Sarawak's main city, Miri. Phil and Brian's job was to get shots of the giant mahogany trees being felled by the loggers. Ours was to venture some 200 miles into the jungle to meet with the Penan, show their way of life, and profile their struggle for survival.

Our journey began on a road running parallel to the Baram River and, within an hour, we had entered a place of almost indescribable beauty. There are more species of trees in Sarawak than anywhere else on the planet. Look in just one of the stumps and there'll be more types of ant than in the whole of the British Isles. A forest so diverse is full of amazing sights and sounds. Along with the screeching of monkeys, we could hear the piercing call of the native hornbill bird. There were wild boar running through the forest, while all around us hovered the most spectacularly coloured butterflies.

But we also came across the first signs that this paradise was in trouble. Lining the road were rows of huge logs which, our guide explained, were the remnants of trees that had been rejected by potential buyers. Some of them had been growing for centuries, reaching heights of over 100 feet and widths of three yards. But the chainsaws had brought them crashing down in less than a minute, and now they were being left to rot. As for the river, it was once one of the cleanest and purest to be found anywhere. But now it was polluted by the logging industry's waste, and soil erosion caused by the tree felling meant tons of dirt had poured into the river, blackening its crystal clear waters.

As dusk fell we prepared for the second leg of the trip. A

four-wheel-drive Nissan was to carry us 2,000 feet up a mountainside to the village of Long Ajeng. The journey took around seven hours as we drove through denser and denser jungle. It was hot and humid but the November monsoon rains kept crashing down, making it ever more difficult for the driver to navigate. Flooded pathways became impassable and hillsides too boggy to hold any weight. When we finally arrived it was way beyond midnight. We were dripping wet as some of the villagers approached us with lanterns, then led the way to the home of their headman.

As we drew nearer we could see that his house was on stilts, with the living and sleeping quarters around nine feet above the ground. Walking up the makeshift ladder I could make out the remnants of the evening fire just beginning to fade. Inside, I noticed that the children under their blankets were watching us with one eye – to be closed immediately whenever we caught their stares.

In Penan culture, there are no social classes or hierarchies. There is no relative wealth or poverty, and all food is shared. The headman in each village has no actual power but instead acts as a spokesman for his people. Talking through our translator-guide, Don spent an hour explaining to Long Ajeng's headman who we were and what we wanted to do. He agreed to us spending some time with the tribe and said we could sleep in a disused concrete building a couple of hundred yards away. When we got there we found it formed the start of the Penan's barricade – a mass of logs and branches. We were struck by how flimsy this barrier was. If a logging company wanted to proceed further into the forest, they could have swept it aside with one bulldozer. But the headman told us they had a secret weapon – and that it would be revealed to us the following morning.

As dawn broke we found ourselves in an area of pristine rainforest, surrounded by a people who had remained hidden from modern civilization. The Penan are hunter-gatherers, and their lifestyle is no different from that of our own ancestors thousands of years ago. They had striking faces – chocolate-coloured skin, topped with heads of dense black hair. Strings of beads were draped around their necks, while earlobes had been pierced then jammed with tight spirals of bamboo. As the men went hunting for squirrels, lizards, monkeys and bearded pig, the women made sago dough from the pulp of wild trees. As we sweltered in our Western clothes, the Penan's adults and children went about their business in nothing but loincloths.

The headman took us to the barricade and explained how deforestation was driving out the wild game. Fruit trees were being destroyed and fish stocks depleted due to the river pollution. Plants whose bark and leaves had provided medicines and snakebite antidotes had been slashed and burned. He said the logging activities had become so widespread that the nomadic tribe had almost reached the point of extinction. A Penan mother said that if their blockade didn't work, their ancient way of life would be over for good: 'We don't want the loggers to come as they destroy our land. We are anxious, we are deprived, we are hungry. If they come to destroy the land, to finish off all the trees, my children will face hardship. My children will die.'

The Penan are noted for disliking confrontation. They avoid eye contact with others and never walk directly towards another person. When someone else does pass by they bend slightly, then bow. Anthropologists who've studied them say they are among the most peaceful people in the world. But the destruction of their habitat meant they were going against their nature, and preparing to fight. Along with their traditional spears they were making a stockpile of blowpipes to be used against anyone who tried to tear down the barricade. I was taken into a little hut to film one of the village craftsmen making them. As he carved the blowpipes from jungle hardwood he explained that they were lighter and more accurate than a shotgun. The blowpipe darts were dipped in a lethal poison called tajem, made from the resin of the ipoh tree. If it got into a human's bloodstream it would interfere with the functioning of the heart, causing a lingering and agonizing death. The headman said they were more than ready to use their weapon: 'If they come here to kill us we will blowpipe them. If they try to pass the barricade against our will we will blowpipe them. Once they are caught there will be no escape. They will die here.'

Throughout our two-day stay with the Penan we lived on tins of sardines and corned beef brought from home. We had a little of the local rice and fruit but decided to pass up the delights of roast lizard. We saw enough of life in the village to sympathize deeply with the natives. They were a proud and gentle people who wanted nothing more than to be left in peace. But their entire way of life was being threatened simply because of Japan's insatiable desire for wood. They saw the trees that supported them ending up as furniture, doors, window frames – even chopsticks. What made them angriest was the prospect of trees being made into plywood panels, which were used to mould concrete, then discarded.

When it was time for us to leave we wished the villagers luck with their blockade, then went to meet the driver whom we had booked to take us back to Miri. Five hours later, he still hadn't arrived. As the light faded we discovered that the Nissan wasn't going to make it to Long Ajeng at all. The monsoon downpours had caused a landslip, making it impossible for any vehicle to get up the mountain. Don went to the headman who found four tribesmen willing to guide us through the jungle and back to the river. It was a final kind gesture, and at that moment we were both grateful. But we didn't know we were about to start the toughest journey of our lives.

The first leg lasted roughly eight hours. Initially, it was fine – the straight downhill walk causing nothing more than a little breathlessness. But after a while, we found ourselves following the guides up steep gradients, clambering over fallen trees, and clinging precariously to hillsides with fast-flowing rivers ninety feet below us. Sometimes we would have to get across these rivers, wading through with the water at chest height. Then, on the other side, we would have to climb more hills and negotiate our way through the thickest of forests. I was bathed in a mixture of sweat and rainwater, constantly rubbing my eyes to see clearly, and always on the lookout for the snakes and leeches whose natural habitat it was. Meanwhile the tribesmen were displaying their superior physical fitness along with their awesome geographical knowledge. As Don and I wheezed, they picked up our equipment and breezed on ahead.

About half-way through these SAS-style manoeuvres, we came to a small jungle clearing. As we walked through the last of the trees I could see a Penan family sitting by a fire, its smoke drifting off above the forest. As the woman cradled one of the children, the father stoked the flames. Wild boar ran in and out of the trees and, apart from the birds squawking above, the forest was completely silent. The family – parents, children and elders – were all naked except for their loincloths and necklaces. Illuminated by the shafts of sunlight through the trees, they seemed to belong on a film set. In all the years I'd been travelling I had never seen such a primitive sight. God only knows what they thought when they laid their eyes on me. Living in one of the remotest spots on earth, they probably didn't even know that white people existed.

By the time we reached the river Don and I could take no more. The guides arranged for us to be put in a boat that would take us downstream on the next leg of the journey to Miri. None of them could speak any English, but they somehow managed to explain to us what we were to do next. I took back our bags from them and was amazed to find that they had kept all the recording equipment and batteries safe and dry. I then remembered that, to get home, they would have to turn back and do the same arduous journey all over again. They didn't use money so it was impossible to pay them But I was so grateful for what they had done, I handed over my watch and my prized Swiss army knife as a thank you.

Once they'd gone, Don and I got into the boat. The locals called them 'river taxis', but in reality they were nothing more than hollowed out logs with old engines fixed to the back. The pilot warned us to hold on tight as most of the journey would be free-flowing and extremely fast. He wasn't making it up.

The next couple of hours were spent charging through rapids with huge waves crashing over the side of the boat and covering our heads. I tried my best to protect the camera and could see the pilot standing at the front sticking his huge pole into the river bed in order to maintain some control. Somehow he managed to keep us on course and finally, as the waters calmed, we sailed gently into a small dock that served a small mission station in the heart of the rainforest. We got off the boat, soaked from head to toe, and made for a small post office that had a telephone. From there I was able to call our hotel in Miri, assure Phil and Brian we were safe, and warn them that we'd be another twenty-four hours getting out.

Back at the mission station it seemed to take ages drying off but, once I did, I went straight to bed and fell asleep before my head hit the pillow. The following morning I had a long hot bath and opened up a waterproof bag containing the one set of clothes that had remained dry throughout my time in the jungle. I put them on and looked forward to a comfortable and leisurely trip downriver to Miri. Then, just as I went to step on to the boat, I lost my footing on the riverbank and went head first into the water. It really was that sort of journey.

Despite my own discomfort, I have nothing but happy memories of my adventures in the rainforest. Sadly, since our return, the logging has continued apace, wiping out around 70 per cent of the trees and vegetation. The Malaysian government has resettled many of the Penan, taking them from their traditional homes and building special reserves. But the ancient lifestyle has all but ended, with a recent report estimating the number of truly nomadic tribespeople at fewer than 500. I can only hope that family I saw in the jungle clearing are among them.

CHAPTER 10
ALL CHANGE

As the world around me has altered, so has life inside television. When your work involves haring around the globe getting pictures for transmission, you barely have time to notice the changes that are happening. Then one day you stop and realize your industry bears little resemblance to the one you joined.

Like many people of my generation I first became aware of TV back in 1952. The reason was the Coronation – the first real mass media event in Britain. My parents had a set installed specially, just like tens of thousands of others up and down the land. Friends and neighbours called in to see live shots of the future Queen walking up the aisle of Westminster Abbey to be crowned. Little did any of us realize the vast amounts of equipment and manpower that were making those pictures possible.

By the time I joined the industry just over a decade later, much of the same hardware was still in place. Even small outside broadcasts would involve four vehicles and upwards of thirty people. A simple series of street interviews required us to lump around some 60lb worth of equipment.

My first TV job was with Mancunian Films, a small independent outfit that supplied news crews to the local company, Granada. I had been encouraged to go for it by Peter Wheeler, a Granada news presenter and neighbour of ours in Southport. He fixed up an interview with the company's owner John Blakely, and I was hired as a sound assistant following a lunchtime interview in a Manchester pub.

Working on Granada's regional programmes was exhilarating. The patch was massive, taking in the old Lancashire mill towns along with the woollen capitals of Yorkshire. It included brash and glitzy Blackpool, as well as genteel Harrogate. There were the working-class swathes of Salford that inspired *Coronation Street*, plus the wealthy stockbroker belts of Cheshire, and the trendy creative hotbed that was sixties Liverpool.

Inside the Manchester studios there was a constant buzz. Our magazine programme *People And Places* was a big ratings hit, making local stars of presenters such as Michael Parkinson, Bill Grundy and Brian Trueman. Autograph-hunters would gather at the entrance as famous personalities dropped in to be interviewed or take part in productions, and I loved going in there to witness the energy that went into putting the programmes together.

Out on the road though, it was hard work. Back then, location cameras only worked by taking the power from a 12-volt car battery, and feeding it through a large and heavy converter. As the sound assistant it was my job to carry both, and to make sure that the camera remained powered-up at all times. That involved ignoring what was going on around me and keeping my eyes fixed on the equipment to make sure the film rotated at exactly 50 cycles per minute, 25 frames per second.

Perhaps the toughest test of my stamina came in July 1964 when the Beatles returned to Liverpool for the première of their first movie, *A Hard Day's Night*. The band had just arrived back from their triumphant début tour of America where they had established themselves as the most popular entertainment act in the world. On the streets of their home town, tens of thousands of fans had turned out to greet them.

The day began at the city's Speke Airport as they flew in on a specially chartered plane from London. Standing among the hordes of screaming teenage girls, we got shots of the Beatles touching down, then ran to the VIP lounge. There our reporter Freddy Aspin got our first scoop of the day, beating all the other journalists to secure the first interviews with the returning heroes.

But there was no time to celebrate. As soon as Freddy had done his chat, the cameraman Dave Woods, sound recordist Phil Smith and I sped off towards Liverpool Town Hall, where the group were due to make a public appearance later in the afternoon. By the time we got there, though, the crowds had beaten us to it and the city centre was at a standstill. We didn't have a hope of getting any decent shots of the Town Hall balcony until Dave persuaded a businessman to let us into the office building which stood directly opposite. I lugged the battery, the converter and a box containing the rolls of camera film up the four flights of stairs. After carrying them through the streets for hours I was completely exhausted. But Dave got what he wanted – perfect shots of the group waving and shouting to the crowds below. And Granada got what it wanted, too. The film led that night's news bulletins and was then sold around the world. It was priceless archive material, and it's been making money for the company ever since.

Over the next couple of years there were more advances in technology, revolutionizing film-making and easing the pressure on my arms. The big advance was the Éclair, the first truly portable 16mm camera. It was half the weight of those that had gone before, making factual programmes much easier to shoot. Suddenly it was possible to film inside cars in the middle of demonstrations. And as well as being easier to handle, the equipment was cheaper to operate.

Armed with the new kit, I was asked to work on a new project called *The Headliners*, a current affairs series aimed at young people. We profiled up and coming athletes, examined exploitation of teenage workers, and looked at how the police mounted a search for missing children. This last episode featured the hunt for a young Manchester boy named John Kilbride – who would later be listed as one of the victims of 'Moors Murderers' Ian Brady and Myra Hindley.

My stint on *The Headliners* gave me the chance to work with producers who knew how to craft half-hour films, as opposed to the five-minute items I had been used to. It was also the springboard to my next job – the camera assistant's position on *World In Action*, and the start of the life of which I've already written.

The changes since then have come with ever-increasing speed. There's the technological leaps, such as the switch from black-and-white to colour, and the development of minuscule concealed cameras. Then there was the change from film to tape. Back in 1979 I was covering the nuclear disaster at Three Mile Island in the USA, along with dozens of TV stations from around the world. During a press conference, producer Brian Blake and I looked round the room and saw the massed rows of electronic tape cameras. We were, in fact, one of just two crews still using the old equipment. And, as our rivals fed their tapes on to satellite feeds, we felt like dinosaurs.

Such technological advances have driven down costs and manpower, stripping the TV unions of their once formidable muscle, and shrinking film crews to a minimum. As recently as the mid-eighties there would be six people in a filming unit – cameraman, sound recordist, two assistants, an electrician and the production assistant. Now only the first two remain. Meanwhile many news organizations now employ video journalists who not only find the story and do the interviews – they shoot and edit them, too.

Then there's the massive expansion of the broadcasting environment. When I joined Granada the only stations to watch were BBC1 and ITV. By 1998 there were five terrestrial channels, video recorders, and the virtually unlimited offerings of cable, satellite and digital. This explosion of choice was bound to have an impact on viewing figures. ITV may still have been Britain's most popular channel but its audience was showing a marked decline. As the executives in charge looked for ways to halt the slide they had to take some ruthless decisions about programmes that were failing to deliver big ratings. With an average peak time audience hovering between four and five million, *World In Action* was clearly vulnerable, and as 1998 drew to a close, it was cancelled. On 7 December, the last edition was transmitted. The closing credits rolled with a familiar caption at the head: 'Camera – George Jesse Turner'.

It could have been the end of my life on the road, but within weeks it was business as usual. Granada won the contract to produce ITV's new current affairs series *Tonight*, a mixture of investigations, high-profile interviews and human interest stories. My first assignment was working alongside reporter Martin Bashir, as he landed one of the biggest interviews of 1999 – with the five men widely suspected of being involved in the murder of the black teenager Stephen Lawrence. Over the following few months I was to work in the USA, the Middle East and – for the first time in my career – Cuba. Back in the UK there were many other stories to cover – including the unbelievable tale of Dr Harold Shipman, the family GP who killed dozens of his elderly patients with lethal injections of morphine.

As with all the other changes, the advent of *Tonight* has brought fresh opportunities and challenges. It's exciting to work with reporters of Martin's calibre, as well as other on-screen stars like Trevor McDonald and Michael Nicholson. And it's rewarding to help the new generation of producers and directors to craft their films, sharing the benefits of my own experience.

Those young programme-makers are now starting out on the sort of adventure that has taken me to places I never dreamed of, providing me with memories I'll never forget. I hope that, along the way, I've helped TV viewers gain their own insights into world events. And, with my enthusiasm and energy as strong as ever, I hope I'll continue doing so for many years yet.

Acknowledgements

I wouldn't have been able to write this book had I not spent so much of my life on the road. And I'm sure I wouldn't have put up with all that travelling without the colleagues who helped make it so much fun. Special thanks must therefore go to the five sound recordists who've shared in most of my adventures. They are Alan Bale, Phil Taylor, Dave Hollingsworth, Mark Atkinson and Keith Staniforth.

When it came to writing about those experiences, I was amazed at how many other ex-colleagues were prepared to raid their notebooks and memory banks on my behalf. It would be impossible to list all those who did, but I owe a particular debt to Brian Blake, who gave up a great deal of time, and allowed me to comb through his lovingly-preserved files detailing so much of *World In Action*'s history.

At Granada, my appreciation goes to Susanna Wadeson for all her support and advice during the writing and research; Louisa Flitcroft for many hours spent hunting down old programme scripts and tapes; Neil Marland, Jim Rowan, Ian Cartwright and Murray Cook for their help with the photo research; and Hazel Coe for being flexible with my filming roster.

As I started work on this, my first – and probably only – book, I was cheerfully unaware of how time consuming the whole project would prove to be. Once the initial rush of excitement wore off it was time for the hard slog; time to pore over the scrap-books kept so diligently by my mother, Bessie; and time to rely on the love and encouragement of my wife Jacki, and my children, Joanna and Richard.

Now that the work is over, I'd like to thank Nicky Paris, my editor at André Deutsch, whose helpful suggestions in the final stages made my story much more readable. And finally, a special big thanks to Rory, Ciaran and Rosie Anderson, who put up with their dad's long hours in the study – when they really wanted him to be playing with them.

George Jesse Turner
Manchester, February 2000

INDEX